To Brad Schaeffer, S.J. -
with gratitude for luring me back
into the Jesuit milieu,
And with all good wishes for many
of God's still unmixed blessings.

Heinz Kuehn

October 30, 1992

Mixed Blessings

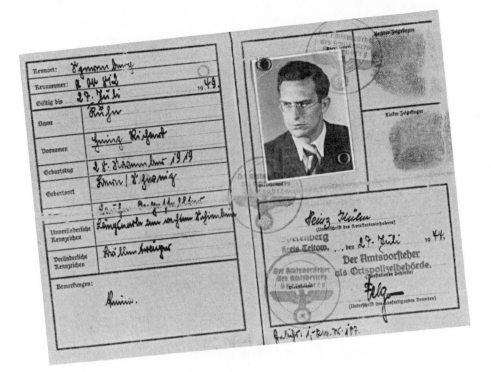

Mixed Blessings

· ·

An Almost Ordinary Life in Hitler's Germany

· ·

Heinz R. Kuehn

The University of Georgia Press

Athens and London

Designed by Sandra Strother Hudson
Set in Times Roman

The paper in this book meets the guidelines for permanence
and durability of the Committee on Production Guidelines for
Book Longevity of the Council on Library Resources.

Printed in the United States of America

92 91 90 89 88   5 4 3 2 1

Library of Congress Cataloging in Publication Data
Kuehn, Heinz R.
   Mixed blessings.

   1. Kuehn, Heinz R. 2. Jews—Berlin (Germany)—
Biography. 3. Children of interfaith marriage—Berlin
(Germany)—Biography. 4. Holocaust, Jewish (1939–
1945)—Berlin (Germany)—Personal narratives. 5. Berlin
(Germany)—Biography. I. Title
DS135.G5K84   1988   943′.155004924024   [B]   88-4744
ISBN 0-8203-1046-8 (alk. paper)

British Library Cataloging in Publication Data available.

Contents

· ·

Contents

Acknowledgments

· ·

The epilogue has been previously published in the *Sewanee Review*, no. 1, Winter 1988. Portions of the text of this book have also been used, either verbatim or in modified form, in self-contained essays published in *The American Scholar*, Summer 1985 and Autumn 1986, and in *Encounter* (London), no. 1, January 1984.

Mixed Blessings

Prologue

. . . .

In the wee hours of a winter morning I stood on a deserted street somewhere in Milwaukee, waiting for a bus. It had been snowing heavily again during the night, but in spite of the early hour a tiny alcove, illuminated by the glare of a nearby street lamp, had been hewn out of a mountain of snow to mark the bus stop. The right-of-way, defined by a double row of lights stretching into the night on either side of me, seemed to have been carved with a knife through a polar mountainscape and turned into a landing strip lying in wait for a plane to materialize out of the black sky. Here and there a window was lit; here and there a column of white smoke rose from a rooftop. I had never seen so much snow; I had never been so thoroughly numbed by cold.

Everything I wore was as new as the snow: gabardine jacket, bluejeans, woolen cap, scarf, steel-tipped boots. For the first time in my life I carried a lunch bucket. In an apartment three or four blocks from where I stood, my wife and two daughters were sleeping, but I did not know in which part of Milwaukee we lived, nor what to expect from the day ahead, except that the bus would take me to the Blatz Brewing Company where I

1

· ·

was to report to work as a dock hand. We had been in the United States for two weeks, and in Milwaukee for three days. It was December 1951; I had just turned thirty-two and was to begin my first working day in my new country.

The silence of the street was so profound that I gave a start when a man stepped into the alcove. I had not heard his footsteps. He was dressed exactly as I, but shabbier; he too carried a lunch bucket. "Morning," he mumbled, and then fell silent. We stood close to each other—there was not much room between the walls of snow that reached up to our hips— like human figures placed without purpose on a forlorn planet. His face, of a bluish color and thin-lipped, looked old and haggard; he trembled with cold. "Where're you headed?" he began the conversation after a few minutes. "Blatz Brewing Company," I replied. I must have pronounced "Blatz" the German way, with a short *a* as in *nuts,* because his next question was, "You from Germany?" I nodded, and we fell silent again. In the distance I now heard the wheezing of a heavy engine, and then, barely visible above the snow walls, I saw the top of an approaching bus. "How long you been here?" he spoke up again. "About two weeks." Now the bus came into full view, and as it entered a circle of light a few yards away I saw that it was crowded with people standing shoulder to shoulder in the aisle. "Let me give you a piece of advice," the old man said without taking his eyes off the bus that had come to a halt in front of us. "Take the next boat back to Germany. I've lived here for thirty years, and believe me, that's the best advice I can give you. Take the next boat home." We boarded the bus, and while I talked to the driver, asking him to signal to me when I had to get off, the old man disappeared among the crowd of passengers. Each weekday for the next two weeks I stood at the same bus stop, at the same hour, waiting for the old man. I wanted to ask him where he had come from, but I never saw him again.

The old man had spoken from a generation's experience of America, an immigrant's experience. I stood at the beginning of my American life, and I had no inclination to heed his advice. If he had asked me why I had left Germany, I would have had to take him back into my past, into the Nazi era and into postwar Berlin. I would have had to disclose to him part of my father's and mother's life. Then I would have had to talk to him about disturbing memories that I hoped would lose some of their strength and vividness in an environment totally different from that in which they were rooted. Perhaps similar experiences had driven him from whichever country had been his home, and he might have understood why I could not take the next boat back.

But let the old man be. What I would have told him, had he asked me, I have tried to express in the pages that follow, for my children and grandchildren, for my friends, for all those who care to read, for whatever reason, about one man's experience of a cataclysmic period in mankind's history.

Part One

....

Confluence
and Disjunction

. . . .

My father's native soil was the Rhineland, the graceful cradle of German culture. My mother's family came from East Prussia, the lonely colony of the Knights of the Teutonic Order, the flat, windswept land that was forever a plot of discord between the European powers of East and West. Father's ancestors were Christians; Mother's, Jews. In the inner vision of my early childhood, Father's world lies West: the sky is bright and hard, the colors are vivid, and the forms are sharply defined. Mother's world lies East: the sky is high and gray, the colors are soft, and the forms are diffused in a warm mist.

Neither of my parents has left me much from which I could reconstruct anything resembling a biography of that period of their life that preceded my recollected childhood. It was not only the instability of their existence, their divorce, the Nazi era, or the devastations of the Second World War that caused my parents' memorabilia to disappear. I would know today a great deal more about Father's life, for example, had we not had a violent argument one day in the summer of 1947. I have long forgotten what caused our quarrel, but immediately afterward he dragged one of the two heavy, battered leather suitcases that were his constant companions out into the garden of the villa in Berlin where we lived at the time, and set a match to the legacy of some fifty years of his life and of German history. From a window I watched how he took piece after piece—letters, clippings, photographs, manuscripts—glanced at each one briefly, and deliberately consigned it to the smoldering heap. After a while I went into the garden and stood silently beside him, but he ignored me. When the suitcase was empty, he watched the pitiable mound until the last shred of paper had turned to ashes. Then, without looking at me, he said, "This was meant for you. But you don't deserve knowing anything about me." I have some photographs of him; copies of three of the nine or ten books he wrote; a scrap of paper on which he had penciled, *In necessariis unitas, in dubiis libertas, in omnibus caritas*—unity in what is necessary, liberty in what is doubtful, charity in everything—and a letter to his third wife. But thanks to one of his cousins, who had been a tenor at the State Opera in Berlin, and whose extensive collection of family documents had by some freak ended up in my possession, I know a great deal about my paternal ancestors.

The Kühn family comes from the good soil of the Rhine country south of the Ruhr region, from that charming stretch of hulking hills and richly wooded valleys that to this day has remained untouched by the noise and dirt of Europe's most heavily industrialized area. In the picturesque villages and on the prosperous farms gracing the highlands of the "Bergisches Land" (a stretch of land once owned by the dukes of Berg) Father's ancestors had been at home since at least the mid-seventeenth century. On his mother's side, they had been *omnes catholici et agricolae*—Catholics and farmers all of them—as a birth certificate from 1816 comments, until her father, a quite prosperous brewmaster, broke with the farming tradition. On his father's side they had been Evangelical Reformed Protestants, members of that branch of Protestantism that was founded by Calvin and Zwingli, and it was that confession which won out, at least temporarily, over the *catholici* when my father was baptized a Protestant. By trade they had been millers or bakers in Solingen on the Rhine, with the exception of my grandfather, who had been a civil servant in that city and at one time was reputed to have been its mayor. A bombing raid on the city during the Second World War destroyed the "Konditorei Kühn" (Café Kühn) that had continued the family tradition.

Richard, my father, was born in Solingen in 1886. His childhood seems to have been a happy one, characterized by the usual privileges and inordinate affections that quickly spoil an only boy growing up among three older sisters. His student years at the University of Giessen, where he studied history and German literature, were typical of the life led by young men of his class during the *belle époque:* drinking, fornicating, and dueling were as worthy of earnest pursuit as the ideals of truth, justice, and beauty. What were the crises of his adolescence? Did he have any? He once fought a duel because of a derogatory remark he had made about Bismarck, but an incident like this—and there were many of a similar kind—merely shows how deeply he and his fellow students felt about the issues of the day. He liked to talk about the "wild student years," about impulsive weekend trips to Rome and Paris "with nothing but a tooth-brush in my pocket," about "the girls we used to sleep with," about bloody brawls at night with young factory workers in the narrow, deserted alleys of the university town. But these were stories meant to entertain, reminiscences about a milieu and a mood he had obviously relished. About his inner world of those days he revealed nothing. Curiously, too, I never heard him speak about his father, and when he talked about his mother, it almost always had something to do with her exceptional piety.

Father left the university without earning a degree. A few years before the First World War began he went to France to do research on the French Revolution, a period in history that fascinated him all his life. In Paris he met and married Gisela Etzel, a German novelist of some repute in the literary circles of that time. The marriage ended with her death a year or two later. Father never spoke about Gisela. As a child I had seen photos of her in my aunts' houses, and I was always struck by the infinite sadness that darkened her young and beautiful face like an impenetrable veil. One of her novels, *Ist Das Die Liebe? (Is This What Is Called Love?)*, stood for a time on Mother's bookshelves. It was a tale of erotic adventures whose vivid descriptions of sexual deviations fired my adolescent fantasies, but at the time I read it I was much too young to understand, let alone judge it. The book later disappeared from Mother's shelves; I never saw a copy among Father's possessions. On the rare occasions when Mother or my aunts mentioned Gisela, they never failed to remark, "She was the only woman your father truly loved." Was this remark meant to explain the failure of his subsequent marriages? Gisela's death may have left him with a wound that never healed completely, and it may explain why friendships with women were indispensable for him until he died. But I don't think that his happiness with Gisela became for him the ideal against which he measured the success of his subsequent marriages. Rather, I believe he was temperamentally destined for a life of solitude, and no marriage, no matter how successfully lived, would have touched the core of his being.

The result of Father's studies in Paris was his translation of Jules Michelet's monumental *Histoire de la Révolution française* (History of the French Revolution). The seven or eight magnificently bound and exquisitely illustrated volumes of the German edition accompanied me throughout my boyhood. I was fond of showing them to my friends— evidence that I not only did indeed have a father, but that he was also a scholar and famous. Then, like Gisela's book, these volumes, too, suddenly disappeared. The outbreak of the war of 1914–1918 put an end to the Parisian episode. Father served as a lieutenant in the infantry, was wounded at Verdun, spent many months in several field hospitals, recuperated in Switzerland, and finally, shortly before the end of the war, was assigned to the German embassy in Bern as an aide to the attaché for cultural affairs. A young Jewish woman, Rosa Heymann, became his secretary. He married her in the spring of 1919, and I was born the following November. A year and a half later, after the three of us had returned to Germany, my sister, Annemarie, was born in Mainz.

Father destroyed the memorabilia of his life in a fit of anger. Mother's disappeared together with the belongings she had saved during her wanderings from Berlin to London and, finally, to New York when the man she had married in New York cleaned out their apartment to the bare walls and vanished, shortly after she was confined to a nursing home. Most of the few documents I have of her ancestors are in Polish; beginning with my grandfather they are in German. But all of them refer variously to "statutes regulating the certification of marriages among Jews" or to "declarations by members of the community of Jewish faithful" and reflect a twofold segregation: as Germans they were separated from the Poles, as Jews they were separated from everybody else. Both my great-grandfather and my grandfather were tailors. Marcus Heymann, my great-grandfather, died in East Prussia. Michaelis, my grandfather, moved to Berlin, where he married Johanna Riese, also a native of East Prussia. Marcus, the "master tailor," witnessed the marriage of his son; being "ignorant of writing," he "undercrossed" the marriage certificate with three X's. The couple moved to Altona, a twin city of Hamburg, where my mother was born as the third of five children, four girls and a boy. The marriage ended in divorce after eighteen years, when Mother was nine.

Grandmother Riese (she assumed her maiden name after the divorce) raised her children in the old workmen's section of Altona. When I was little I lived with her occasionally, just as I used to live from time to time with Father's sisters in the Rhineland. I still see her sitting on a chair in the center of her kitchen—tall, heavy, erect, a loose, light gown covering her enormous body, her hands resting on her knees. From a black stove on curved clawed legs comes a flickering light that makes pots, carving knives, pans, and ladles glow mysteriously like dark gold. In one corner there is a wooden tub held together by gleaming metal bands, in the other a plain wooden table. Grandmother has very long, white hair that cascades over the backrest of the chair. I comb her hair with a heavy comb that threatens to slip out of my fingers when I meet some resistance. Standing on tiptoe, I start at the top of her head, bending my knees as I reach the level of her hips, finally kneeling as I lift thick, shiny strands from the floor planks and curl them around my wrist.

There is another lady in the room. She is young and her large, dark eyes, eyes like Mother's, are full of tenderness. On her head she carries a little tower of black hair that sends out tiny sparks. The two ladies talk and laugh a lot. Grandmother's laugh is deep and resonant, like a man's; it makes her body shake, and then the silvery waves come alive in little nervous ripples. Aunt Clara's laugh sounds like a happy bell. Nobody laughs as merrily as they, and their laughter makes me feel good and warm inside. I don't want to stop combing Grandmother's hair because, when I am finished, Aunt Clara will take a kettle from the stove, fill the wooden

tub with warm water, undress me, and give me a bath. I hate being undressed, scrubbed, and toweled by anyone but my mother. But Mother is
not there. I am waiting for her to come.

Mother's brother, Willi, also lived in Hamburg, and sometimes I would
stay with him and his family. He was married to a Christian and had a
daughter, Ilse. When the Nazis came to power, he emigrated to America,
leaving Ilse and his wife behind. He made no particular impression on me
when I was a child, but when I met him again after the war in New York,
where he was reunited with his family, I found him interesting, well read,
and witty, and I regretted that he had never become a part of my childhood. Yet an isolated memory connects him with an event that, like the
first experience of an air raid, impressed itself on my soul more perma-
nently than any other of the many scenes of public turmoil I observed in
later years.

It was shortly before Hitler came to power, a time when the uncontrollable fanaticism of numerous political parties rent the delicate fabric of the
Weimar Republic and signaled its impending doom. Ilse and I had gone to
a railroad station to pick up Uncle Willi, who was returning from work.
On our way to the station we had noticed that the street which was our
familiar route had been noisier, more crowded, more agitated than usual,
and at one intersection we had slipped through a cordon of policemen and
raced across an empty right-of-way, only to be stopped on the other side
by a policeman who had caught Ilse in his arms, held her high up in the
air, and given her a good-natured scolding. I felt that something ugly and
ominous was in the air. The moment Uncle Willi emerged from the station
building he knew what was about to happen, and his smiling face turned
grim. He took us by the hand, on either side of him, and without saying a
word began to walk rapidly away from the station square, which by now
was packed with people. At one moment during our breathless walk I
noticed that he displayed on his coat lapel an emblem that had not been
there when he had greeted us a few minutes earlier: a sign that looked like
three parallel streaks of lightning, the badge of the "Iron Front," an um-
brella organization of various political parties, with the specific aim of
opposing National Socialism. This was the first time—and it remained the
only time—that I had seen a member of my family, East or West, display

. . . .

the sign of a political organization, and for some unexplainable reason the
fact delighted and excited me. Somewhere we got caught in the crowd. I
was trapped by clothing that smelled of work and smoke and poverty, my
only link to a familiar reality the warm, strong hand that gripped my wrist,
and I experienced the surging panic of claustrophobia, the fear I would get
to know so well in the bomb shelters of Berlin. Suddenly, from a rooftop,
a machine gun began to fire. Piercing screams went up from the crowd,
and a man close to us shouted, "The Nazis!" It was the first time in my
memory I had heard that word. As we crouched in some dark gangway,
pressed hard against the wall of a building, I saw appear on the suddenly
empty street, on that short stretch that was visible to me, a cluster of men
in workmen's clothes, walking slowly and without concern, out of whose
midst three huge, blood-red banners unfurled merrily in the evening
breeze.

Against the vividness of such impressions, my memory of my stays
with my aunts and uncles in the Rhineland has paled. The pictures of the
streets of Hamburg, of Grandmother's apartment, imprinted on my soul so
forcefully at such an impressionable age, have remained indelible. In time
they became counter-pictures to my childhood impressions of Father's relatives: *their* rooms are sunlit, spacious, comfortable; *their* streets are
quiet, tree-shaded, wide; *their* day is ordered: a father goes to work, a
mother cooks, a child goes to school. There are pets, books, a piano,
games. When I think of *them* I see the waters of a majestic river, white
boats, cathedrals, high bridges of massive stone, green hills, sedate cafés
and stores. In Hamburg the streets are narrow, crowded, noisy; in Grandmother's apartment the floors creak, and the rooms are gloomy. After
dark, Aunt Clara lights a lamp that has a heavy shade of milky glass. The
smell of kerosene fills the adjoining room where I lie in bed. The door is
ajar and I can hear the soft murmur of the two women. I feel comfortable
and reassured.

The various places where Annemarie and I lived together with our
parents have left no trace in my memory, except for one apartment in
Berlin. It must have impressed me because, unlike any of my relatives'
homes, it had sky-high ceilings from which hung enormous crystal chan-

deliers; slippery, mirrorlike parquet floors on which I was forbidden to run and permitted to walk on only with my shoes off; and walls covered with large, dark paintings in heavy, gilded frames and with bookcases that reached from floor to ceiling. An endless source of delight for Annemarie and me, the place had some system whereby one could set off from each room a bell in any of the other rooms, at the sound of which a square in a little box mounted next to the door would light up, indicating in which room the bell button had been pushed. Most wondrously of all, there also was a maid, a heavyset woman whom we called Berta, who always wore a black dress, a white cap, and a little white apron, who took Annemarie and me for walks, and who tucked us in at night.

I also hear Father's voice in that apartment, his soft, gentle voice reciting a poem and creating a cozy little space in that cavernous place as he holds me on his lap. Father's store of poems he knew by heart was inexhaustible, and prompted by mood or circumstance, he often broke into verse. Heinrich Heine was one of his favored poets, and whenever I think of that apartment in Berlin and hear Father's voice, there comes to my mind, for whatever reason, Heine's short melancholy poem that goes like this:

> There was a king high up in years,
> Of heavy heart and graying hair.
> This king, oh pity, married
> A woman young and fair.
>
> There was a handsome page-boy—
> Golden his hair, his heart was light;
> The silken train he carried
> Of the queen so gay and bright.
>
> This age-old song—you know it?
> So sweet the sound, so sad the knell!
> Death was the lovers' fortune
> Because they loved too well.
>
> > (My translation)

Does my memory of the apartment evoke this melancholy poem of love and perdition because in its rooms I also heard other voices and sounds, the ugly voices and sounds of domestic quarrel? My love of German poetry began in that elegant home in Berlin, but also my apprehension of raised voices and of arguments.

At that time, in 1925, Mother obtained a divorce, and that same year Father married Edith Freudenheim, an actress. My sister and I were given into Mother's custody. Mother was thirty-two then; Annemarie was four and I was five.

A Portion
of Jewishness

· ·

Annemarie and I grew up in Berlin, in an area intersected by the Kurfürstendamm and the Tauentzienstrasse, the two wide boulevards where expensive stores and restaurants, sumptuous movie theaters, and pleasant sidewalk cafés alternated with stately hotels, fine townhouses, and nightclubs to create that impression of cosmopolitan élan and elegance that Berliners meant when they spoke of "West Berlin." The hub of the two boulevards was the Kaiser Wilhelm Memorial Church, a monumental edifice in simulated Romanesque style, whose tower looked with frosty Protestant disapproval at the bustle and frivolity at its feet. That tower was the point of reference for the Berlin of my childhood. It threw its shadow on the Zoological Gardens and on the Zoo station, where Mother usually met her dates, and it remained visible even from the graveled walkways, the oak groves, and the lagoons of the Tiergarten, where we took our Sunday afternoon strolls.

Beyond these fifty acres of wooded parkland, beyond the Brandenburg Gate at their northwestern edge, lay a city I did not know as a child. Occasionally Father would meet me at the gate, and we would walk along the Unter den Linden, the spacious double avenue with its gracious center promenade lined with lime trees; its grandiose government buildings in the neoclassical style of Prussian arrogance; its royal palace, opera house, and university; and its numerous embassies and office buildings. Here, at the center of Prussian and Imperial German history, Father was in his element. But for me the memory of this stylish street is embedded in the memory of a more agitated, more violent time. It has merged with the remembrance of cheering, screaming masses, of endless marching columns, of cavalcades of black limousines, of two faces, side by side, the Führer's morose, the Duce's impenetrably grim, of an endless replication of swastika flags, wiping out the disciplined features of the avenue in a blinding burst of vulgar brazenness, and it has merged, finally, with the memory of a silent field churned up by huge craters, a no-man's land lined with towering fragments of blackened façades and strewn with twisted skeletons of steel.

Nor did I know anything, as a child, of that vast, amorphous, bleak city where most of Berlin's four million residents lived—East Berlin, predominantly ugly, predominantly sad, the Berlin of the factory workers, of huge industrial plants, of stockyards, of narrow alleys and gloomy rental barracks, of sunless labyrinthine back courts and cavernous, soot-blackened railroad stations. Later, as an adolescent, I would get to know a little of the other cities within the city: the Berlin of the Hohenzollern court, the Berlin of Käthe Kollwitz and Bertolt Brecht, of the compassionate physician-writer Alfred Döblin and the communist revolutionary Karl Liebknecht. I would walk through the self-contained quiet villages with their cobbled streets and old, sagging frame houses built along a narrow canal, the villages around and between which the modern city had grown up like a poisonous weed, and I would become a steady visitor to the Berlin of the nouveaux riches who lived in the southwest in white, secluded villas whose spacious, fenced-in grounds bordered on woods and lakes. Later still, living in the United States, I would read avidly about the history, the architecture, the writers, artists, politicians, and demagogues of a city that for the last two hundred years had been the fate of Europe, trying to fill in the gaps in my knowledge of the place I once called home. But by then many of the sites I had known had been destroyed or, having been rebuilt, had become unrecognizable, while others, those of which I had known little, and remembered less, had been turned into a foreign city behind The Wall.

Although we changed apartments several times during my growing-up years, it seems as if we lived always in the same place. I would turn from the Kurfürstendamm into a side street, and suddenly I would hear above the quickly fading noise of the boulevard the laughter of children, the ringing of bicycle bells, the thump-thump of balls, and the chirping of birds. I would enter a spacious, ornate lobby, traverse it past the wide, carpeted marble staircase, the polished mirrors in gilded frames, the alabaster statues of nymphs and fauns, and walk down a dimly lit, narrow hall at whose end a door led to an inner court. Unlike the notorious bleak backyards of the inner city—weed-grown, trash-strewn, poisonous playgrounds for children who had nowhere else to go—the court was light and clean, the trash cans were hidden behind an enclosure of greenery, and the carpet rails in the center were encircled by flower beds and shrubbery. I would enter a rear building through a door marked "Erster Aufgang"— First Entrance—and climb the steps to the second floor. Up to the second floor the elegance in the front building would still be mimicked by touches of bourgeois respectability, but from the second landing up the stairs were bare, the ornate wall covering changed to painted plaster, the crystal fixtures to porcelain receptacles, and the door-bell casings from brass to wood. In West Berlin, carpeted stairs and social acceptability ended on the second floor of the First Entrance.

In her short married life, Mother had relished the prestige of living "in front" as much as she had savored all luxury, all elegant and expensive things. Living on the second floor of the first rear building meant the limit of the concessions she was willing to make to her status as a divorced woman supporting herself and two small children. A snob by temperament, but guileless in a touching way, she would not have condescended to being friendly with the tenants of the two or three floors above, nor with the people hanging their wash from the windows and balconies of the buildings that formed the other, interconnected courts. She was seldom at home. In the morning, when Annemarie and I left for school, she was still asleep, and when we returned in midafternoon she was still at work. She would come home at suppertime, hurriedly prepare some sandwiches for us, change into an evening dress, and then leave again for whatever engagement she had that night. She was never more beautiful, more radiant than in those moments of leave-taking that set the pale, delicate skin of her face aglow. Her dress, her jewelry, her gloves were chosen with impeccable taste to emphasize the small waist, the full bosom, and the raven hair, and her large, brown eyes sparkled in nervous anticipation of what the evening promised. She did not know how to kiss or hug perfunctorily. Impulsive, passionate, sensual, she would turn each goodbye into a small drama of tears, kisses, and long embraces, undoubtedly sensing our jealousy of whomever she was going to meet and our unspoken misgivings about another night alone in the vast stillness of the apartment.

Undoubtedly, too, she felt guilty about leaving us. She was too sensitive a person, too loving a woman, and too responsible a mother not to suffer from her insatiable hunger for pleasure, diversion, and, most of all, admiration, a hunger that made her unable to endure a long evening at home in the sole company of her children. There was in her nature a restlessness, a streak of the grande dame, of the adventuress, that made her flee from whatever smacked of confinement and solitude. The "up front" apartment *was* her proper milieu. She cooked for us, she sewed, she cleaned, she saved sporadically, but some irresistible impulse always drove her "out," among people, into the glittering make-believe world of the Kurfürstendamm, into shops and restaurants too expensive for her secretary's income. These were the years when the Weimar Republic was thriving under its brilliant secretary of state, Gustav Stresemann, and Berlin had once again become a European capital for entertainment, amusement, and the arts. Theaters, opera and concert houses, cabarets, and nightclubs flourished, and their lure was compelling.

Annemarie and I were, of course, too little to have any part in the nightlife of the city, or in the frivolous or decadent amusements it offered in such abundance in the mid-twenties. We envied her the nights and weekends filled with fun and excitement, while we were left to our games or books, or had to go to bed. Sometimes, after Mother had left, we would slip out of bed, put a record on the gramophone, and, in our nightshirts, play Esplanade or Adlon, or, if we were in a more enterprising mood, get dressed up with Mother's finery, and play Scala or Apollo. Esplanade and Adlon were the names of two fashionable hotels where Berlin's café society mingled with the demimonde at elegant dances. Scala and Apollo were variety theaters that offered a mixture of lush productions ranging from political satire to burlesque. But if we had hoped that someday we, too, would get to know the real world of laughter and beauty and happiness, we were to be cruelly disappointed. By the time we were old enough to experience that side of the Berlin of the twenties, the Third Reich had sterilized elegance and entertainment and had driven frivolity and decadence underground. All we remembered of that period was that Mother, like the city, never knew a pause, never stood still, never looked back.

And yet, as restless, as unpredictable, as tense, and, at bottom, as unhappy as she was, there was in Mother, perhaps as an indestructible legacy from Marcus the Master Tailor, an uncanny instinct for the goodness, the redeeming force of the ordinary: it was from her that I learned to cherish the consolations of a good bed and a good book, of a leisurely bath and a quiet evening next to a reading lamp, of a bunch of flowers on a windowsill, of a nice meal and a stroll in the park. Mother was an avid, if indiscriminate, reader; a love of books was one of the few things she had in common with Father, and she treasured the stately mahogany bookcases that contained the library of their years of marriage. These books were the companions of my early childhood, and some of them etched the tabula rasa of my young mind with indelible images: the fairy tales of the Brothers Grimm and of Hans Christian Andersen; the Wild West stories of Karl May, the German writer who had never set foot on American soil until after his immensely popular books, which profoundly influenced my and my generation's view of America, had been written. The adventures of Robinson Crusoe and the heartache of *Uncle Tom's Cabin;* the pranks of the cartoon urchins Max and Moritz and the legends of the Nibelungen and of other heroes of the age of chivalry and romance. Those were the "children's books" of my time. But most of those I read were beyond my grasp and should have remained locked up behind the stained-glass doors of their cases.

I read without direction, often without understanding, overwhelmed and blinded by writers too powerful for a tender and still unformed mind. I read in solitude, too much too early, and there was nobody with whom I could talk about the images, the feelings, the desires and dreams that obsessed me. These books filled the void of Sunday afternoons, kept the threatening silence of interminable evenings at bay, helped me to deal with the problem of time. Alone in the apartment, with Mother and Annemarie occupied elsewhere, I would lie flat on my stomach, next to a bookcase, elbows propped up, chin resting in hands, engrossed in the book that lay before me on the rug. What did I read besides those "children's books"? On a shelf in my study stand six books I salvaged from Mother's belongings, books that had once belonged in the apartment in Berlin: two novels by Jakob Schaffner and one each by Hermann Hesse, Hermann Sudermann, Hans Carossa, and Selma Lagerlöf. They were all serious, high-minded writers, humanists whose works could be found in any "good house" of the German middle class of my youth. Hans Carossa, a practicing physician, was befriended by and influenced the writings of Thomas Mann, Rainer Maria Rilke, and Hermann Hesse. Selma Lagerlöf, the Swedish novelist whose *Gösta Berling,* a novel about a wayward priest, created a sensation in Europe, was a Nobel Prize winner, as was, of course, Hermann Hesse, the most enduring and influential among the five. Hermann Sudermann, one of the purest representatives of naturalism, had been a brilliant dramatist who castigated in his plays the mindlessness of the Prussian aristocracy's code of honor and the moral corruption of Berlin society during the kaiser era. Even Jakob Schaffner, the Swiss writer who lived in Berlin and in his old age supported National Socialism, was a man of pure motives and high ideals: to give an articulate and persuasive voice to the aspirations and values of the "little man," to those ignored and forgotten by the smug bourgeoisie of the turn of the century.

The books had accompanied Mother when she fled to England in 1939, and again when she moved to New York after the war. Three of them she inscribed with her name and one of them bore a date: 1930. I was eleven years old then. Herbert Hoover was president of the United States; Heinrich Brüning, chancellor of Germany. The Weimar Republic, rent by political turmoil and economic distress, was fighting for survival. Nazis and Communists owned the streets of Berlin, shooting each other up. In another three years Hitler would assume absolute power. But that was not the real world for me—not yet, at any rate. My real world—and the real world of millions of middle-class Germans—was in the kind of books exemplified by these six volumes. By Sudermann's *Lithuanian Stories,* for example, one of the books Mother had inscribed with her name. The *Stories,* according to a list of Sudermann's works at the back of the book, had first been published in 1917, and at the time Mother bought it, in the mid-twenties, 70,000 copies were in print. I also learned that, of the dozen or so novels Sudermann had written, his most famous one, *Frau Sorge* (Frau Sorrow) had reached in Mother's time a printing of 295,000.

Lithuanian Stories is a handsome volume, a selection of the Deutsche Buchgemeinschaft (German Book Association), a refined version of today's book clubs. The red-leather spine shows a stylized tendril of leaves and blossoms, cut in gold. Scenes of peasant life, traced in fine, chalklike outlines, adorn the gray linen cover: a cottage, cattle and dogs, a hunter, a man in a boat, a couple in embrace. The heavy paper shows no trace of yellowing, and the type, a German Gothic face, is pleasingly decorative and still crisply black. A bound-in silk ribbon serves as bookmark. One of the things that makes the bookcases in the apartment of my childhood unforgettable is the remembrance of aesthetic pleasures: each volume had reflected *Buchkunst*—book art—a term denoting excellence in book production and taste in book design. My mind may have forgotten titles and contents, but my eyes and hands still happily remember the sight and touch of these books.

Books were my link to Father. They were his substitute in the apartment and a never-ending topic of our conversations when we visited, and the strongest means he had to exert his influence on my development. Before the strength of his presence in my inner world, Father's substitutes in the real world, the world of things and people, seemed hollow, lusterless: the "uncle" who would come to dinner bearing flowers for Mother and coloring books or toys for Annemarie and me, take us to a movie on a Saturday afternoon, or accompany us on an outing to the zoo. None of the courting men who came and went ever became a substitute for Father, but Mother's sisters, Aunt Minna and Aunt Walli, took his place in many ways, and in some they were a substitute even for Mother. Aunt Minna, Mother's younger sister, was a self-effacing woman. When the apartment became crowded with people, she liked to sit apart, smiling and chain-smoking Turkish cigarettes, her quiet, pleasant voice ignored. But in her absence, the light seemed dimmer to me, the temperature frostier, and Mother's voice harsher. Her two words, "But Rosa . . . ," the words I remember so vividly with their peculiar cadence of disapproval and regret, restored, if not tranquillity, at least a temporary truce in the apartment whenever one of Mother's frequent outbursts of wrath had run its course.

Of her life I know virtually nothing. In Berlin she worked as an office clerk at the Telefunken company, and later, in New York, she had some menial job in a ribbon factory. She was addicted to detective stories, but what inner life she had she kept to herself as long as I knew her. Like her brother, Willi, she had a keen sense of humor, but whereas her brother's wit could ridicule and hurt, hers soothed and restored. Like Mother, she was almost always in the company of an "uncle," but true to her own imperturbable reliability, Minna never changed her companion until she left Germany: Uncle Robert, well-dressed, well-mannered, like Minna an unobtrusive, comfortable presence. They never married, and Mother and Minna remained inseparable. She followed Mother to England and died in Mother's apartment in New York. I stood by her deathbed, in her small room illuminated only by a table lamp over which Mother had draped a towel to dim the light, listening to her labored breathing and lost in the images of a world that had ceased to exist. What had been the source of her patience, I thought, of that quiet charm that seemed especially attractive to those familiar with suffering and grief? Was it that God, of whom she never spoke, favored her for reasons of his own, and through her life spoke of his mercy? Suddenly I felt that she was looking at me. I bent down and took her hand. "You are a good boy," she said, clearly and loud enough so that Mother, who sat in a chair in a corner of the room, could hear her. "He is a good boy, Resy," she said again, addressing Mother with a name Mother had not used in decades. These were her last words to me. In these words lay the gift of her humble life, the gift for me, for Mother, for my sister, for everyone who had ever come near her: don't fret, her life had said, you are good, you are good.

Aunt Walli's gift to me was of a different, more easily fathomable nature. Mother's older sister had none of Mother's impulsive warmth, none of Minna's equanimity, or of her brother's gift of irony, yet I sensed in her something that, much later, I came to realize as my own: a certain proud independence, a melancholic solitude, an aloofness from the trivia of the marketplace, a dislike for all-too-readily displayed emotions. She lived with Aunt Minna in an apartment in the shadow of the Kaiser Wilhelm Memorial Church, drawing some income from the estate of a deceased husband. The apartment was, of course, in a rear building, but, an unusual convenience for tenants living "in back," you could ride up to her floor in an elevator, a narrow cage of black-iron grilles that never failed to awaken in me dim pictures of a terribly remote time, a time when Mother and Father and I rode an elevator to *our* apartment, past thickly carpeted landings and alabaster-white railings, when the door to *our* apartment was opened by a lady all dressed in black except for a tiny white apron and a tiny white cap. Her apartment was high and light and sparsely furnished; I liked its cool spaciousness because it made me feel taller and freer than in the cloying coziness of the places in which most of Mother's friends lived. She kept a canary that perched on her shoulder when she stood by the stove or sat mending by the large window of the living room, and when I was alone in her apartment, I played with the loaded revolver she kept in a drawer of her nightstand.

Perhaps I was drawn to this stately, taciturn woman with the rich blond hair and the proud gray eyes because she was different, apart from the rest of Mother's friends and relatives, who looked on Walli's eccentricities (as they saw her way of living) with misgivings and rarely included her in their endless whirl of parties, kaffeeklatschs, visits, and outings. They were the people for whom Mother, with a touch of contempt, used the Yiddish word for "clan": *Mischpoke.** They formed that churning sea of cousins, second cousins, friends, and neighbors that surrounded the famil-

---

*The Yiddish spelling is *mespocheh* or *mishpocheh*. Used in Germany by Jews and non-Jews, the word was spelled *Mischpoke* and pronounced *mish-pō´-kē*.

iar island of the apartment, was apt to flood it at any moment, and filled it with a perpetual roar. There were Hulda, Hilde, Gerda, Rebekka, Ilse, Marta, Helen, and countless other women whose names and faces I have long forgotten. Except for "uncles" who came and went, there was not a man among them, none I can remember. They were a good-looking lot, these women: dark-haired, large-eyed, full-bosomed, slim-waisted, sparkling with a *joie de vivre* that made even their complaints and arguments sound triumphant. Some of them had children, but none was married. Single, separated, divorced, or widowed, they lived within walking distance from each other, in small or large apartments that looked and smelled alike, worked in offices, visited back and forth, smothered me with wet kisses and long embraces, and filled the air with the sound of their laughter, the harsh whisper of their gossip, the bitterness of their lament, and the aroma of their cakes and cigarettes.

I longed for the cool, reticent affection of a man, of a father, for a presence in that apartment which quietly encouraged and confirmed my sense of order and guided the uncertain instincts of an eight- or ten-year-old: a curiosity about books, a need for solitude, a hunger for knowledge. I resented the intrusion of the Mischpoke into my life, their claim on Mother's time and affection. Yet the swarm of the Mischpoke gave to my childhood what they had, and I know today that it was much. Their daily work was tedious, and the marginal jobs they held were threatened as much by the prejudices of their fellow workers as by the uncertainty of the times. They knew by heart what every piece of jewelry would fetch at the pawnbroker's, and they used this source of temporary solvency with the same regularity with which others used their savings accounts. There was tragedy in their lives, and grievous sin, and sickness, and suicide—things I sensed keenly then but understood only much later. But their affection was genuine and spontaneous, their pleasures were innocent, their sorrows real. They had an instinct for goodness, an innate sense of truth and beauty, the fierce Hebrew sense of justice, and above all an indefatigable effervescence. If their tastes were unschooled and their interests in the arts did not extend beyond the movies, a promenade concert, or an operetta, they were by no means superficial: something—whether a memory of more elegant, less careworn days, the unforgotten influence of a husband or a lover, or simply a primeval genetic disposition—made them uncommon and interesting, and much more arresting than Father's relatives.

Religion played no part in the lives of Mother and the Mischpoke, neither in faith, nor by habit, nor as custom or tradition, even though Mother converted to Catholicism when I was in my teens. They bandied the word *God,* but this God, their expressions taught me, was merely a being that meted out reward and punishment, and to whom one turned when the fulfillment of a wish, no matter how trivial, was at stake. "I pray to God . . ." was Mother's favorite expression, and with the same fervor with which she implored him to strike down the witch who had stolen her husband, she invoked his name when a cloudy sky threatened to ruin an outing to the Tiergarten. God did not make her happier, or more content, or more resigned than others.

Yet my childhood was not devoid of strong religious influences, as confused and diverse as they were. I saw on my walks with Father through the cathedrals of the Rhine the signs and symbols, the rituals, of Catholicism, felt the mood of sacred space. He had insisted that Annemarie and I be baptized as Catholics. "If the children are to be baptized at all," he had said, according to Mother, "I want them to be Catholics. No other religion makes sense." But in Berlin, Annemarie and I went to state schools that were universally Protestant, and Mother was adamant that we attend the religion classes of these schools. Under their influence I once joined the YMCA in an attack of puerile religious fervor that was short-lived. At our weekly prayer meetings we were supposed to proclaim publicly whatever came to mind under the prompting of the Holy Spirit—in our group mostly self-reproaches for offenses against chastity. Kneeling on the floor in a darkened assembly hall, my arms outstretched, I listened with painful embarrassment as the boys around me fitfully called out their secret thoughts and deeds. After suffering that agony a few times, I quit the organization, carrying away from the experience a lasting and profound distaste for religious exhibitionism.

Another experience proved more wholesome, a brief experience of living faith that did not mean much at the time, but to which I owe indelible sentiments of affection and reverence toward the rituals of Orthodox Judaism. Annemarie and I used to spend our summer vacations with either Father's or Mother's relatives, and on two or three occasions Mother sent us to the East Prussian town of Gilgenburg where my great-grandfather, Marcus the illiterate master-tailor, had died, and where one of his sons, Mother's uncle Markus, still owned a dry-goods store on the cobbled square encircling the town hall of the drowsy little place. Gilgenburg is a memory of the excitements of which a child's dreams of vacation time are made: of wading against the icy current of a spunky creek shaded by enormous weeping willows; of climbing the ruins of the wall with which the Knights of the Teutonic Order had surrounded their fortress in the twelfth century and which the Poles had destroyed in the fifteenth; of breathlessly riding bareback across an open field; of roaming the cavernous mansard of the store, dizzy from the scent of dusty bolts of cloth and old wood, and of listening to the rain drumming on the flint-tiled roof. Annemarie and I came to know more about the sites, the history, and the people of Gilgenburg than we knew about our own neighborhood in Berlin.

Yet these memories would have paled over the years had they not been borne by a deeper and richer experience that has remained unique in the course of my life. As Orthodox Jews, Markus and his family may have resented Mother's indifference to her religion, but they treated Annemarie and me as if we had been their own children. They included us in the routine of a life where nothing seemed ultimately important but where everything appeared in some indefinable way joyfully solemn. The freedom we were permitted in their house, their town, was not the kind of moody, lonely freedom that weighed on us in Berlin. Here, the day's tasks and affairs were set into a frame of rituals and habits that brought moods and thoughts home, from wherever they had strayed, to a shelter of serenity, and a mystery I could not name gave a tone of freshness and a ring of happiness to even the most ordinary household chores. Here, it was not the Paradise above a soaring Gothic portal but the *mezuzah** on the doorframe of Markus's house that closed off a sacred space from the intrusions of the marketplace. Here it was not the chanting of the canons but the

*Among Orthodox Jews, a piece of parchment with biblical inscriptions, rolled up in a small container, and attached to the doorpost as the biblical passages command.

voice of Markus, his rapid, plaintive singsong that, awakening Annemarie and me, gave an air of festivity to the breaking day. Here, sitting at a table covered with embroidered linen and set with things of silver and precious-looking china, breaking the brittle disks of matzo by the light of candles, I was not a spectator but a participant drawn into an inexplicable and deeply exciting ritual. I was too young to understand what I saw and felt, but I sensed that these prayers, these rituals, this table, this meal were the source of the lightheartedness, the smiling openness, the spirited gaiety that drew me to this couple. I knew homesickness—I would know it throughout my childhood—but in Gilgenburg I had no thought, no longing for Father or Mother, or for Berlin, the city where I belonged.

Long before I could distinguish between Jews who lived their faith and those who were indifferent to their religion, I sensed that Mother and the Mischpoke bore the mark of the Chosen People. Perhaps it was their clannishness; or the Yiddish words with which they sprinkled their conversations, and which I grew up using as part of my natural vocabulary. Perhaps it was their bearing, or the ring of faint contempt with which they spoke of "goys." Whatever it was, I felt a barrier that separated them from my classmates and my teachers, from the people who lived in the apartment across the hall, from the world of aunts and uncles in the West, from the world of Father. They were restless, rootless people, she and the orbiting Mischpoke, people without a home for the soul. On the other side, in the West, in the Rhineland aglow with the brilliant flowers of a sacred history, there was among Father's relatives a rootedness, a stability that drew a firm, if somewhat cold and rigid, dignity from a still-keen sense of the respectability of family life, from pride of country and region, from a sense of obligation toward inherited rules, customs, and forms. In Berlin, the Mischpoke had cast off from their homelands generations ago. East Prussia, Silesia, Poland, Russia were words I heard occasionally mentioned, but they had no relation to and no relevance for the living, nervous, ever-changing reality of the streets and apartments of West Berlin.

And yet, I wonder if Mother's life—the life of a woman who had been driven from apartment to apartment, from job to job, from country to country, from love to love—if that life had not been one search for an inner core nourished, invigorated by the springs of a sacred legacy hidden deep beneath the surface of daylight feelings and conventions. She could have found that spring when she converted to Catholicism. But that conversion, a noble deed of love, a gesture she hoped would reconcile her with Father, remained for human eyes a sentimentality. When, in her early seventies, she married again, I visited her in the apartment in the upper Bronx where she lived with her new husband. I hoped that, after so many decades of loneliness, she might finally, in the twilight of her life, have come to peace with her self. But the uncouth loudmouth who greeted me at the door and whose gushing sentimentalities were belied by the cold shrewdness in his eyes was again the wrong companion; the apartment that overflowed with the ugly knickknacks, the cheap prints, the fake antiques he called his art collection was, again, the wrong apartment; and the Bronx with its colony of sad-eyed Jewish refugees from Germany was altogether the wrong milieu. In spite of her obvious pride in her home, in spite of the fine dinner she cooked herself and served elegantly, in spite of a new vocabulary that now included the words "my husband," "us," and "our," there was, still, that old, familiar restlessness, that urge to be "out," to go for a ride, to see a movie, to visit friends, to be noticed and admired. Here was again—in a cheaper, uglier, darker, sadder version— the apartment of my childhood. And when, during a brief absence of her husband from the room, Mother quickly whispered into my ear, "I think Harry is seeing another woman," I heard in her words again the old bitterness about "the witch who stole my husband," and I knew that nothing, nothing had ever changed for her.

It has been more than fifty years since I lived with Mother and the Mischpoke. What has been their legacy to my childhood? It was not a legacy of tradition—of family, profession, estate, country, or religion—but Mother and her sisters, Annemarie and the Mischpoke, were the only people to whom I ever belonged, belonged in a sense I had not belonged to Father or his relatives, or anybody else since. The Mischpoke had meant intimacy, an intimacy that was the mysterious composite of human warmth, tenderness,

and gaiety, of squabbles and domestic violence, of the aroma of Turkish
cigarettes, of Sunday rituals centered on home-baked cakes and "real coffee," of penny-pinching thrift one day and squandering generosity the next,
of fears without substance and happiness without reason, and of the sus-
penseful wait for Christmas Eve. Not more, not less. Mischpoke had been
home.

Visits
with Father

· ·

Father does not belong in the apartment of my childhood. He never visited us, but I felt his presence among the silent and yet so eloquent witnesses of a happier and more prosperous time in his and Mother's life: the massive, elaborately carved chairs and table in "peasant style" that crowded the dining room; the cut-crystal glasses that shot sparks of violet light; the coffee table of inlaid mosaic, the smokers' set of heavy silver. I sensed his taste and preferences in the faded Gobelins with their moody scenes of shepherds and shepherdesses, fauns, and nymphs; in the oriental rugs; and most palpably in the high, glass-enclosed cases filled with books from what once had been his library. These things expressed him as I knew him, and if I resented Mother's dates, the "uncles," it was not because they claimed Mother's attention and love, but because they occupied and made themselves at home in a place that I felt was rightfully Father's, and Father's only.

I saw him periodically but by no means regularly; Mother bitterly resented our visits, and she would make me pay for them dearly, with either tears and outbursts of hatred, or with a stony silence. Sometimes our visits would last for only a few hours, sometimes for a weekend or several days. Edith, the actress Father had married after my parents' divorce, would usually withdraw to her quarters when I arrived, but she remained an elusive and disturbing presence. Did she sense and was she embarrassed by my fascination with her? From the moment I first met her, I was drawn to her, spellbound, overcome by feelings that, had I been an adult, I would have recognized as the first alarming manifestations of a strong erotic attraction, but that, at age seven or eight, only threw me into a turmoil of fright and suspicion. Most perplexing—and something of which I gave no account to myself at the time—was her resemblance to Mother: Mother in a lighter, airier, fresher, crisper rendition. Both women had a voluptuous figure, but whereas Mother's hair was raven, Edith's was luxuriantly reddish blond. Both had a fresh and rosy complexion and large, sparkling eyes, but whereas the light in Mother's eyes seemed a reflection from a source outside herself, Edith's shone from natural inner happiness. Both were vivacious and temperamental, but where Mother's liveliness, even in moments of joyous exuberance, always seemed to be somewhat forced and overshadowed by a cloud of sadness, Edith's was spontaneous, resolute, and free from any affectation. Her father was a Jew, but I never noticed that she cultivated her Jewish legacy in any way: I could not picture her among the Mischpoke, but I could easily imagine her as a perhaps sometimes provocative but always animating guest in the respectable, well-mannered, well-ordered homes of Father's sisters. As I grew older, our relationship became more relaxed and gradually turned into friendship. I was to see her marriage to Father deteriorate and finally come apart, but our affection for each other remained intact until, during the first year of the war, she too left Germany.

The various rooms where Father and I visited over the years always seemed to look and smell alike: a desk or writing table on which a neatly stacked pile of manuscript, a pocket watch and a cigarette case of heavy silver, ashtray, blotter, and inkwell were arranged in meticulous order; books on every surface that would support them; a chair or two, and a sofa that could be converted into a bed and that he covered during the

day, as long as I knew him, with the same heavy blanket of camel hair. A
bluish haze filled the room, and the aroma of Turkish tobacco sweetened
the air. We played a game or two of cards or checkers, or just talked.
Father was not a fluent or articulate talker, but his low, soft voice was
pleasing. Impeccable in manners and immaculate in appearance, he had a
natural charm of whose almost erotic quality I was already aware when I
was still quite young. His movements were deliberate and had about them
a reflective uncertainty—the hesitancy that characterized his speech
seemed to transmit itself to the movements of his slender, almost effemi-
nately elegant hands and his tall, angular frame. But whatever his words,
his movements, his gestures were meant to convey, his inner self was most
eloquently revealed in his face: in the wide mouth with its full, sensuous
lips; the strong, fleshy nose; the high forehead with the sharp furrows
between the brows, and, most strikingly, in the eyes that seemed forever
held by something, somebody, unseen by the world around him. Even
when he listened to me—and Father was a superb listener—there was in
his expression a last line of defense, a holding back, as if he knew that his
eyes could give away whatever secrets he wanted to protect, and that the
veil he had drawn across these portals to his soul would tear at the slightest
pressure.

Father was good at playing cards and checkers; he also taught me how
to play chess, which became our favorite game and with which we were to
while away the endless hours in the bomb shelter when, during the first
couple of years of the war, a single British reconnaissance plane would
send the whole population of Berlin into basements and shelters for half
the night. But whenever the weather was favorable, he would reach for his
walking stick and we would set out for a park, a forest preserve, or a quiet
suburban boulevard. Father was a tireless walker who loved walking simply for the sake of walking, and who thought nothing of spending two
hours on his feet each way to visit a friend or a publisher's office, in
preference to taking a bus or a streetcar. He always carried a book in his
coat pocket, and when he walked by himself, he would read, stick in one
hand, book in the other close to his face, oblivious to the stares of passersby. But when we were together he would talk. Or rather, he would talk

and I would listen as best I could, trying to keep up with his pace that became faster the more he became engrossed in his monologue, oblivious then even to *my* company.

What would we talk about? What was on his mind? What formed the substance of his life during the two decades that lay between the end of one world war and the outbreak of another? Stephen Spender, the British poet, once wrote about the *entre deux guerres* generation:

> Who live under the shadow of a war
> What can I do that matters?

There were many things that mattered to Father. Among the words I picked up as a child from our conversations or his frequently vehement discussions with others were words like *separatists, French revenge, Dawes plan, socialism, League of Nations, reparations,* and others reflecting the tumult and the issues of the first decade of the Weimar Republic, but I was much too young to attach any meaning to them or to understand where he stood on the questions that moved the German intelligentsia of his day. I knew, however, where he stood on Adolf Hitler almost from the moment that name crept into the vocabulary of political discussions. I was about eight or nine when, during a stroll along Berlin's Unter den Linden, he spotted on an advertising pillar an election poster showing the mustached face of the Führer. Father stopped before the poster and, to give his words emphasis, lifted me up until I was face to face with Hitler's grim visage. "Remember this face," he said. "This man will some day destroy Germany." By the time I was old enough to discuss issues of public life, Germany's destruction had begun and the things that had moved the minds of Germans during my childhood had lost their actuality.

Sometimes we would talk about the book on which he was working, about the stacked manuscript on his desk. I never knew Father to be anything but a writer, although my parents' divorce papers list him as a "merchant." There was, after all, on the bookshelves in Mother's apartment, his German translation of Michelet's history of the French Revolution, those beautiful volumes I was fond of showing to visitors and friends. He may have done different things at different times when I was still a child, but in my memory he seemed forever to be filling page after page with his small, elegant, almost calligraphic script. Most of his literary production during the late twenties and early thirties consisted, I believe, of book and theater reviews and of feature articles for liberal newspapers and magazines. Occasionally he referred to this period of his career as his "journalistic war years," and he used to tell me—with an air of smugness he rarely displayed—how the press of the Left and the press of the Right had closed ranks in denouncing him for his liberal humanism. Whenever the conversation, during the Hitler years, turned to the problems and eventual demise of the Weimar Republic, he heatedly insisted that the press on either side of the political spectrum had been in collusion against their one common and most dangerous enemy: the voice of reason and moderation.

After Hitler came to power and silenced the free press, Father turned to editing and translating, and to what he considered his true vocation: writing books. He talked with never-diminishing enthusiasm about plans for this or that book, about meetings with publishers, about how the book that was nearing completion would once and for all put an end to the confusion and uncertainty of our lives. But the books he did succeed in getting published brought him neither fame nor even temporary relief from money worries. "Your father didn't give me any money. Ask him," was Mother's refrain when I asked her for something other than a bare necessity. Most of the time, whatever money paid for his food and rent either came from Edith's wealthy parents or from one or another of his sisters. Whenever he did get paid for something he had written, translated, or edited, he made good on a debt or gave the money to Mother.

Father was generally nonchalant about the books he had written, and he was particularly reticent about those he wrote because his publisher thought they had a ready market. *Letters of Court Ladies* was one of them. It was a collection of personal letters written by young noblewomen serving at the imperial court of the Hohenzollern during the Bismarck era. Another of his books I discovered accidentally early during the war when he asked me one day to work for a few weekends in his publisher's bindery, which was then short of help. The book being bound was titled *Woman Among Civilized Nations*—a large, expensive-looking volume lavishly illustrated with gravures of nudes. When I walked into the small shop I was embarrassed at seeing it littered with stacks of these illustrations, but my embarrassment turned to shame and something amounting to helpless anger when I discovered Father's name on the cover. I didn't mention the incident to him or question him about the book. He never told me he had written such a book, and I never saw a copy in his library.

There was one book of which he always kept a copy among his possessions: a biography of Greta Garbo. The book was the result of his brief affiliation during the late thirties with the UFA (Universum Film Aktiengesellschaft), for which he read French novels and plays to extract from them story material for motion pictures. None of his ideas was ever turned into a film, but having access to the archives of Europe's largest film producer, he used the opportunity to write the story of a woman whom he admired, not because she was a great actress (he didn't think she was), but because he saw in her one of those rare actresses who are persuasive and arresting because they remain true to their soul in every role they play. *Woman Among Civilized Nations* had exploited Father's talent and poverty for the publisher's gain, and I am certain Father disavowed the book the moment he turned in the manuscript. *Greta Garbo: The Life of a Woman and Artist* he had enjoyed writing. It bore the dedication "For Mrs. Edith Kühn," although when it was published in 1941, Edith, the actress he had married, had already left Germany and their separation had become permanent.

Edith once told me that Father was still an agnostic when he married her; he was then forty years old. What had drawn him to Christianity, and why did he convert to Catholicism? Perhaps because of his mother's influence, Roman Catholicism had always had an attraction for him, accounting for his insistence that Annemarie and I be baptized as Catholics. I was still quite small when he first exposed me to the romance and grandeur of Roman Catholicism. Whenever I stayed in the homes of his sisters in Cologne or Mainz, and he happened to visit there, we spent hours walking through the cathedral and medieval churches of these cities, and we sometimes took long excursions along the Rhine for the sole purpose of visiting a church of which he was particularly fond. He knew the story of every stained-glass window, every statue, every tomb, every patron saint, and although his rapid and enthusiastic recital of names and dates and events often confused and tired me, I perfectly understood, as young as I was, that he talked with the tongue of a lover, not with the tongue of a historian. Father's excited whisper; the cool, dark solemnity of these sacred vaults; the embarrassingly irreverent echo of my hobnailed boots; the mysterious glow of soaring windows; and the wintry smell of granite tombs—these impressions are as indelibly a part of Father's picture as are his desk, his books, his cigarettes, and his tattered suitcases.

As a historian, Father was of course particularly receptive to the architectural and artistic manifestations of Catholicism in history, but the intellectual impetus to his conversion came from books. I suspect that many of the authors who had a strong religious influence on him and his generation are by now largely forgotten. "The history of literature," Heinrich Heine says in his *Romantic School,* "is the great morgue where everyone seeks out his dead whom he loves or to whom he is related." Theodor Haecker, for example, now rests in that quiet place. A contemporary of Father's generation, Haecker was a German Protestant philosopher who translated and wrote about Cardinal Newman, Kierkegaard, Vergil, Hilaire Belloc, and Francis Thompson, and whose conversion to Catholicism decisively influenced Father's own conversion. I was in my late teens when I first read him, and I still remember the power, lucidity, and poetic fervor of his language. Yet when, in the spring of 1971, I visited a friend in Berlin and, having come across an edition of Haecker's works in his library, asked him, "What does one think of Haecker nowadays?" he replied laconically, "Nobody reads him."

Perhaps Ernest Hello (1828–1885) is another inhabitant of that morgue. Father translated his *Physiognomies des Saints* (Portraits of Saints) and *L'homme* (Man) into German, and the two books are now on my shelves among the volumes I have salvaged from the apartment of my childhood. Hello was a French critic and lay theologian who in his books and philosophical and critical essays revealed and castigated the intellectual dishonesty and shallowness of nineteenth-century rationalism and positivism, and whose critical essays on Victor Hugo and Shakespeare have a permanent place among this genre of literature. But Hello was above all a mystic for whom all problems of man and society converged in what he called "the problem of adoration." In him Father found the articulation of what he knew to be the driving force in his own life. Father talked frequently about "the problem of adoration"; it was, in fact, the central theme of all his favorite authors, no matter how sharply they differed among each other on specific religious, social, or political issues.

Besides Hello, the three writers I remember best from our conversations are Görres, Brentano, and de Maistre. Joseph von Görres, the most influential German writer and political publicist of the Napoleonic era, was Catholic, liberal, passionately anti-Prussian, and cosmopolitan. On the other hand, Clemens Brentano, the novelist and poet who wrote some of the finest lyrics of the period of German romanticism, was a convert to Catholicism, a sentimentalist in his personal conduct, and politically naive. Joseph de Maistre, their French contemporary, was a traditionalist historian and philosopher, a political polemicist, and ultraconservative in his religious views. But all three of them had the talent, the gift of mysticism, to see in a personal God the source, the unifying and vivifying principle, and the fulfillment of everything that is.

More important, for these writers God had irrevocably become a participant in the bloody, violent history of his creatures, and it was for them unthinkable to speak about social, cultural, or political reforms without speaking in the same breath about God. Their vision spoke powerfully to Father's instinct as a historian. Long before he became a Christian that same vision may have drawn him to Michelet. As a historian, Michelet is notoriously unreliable, but his visionary qualities, his deep insights into the creative forces of history, his perception of the demonic and the divine in the life of nations make him the most stimulating writer in his field. Michelet remained one of the favorite guests in Father's intellectual household, as did, for example, Heinrich Heine, whom he considered an Israelite of the Old Covenant at heart, or Nietzsche, who strongly influenced him in his youth and whose unredeemed mysticism he took seriously. But he scorned (a contempt that had already caused him great difficulties in his student years) most of the textbook heroes of German literature and history: Goethe, Richard Wagner, Frederick the Great, Bismarck, Rilke. "They are Teutons," he used to say. "They brood too much." Had he not found his way to Christianity, I suspect he would have chosen Heine as his literary patron saint.

Much of what Father and I talked about during my growing-up years, or what I sensed without words, I understood only much later. I grasped, though, what mattered to him, and I felt that the world he loved and in which he was at home was crumbling all around him. The Weimar Republic, in which he had fervently believed as the only hope for a democratic system that would work in Germany, had disintegrated. Secular humanism, the worldview built on the great ideas and traditions of the Enlightenment and the French Revolution, no longer furnished him with the visions he needed to nourish his inner life. Roman Catholicism attracted him irresistibly, but his divorce from Mother and his marriage to Edith, the precarious nature of which he had undoubtedly realized almost from its beginning, offered formidable obstacles to his acceptance into the Church.

Yet I felt that there were roots, deep and strong, that kept nourishing him, no matter how restless his outer life may have been, or how turbulent his inner world. The cities of the Rhineland where his sisters lived with their families—Cologne, Mainz, Düsseldorf—may have been too provincial for him to settle there, but he often visited them, and he particularly loved that region where his parents and ancestors had lived. He was at home in its history, he was fond of its foods and wines, he knew the customs and various dialects of its people, he sang its songs, and he could retell its legends and fairy tales. As much as he admired the French and may have thought of himself as an intellectually displaced Frenchman, he was as emphatically and visibly a German of the Rhenish persuasion as the Rhine itself. For most of his life it was his fate to be homeless in the literal sense, but unlike Mother and the Mischpoke, he never appeared rootless or a stranger in his own country. His was a solitary existence by temperament and circumstances, but he never appeared lonesome. He strayed often from what he knew to be his road, but he never appeared to have lost his way.

My visits with him were indispensable for me and, I am sure, also for him. He was my only guide. If nothing else, I needed him to talk about the books I read, about Mother and the Mischpoke, about my visits with the aunts and uncles in the Rhineland, about my teachers and classmates, about my hopes and fears and longings. There was not much he could *do;*

we met, talked for a while or played a game, perhaps enjoyed a few days
of growing intimacy, and parted again for weeks or months. Living each
in a world that was radically different from that of the other, we had to
renew, at every visit, that familiarity, that closeness we had felt when last
we had parted. Perhaps he helped me most during my growing-up years by
being who he was: a man I loved and respected, indeed admired, and
whom I sought to emulate. There were in my world many voices, too
many, claiming my attention, my love, my respect, and my obedience.
His was the only one I longed to hear, I wanted to listen to. But now there
would soon be added to these voices another voice, a voice that drowned
out all others, and sometimes even his, a voice that screamed of race and
blood and honor, and of Jews.

Different Drummers

· ·

When did I first realize that the people among whom I grew up were first of all Jews before they were anything else; that this fact, and this fact alone, isolated them from many and made them despicable to some, and that I shared to some degree their acknowledged or unacknowledged isolation? That Judaism was a religion different from Christianity or, for that matter, from Buddhism, I had known from the time one learns such things in grade school, but what I now came to learn was that Jews were set apart as people, as citizens, or—by the definition of a voice that sounded ever shriller in the marketplace—as a race.

If I have to date the beginning of a rising consciousness in me that I was Jewish, it was probably in 1930, when that voice began to be heard and to be taken seriously. Until then, that voice—that howl, that shriek—had been just another sound in the cacophony of voices clamoring for attention. Father had lifted me up, when I was still little, to a picture of the man, pasted on an advertising pillar, and prophesied the catastrophe of the Third Reich. But Father was a prophet, and being a true prophet he went unheard. Of course, I saw the Brownshirts marching down the Kurfürstendamm, watched them ride by in open trucks decked out with swastika banners, singing, and bawling "Juda verrecke"—Death to Judaism. Of course, I met them when they, tin can in hand, arrogantly pushed their way through the tables of a sidewalk café to collect money for their cause, or when they stood threateningly in front of stores owned by Jews, glowering at Mother and me when we dared to enter. But others, too, marched, collected, sang: Communists, Social Democrats, German Nationals, Liberals, dozens, scores of noisy throngs parading *their* uniforms, waving *their* banners, shouting *their* slogans. To me, to Mother, to the Mischpoke, and to almost everybody else I knew they were part of the familiar, common *Strassenlärm*—the Noise of the Street—to which we were accustomed and which we ignored unless a bloody brawl developed or the sound of guns made people scatter. At home, at school, I heard few people talk about politics. Father did incessantly, but he also talked as vehemently about books, religion, philosophy, and history, and much of what he said was above my comprehension. Father talked about anti-Semitism, too, and I believed him when he said that he feared for his Jewish friends. But where I lived, in the apartment, among the Mischpoke, the word was rarely mentioned. Hitler, in the words of Mother and her friends, was a tomfool, a clown, an idiot, a monkey. It would be some time yet before they would call him a criminal.

In 1930, Hitler's voice became distinctive, drowning out all other voices. That year, when I was ten, I entered a boarding school in Potsdam as a gymnasium freshman. The school, the State Institute of Education, had been a prestigious military academy in the kaiser era; it was still run like a military academy and for the most part attended by the sons of families who would have wanted their children to choose an officer's career had a German army then existed. I don't know who chose the school for me nor who paid the substantial tuition, but the result of this brutal separation from my environment, this assault on everything I knew to be my true, my own nature, should have been predictable: for three years I was in a state resembling shock. The day Mother walked with me through the forbidding portal set into the endless, high brick wall surrounding the spacious grounds, my childhood ended. Whatever had happened before that day, whoever I had been before that day, has, in my memory, the fine, mysterious flush of childhood. Whatever happened afterward, whoever I became afterward, lies in the cold light of a well-remembered past.

The experience of those three years I spent in Potsdam was the all-too-common experience of a sensitive, somewhat spoiled, emotionally unstable child who, having grown up in the company of women, is tormented by the regimentation, the harsh discipline, the total lack of privacy in vast dormitories and crowded study halls, and the locker-room atmosphere of a boys' boarding school: I was desperately homesick. Our teachers and headmasters were of different political persuasions, of different party loyalties, and although some of them occasionally used the classroom or the dining hall to break into political oratory, by and large they respected the rule that politics was not to be discussed at school. They were knowledgeable and devoted; the curriculum was demanding, and time-off was scarce. Among my fellow students, politics was talked about the way boys in their early teens talk about such things, but I don't recall that I ever became the target of anyone's hostility or, for that matter, that anyone except a few teachers knew that my mother was Jewish. I felt isolated and was lonely, not because anyone saw behind me the *Judenfratze,* "the ugly grimace of the Jew," but because I did not want to—did not know how to—mingle; because I loathed a life stressing physical prowess; and because I was in constant fear of the brutal beating—"lower your pants, bend down"— handed out for the slightest infraction of a rule. "Judenkühn" (Jew Kuehn) was a taunt I did not hear until, years later, I had entered a Catholic boarding school.

During the three years I spent in Potsdam—from 1930 to 1933—Berlin turned into a battleground where Nazis, Communists, and half a dozen other parties fought each other for supremacy in the streets. The school permitted us, as a matter of course, to visit parents or relatives in Berlin once a month, but as the tumult increased and bloodshed became increasingly frequent in the city, we had to obtain from the person we wanted to visit a special request for such a weekend leave, absolving the school from all responsibility, and on our return to school we had to produce a signed slip that we had, indeed, spent the weekend with that person. The school did its best to protect us from bodily harm, but it could

. . . .

not protect me against the Strassenlärm that now thickened to a roar of
hate pierced incessantly by the word *Jews,* as a shrill bell pierces the din of
a vicious storm.

At what moment, and by which process, does one know, at any stage in
one's life, with sudden certainty that one is linked forever, bound insep-
arably, to something, somebody? That one has lost the freedom to say yes
or no to a person, a situation, a condition? At some time during those three
years at Potsdam, one morning, one evening, one Sunday afternoon, I
knew, I saw with clarity, that I was linked to a people who aroused antag-
onism, suspicion, fear, and hate in others. Was that the "difference" I had
sensed all along but never grasped? I began to realize that my mother
could be despicable to someone, not because of something she had said or
done, but because of something Jews did to Germany, and that I, because I
was her son, shared in that despicability. The voice was ubiquitous and
trenchant, repeating its simple message with a hypnotic monotony. Even a
confused twelve-year-old quickly understood what it said, what was at
stake. The radio, the loudspeakers in the streets, the placards, the leaflets,
the graffiti, allowed no room for intellectual or emotional equivocation:
Jews, the voices screamed, are a culture-destroying race, hook-nosed
greedy hunchbacks, parasites sucking the lifeblood of an unsuspecting
Germany. They must be eradicated.

On January 30, 1933, the aging and by then virtually senile President von
Hindenburg appointed Hitler Reich Chancellor. A few weeks later, on
March 21, I was among the throng of spectators surrounding the square of
Potsdam's Garrison Church where Hitler and Hindenburg, in a symbolic
show of unity, were to celebrate the rebirth of a united Germany under
Hitler's leadership. As the procession of dignitaries approached the church,
I saw for the first time the man whose voice I had long come to fear: the
puffed-up face, the sallow skin, the darkly veiled eyes, the fleshy nose
supported by a dark bristle that, close-up, looked artificial and faintly
ridiculous. It was a disappointingly ordinary face. Stony, expressionless, it
reminded me of streetcar conductors, factory workers, and policemen, and
its insignificance was not redeemed but rather accentuated by the stiff white
collar, the black swallow-tail, the striped trousers that, incongruously,
draped the stocky figure. At his side, like a giant who had stepped out of the

pages of an illustrated text of Prussian history, towered the ancient President von Hindenburg in the gala uniform of a Prussian general field marshal of the kaiser era, complete with piqued helmet, droopy mustache, shiny hip boots, sash and saber, and bemedaled breast. I may not have appreciated fully the striking symbolism of the two figures, but their significance was so obvious, so forceful, that a boy next to me began to giggle, and when I looked at him he whispered, "I think they borrowed the old man from some museum as a decoration." In historical perspective, it turned out to be an uncanny remark.

Shortly after this event the school was turned into a National Political Training Institute, one of the boarding schools personally selected by Hitler to educate and train a generation of elite Nazi leadership. When we were put into smart brown uniforms, Father, knowing that my expulsion would be only a matter of time, took me out of the school. I lived again with Mother and Annemarie in an apartment in West Berlin—some apartment within walking distance from the Kaiser Wilhelm Memorial Church—but it was no longer the place of my childhood, and Mother and the Mischpoke were no longer the human cocoon that once had given me a measure of warmth, love, and security. Berlin resembled a city occupied by a foreign power: the flags, the uniforms, the insignia, the hymns of the victors were everywhere. Yet few sensed as yet the brutal will, the deadly aim, under the camouflage of festivity. "The students burned a lot of books last night in front of the university," Mother said one morning at breakfast. "Good God, kids really are getting out of hand these days." Mother could not be blamed for being casual about the affair. The Burning of the Books, which occurred on May 10, 1933, had been staged by the Nazis to symbolize the end in Germany of Marxist, Jewish, and other "degenerate" literature that included authors such as Heinrich Heine, André Gide, and Erich Maria Remarque, but the press and the radio, on instructions from the Ministry of Propaganda, had played the incident down. I would have forgotten Mother's comment had I not discussed the conflagration with Father. He had been outraged by it—and by Mother's remark. "Just because Berliners are tolerant of Jews and think the Nazis are a nuisance doesn't mean that the Nazis will leave the Jews alone," he said, his face revealing clearly his anxiety about the fate that threatened

Mother and her sisters. "The handwriting is on the wall, but, as usual, your mother lives in a make-believe world." Perhaps she did.

Outwardly, life in the apartment went on as it had during my childhood. The sign *Juden unerwünscht* (Jews unwanted) that now appeared on the beaches, in the parks, on the doors of restaurants, shops, and theaters, did not exist for Mother. "Am I really unwanted?" she would laughingly ask the young man in the cashier's booth of the neighborhood theater. My heart would pound, but Mother would nonchalantly stride to her accustomed row. The whirl of the Mischpoke continued unabated: shopping along the Kurfürstendamm, evenings out on the town. Yet underneath the laughter, the nonchalance, I sensed a growing uneasiness. They had become people who woke to a new day with doubt, who seemed to walk the street as one walks in enemy territory. When we sat in a sidewalk café, their smiles seemed contrived, and they had lost their zest, their pleasure in planning an outing to the zoo or a New Year's celebration. They delighted in telling jokes about the Nazi leaders—this was the time when such jokes proliferated like mosquitoes in the sultry air before a storm—but when a stranger came within earshot, the conversation ceased. Occasionally there was talk of someone who was selling the family jewels to raise money to go to China or America, or Mother gave a farewell kaffeeklatsch for a cousin or a friend. But she did not talk about America or China; the old concerns of my childhood remained her real concerns: the court bailiff who would come to claim the furniture because she could not pay the rent; Father, who failed to pay his alimony; or an "uncle" who had proved a disappointing companion. I saw that her world was shrinking, that her life was aimless, and I became restless in an apartment where the air was stifling, but Mother seemed to pay no heed.

Annemarie and I suffered no restrictions. The gymnasium I now attended—an institution founded in the kaiser era—was known for the excellence of its curriculum, and our teachers did not compromise its reputation. They maintained discipline effortlessly, kept us to our books and papers, and dismissed us with a staggering amount of homework. On the walls of the classrooms there was a picture of Hitler next to one of Hindenburg, and some of my classmates showed off the uniform of the Hitler Youth, but aside from these few outward manifestations of the new order of things, nothing else made school more difficult than I had always found it to be. When it was announced one day that "Heil Hitler" would now replace the "Good morning" with which teachers and students customarily had begun a class, most of my teachers ignored the order or kept silent altogether. Once, in biology class, the teacher called me to the blackboard and asked that I show the class my profile, to demonstrate the shape of a typical Aryan skull. The incident amused Mother and the Mischpoke but annoyed me; I suspected that the teacher knew perfectly well how much of an "Aryan" I was, and that he had used me to show his cynicism about the doctrine of races he was forced to include in his curriculum.

Intrusion of the ideological dictates of the Third Reich jeopardized in particular that curriculum for which these dictates had been defined most sharply and where any disregard of them could have had the gravest consequences for the teacher, including deportation to a concentration camp: Germanics—German literature and history. *Deutsch* took the greater part in the humanistic branch of higher education I had chosen, and for nine years I was drilled in a thorough knowledge of the giants of the German tongue. The demands of a German gymnasium were high: in each of the four I attended between 1930 and 1938, classes began at eight in the morning and ended at two in the afternoon, except on Saturdays when school let out at one. The afternoons, much of most evenings, and frequently a part of Sunday were taken up by homework. I learned quickly, remembered easily, and preferred Deutsch to any other subject, but even I found it difficult to keep up with the pace. We read and discussed the German classics, wrote lengthy compositions about them, and, most important, learned by heart many of the best, or most famous, things the authors had written. More than forty years after I was graduated, I still know by heart numerous passages from Goethe's *Faust* and from his other works, whether in prose or rhyme. I still have the same recall—which may not be instant any more but quick enough, given a bit of thought or, even better, a glass or two of good wine— of many of the poems, songs, and lines of plays by such favorites of mine as Schiller, Ludwig Uhland, Friedrich Klopstock, Heinrich von Kleist, Joseph von Eichendorff, and Heine. This heritage, taught persuasively if sometimes pedantically by teachers who knew their stuff, believed in what they taught, and loved it, has endured and retained its vigor and perennial freshness under the vicissitudes of my life.

Perhaps this is the secret of why I not only remember the classics of German literature but why so much of what such authors wrote still sustains me, often at moments when I least expect their intrusion into my thoughts and feelings. My teachers themselves lived out of that immense and immensely rich treasury of the German language, and today I know that they wanted to transmit to us not merely knowledge, an obligatory curriculum, but survival rations for the road ahead. And perhaps more: a vision of Germany and of things German that was in desperate peril. The last six of my nine years at the gymnasium fell in the time of the Nazi regime. As a half-Jew I was perhaps more sensitive to the outrages of that ideology than most of my classmates, but I recall nothing from all those years that smacked of the "guidelines" put out by the Ministry of Education. We were taught literature, not the social merits or abuses of literature. For my teachers—gray-haired *Studienräte* (professors) most of them, who had survived the First World War and had made their careers under the Weimar Republic—language mastered by genius was intrinsically beautiful and valuable. Whether a poem, a novel, or a drama confirmed or denied, supported or attacked, an ideology, a belief, or a conviction was the listener's or reader's task to decide—not the teacher's or, least of all, the state's. I suspect my teachers became all the more scrupulously objective the greater the restraints that were forced on them by the state-approved curriculum. Were they hiding their abiding distaste for the regime behind the mask of an impeccable objectivity? "This poem reflects the sentiments of the romantic school"; "This drama is in the vein of the New Naturalism"; "Here we have one of the finest examples of an expressionist novel"—our teachers should have told us that romanticism was highly suspect, that individualism and expressionism were incompatible with the new consciousness of *Volk,* of nationhood, of blood and soil, and of a German destiny. They never did. They would have choked on the very words.

One of the few books that have survived the destruction of my own library during the war is Paul Fechter's *History of German Literature.* Fechter was one of the most renowned literary critics of my parents' gener-

· ·

ation. He became a Nazi sympathizer and in the 1940 edition of his *History* revised his views on German literature to accommodate the Nazi doctrines. In that edition he devotes two chapters—"The Great Turning Point" and "The New Age"—to the writers in whom, according to the regime, German literature had attained its zenith. He reviews at length some thirty of these men and women. All of them wrote at the time I went to school, but I never heard of their existence.

What *did* teach us the spirit of the new age was something else: the sharply, painfully felt contrast between the world of great German literature and the vulgarity of the new German reality. We would be sitting in class, for example, the windows open to a blue sky and the fresh green of spring, listening to the teacher's or a classmate's recital of a poem. It could have been any poem by any of the classics. Perhaps it was one of Friedrich Hölderlin's, perhaps his *Menschenbeifall* (Crowd Applause):

> Ist nicht heilig mein Herz, schöneren Lebens voll,
> Seit ich liebe? warum achtetet ihr mich mehr,
> Da ich stolzer und wilder,
> Wortreicher und leerer war?

> Ach, der Menge gefällt, was auf den Marktplatz taugt,
> Und es ehrt der Knecht nur den Gewaltsamen;
> An das Göttliche glauben
> Die allein, die es selbst sind.

> [My heart, is it not holy, full of life still more beautiful
> Now that I love? Why did you pay me greater respect
> When I was prouder and wilder,
> more loquacious and emptier?

> Alas! it pleases the crowd what is fit for the marketplace,
> And the serf honors but him who is brutal;
> Those only believe in the divine
> Who are divine themselves.]

(My translation)

And while we listened, attentive, perhaps entranced, we would hear, suddenly, the beat of combat boots on cobbled pavement, muffled at first, then growing louder, and then a song would rise up and shatter the stillness, silence the voice of the reader, destroy feelings and images. It could have been any of the marching songs that reverberated in the streets of Berlin in those days. Perhaps we heard:

Es zittern die morschen Knochen
Der Welt vor dem grossen Krieg.
Wir haben die Fesseln zerbrochen.
Für uns war's ein grosser Sieg.
Wir werden weiter marschieren
Bis alles in Scherben fällt!
Denn heute gehört uns Deutschland*
Und morgen die ganze Welt.

[The world's brittle bones tremble
Before the great war.
We have broken the chains.
A great victory was ours.
We will march on
Until everything lies in ruins!
Because today we own Germany
And tomorrow the whole world.]
                                        (My translation)

Whether the incident happened exactly as I describe it, whether it happened at all, doesn't matter. The time was full of such tearing contrasts—in sights and sounds, in thoughts and feelings. Still in our malleable years, we lived in a world of tension and conflict, too young to escape into compromise, as did many of our elders. We were young enough to choose sides without probing, and some of us did. We were young enough to ignore conflict and questions, and many of us did. But those of us who were sensitive to such things kept asking, "What is true? The Germany of great literature that seemed to have no spokesman in the marketplace, or the Germany of the streets, the radio, and the public press?" On that question, our teachers had to remain silent. Answering it would have been

*The original text of the song reads: "Denn heute *hört* uns Deutschland" (Today Germany hears us). However, *hört* was commonly sung as *gehört*, meaning "own" and changing the text as it is rendered here.

tantamount to a political confession. What they did was to give us the stuff from which we could, if we cared, form an inner core of knowledge and perception that was unassailable by the new masters of our social existence. Whether we would accept their gift, and how we would use it, was up to us.

For Father, my higher education had always been a prime concern, and he carefully selected each gymnasium I attended. Mother could not afford to send me to a gymnasium, and Father, himself chronically penniless, frequently begged the tuition, which was substantial in case of a boarding school, from one or another of his well-off sisters. Now that I was in the last years of the gymnasium, in my mid-teens, and able to hold my own in our conversations, he took a livelier-than-ever interest in what I was being taught. My own conversion to Catholicism (which, since I had been baptized a Catholic as an infant, was more in the nature of a promise of allegiance to the teachings of the Church) followed naturally and effortlessly from our discussions at that time. One Sunday morning in 1934, when I was fourteen, he asked me to accompany him to mass. Afterward, at breakfast, he simply asked, "Did you like it?" I said I had. It had been my first attendance at mass, and his invitation had come without forewarning, but the experience, far from taking me off guard, had touched me as though it were something I had expected for a long time, had, indeed, waited for as one waits for the final explanation, the final clarification in a leisurely conversation. A year later, I was received into the Church.

Annemarie, too, took lessons in the Catholic catechism, but she held to the faith she had been taught in Protestant schools more stubbornly than I. We still shared a bedroom then, and often, after Mother had kissed us goodnight, we would argue in the darkness about the slyness of the Jesuits or the cold impersonality of a Lutheran service. On the day of our first communion I walked with burning embarrassment among a file of children two heads smaller than I, and afterward Mother had a kaffeeklatsch to which she had invited the priest and the Mischpoke. She was genuinely happy when I became an altar boy; she helped me memorize the Latin responses and even accompanied me occasionally to a mass at which I served. A year or so later she herself became a Catholic. But if she had hoped that this step would clear the way for a reconciliation with Father, she was to be bitterly disappointed. Father's decision to take up the burden of that gospel whose manifestations in history he had for so long admired and loved may have given him a share of that peace which the world cannot give, but that same decision had harsh consequences for Mother and Edith.

I attended the hearing at which my parents' marriage was dissolved by the Church by virtue of the Pauline Privilege that, under certain conditions, makes it possible for converts to remarry while the former partner is still alive. I remember a large, gloomy room whose wooden floor was bare and highly polished. On one wall hung a tall white crucifix. Father, Mother, Annemarie, and I were sitting on chairs, far apart from each other. An old man (whom I didn't recognize as a priest then) with a mane of white hair faced us across a fortresslike desk that seemed to occupy half of the room. Mother and Annemarie were sobbing. Whatever was on that day set in order in the eyes of Father and the Church, it caused only profound misery for both women. For Mother, it destroyed any hope that Father would one day return to her and his children. For Edith, too, Father's conversion set an end to her hopes for a permanent union. After the Church had sanctioned my parents' civil divorce, Father could have had his marriage to Edith sacramentally validated by a remarriage in the Church. Yet he never took this step. Instead, they separated, although they continued to see each other frequently, and periodically even lived under the same roof. Whatever treasure Father had found by becoming a Christian had remained hidden from the women who loved him. They experienced only the sword of the kingdom.

Shortly after my conversion I joined a Catholic boys' organization. Neudeutschland (New Germany) was a Christian-Catholic version of the youth movements that had sprung up during the neoromanticist era to nourish a love of nature, community, tradition, and fatherland amid an environment that became increasingly technological and dehumanized. Founded by the Jesuits, it professed the reformation of German life in Christ. Its political purpose was to prepare young Catholic men in gymnasiums and universities for strategic positions in academia, industry, and government. Our motto was *mens sana in corpore sano* (a healthy mind in a healthy body); our emblem, a black Chi-Rho on a silver background. We wore black uniforms—from black velvet jackets and shorts to black socks and black hobnailed boots—and when we marched in the streets to the reverberating, spine-chilling sounds of numerous snare and kettle drums, we were led by huge banners emblazoned with the multicolored heraldry of German medieval imperialism. It was a time for uniforms, for marches, drums, and banners. Of course, only one uniform counted, only one ideology had power. Sometimes our march was blocked by Hitler Youth; occasionally, on a camping trip, our tents were set on fire. But as long as we had the opportunity to parade our beliefs in public, we did not shy away from a fistfight or a bloody brawl.

For the first time in my life I experienced the elation of belonging to a community of young men bound together and inspired by common ideals; for the first time I had a sense of liberation from the old, familiar anxieties. In school, when the Nazi regime decreed that physical education had to take precedence over anything else in the curriculum, my love of sports had turned into hatred for the brutal and mindless glorification of physical prowess. For Neudeutschland, sports was the training of the body for the rigors of a crusader's life, and the image called up before us by our group leaders was that of Saint Paul the missionary. This was a language I understood; sports now had a meaning and a purpose independent of the acclaim of "the world."

At home, books, as often as they were refuge, consolation, and inspiration, just as often were the source of confusion, secret desires, and bad dreams. Now, read aloud beside a softly crackling campfire, or recited to the muted strains of a flute or guitar, in a room lit only by wax candles whose sweet fragrance was a token of peace and fulfillment, books became songs, sparks that lit up the dark landscape of a hidden and beautiful reality, reassurances that dreams were to come true—that indeed they had come true—that, yes, chastity was possible, virtue was alive, God was in the cool morning breeze and in the fire on the mountaintop, and that the "world" belonged to "us." Uniforms, the despicable symbol of conformity and faceless power, now were a sign of "our" unity, a public proclamation of the truth and of our readiness for martyrdom. Often, walking home after an evening group meeting, dressed in my black uniform, I would purposely choose a route that would take me along the brightly lit, busy Kurfürstendamm or other crowded streets. Imagining admiring glances from startled passersby, I would hold my head high, throw out my chest, and hum a song that spoke of Christ's victory over darkness, sin, and death, until suddenly my knees would weaken and my hands turn clammy from the desperate effort to hide my embarrassment and self-consciousness. I was not given to ostentation.

Perhaps in those moments my body told me something that my mind came to understand and accept only years later: the complexities of my life could not be resolved by easy camaraderie, uniforms, campfires, and the romantic notions of a "New Germany in Christ." While we sang of the blue flower hidden under the snow on the mountainside, of knights in black armor and castles with golden gates, other thoughts and images kept intruding: Mother and the Mischpoke selling their jewelry to raise the money that would help them to escape Germany and the concentration camp; Father withdrawing from Edith into the unapproachable solitude of a hermit; friends and neighbors, in dreadful defection from life or integrity, committing suicide or making dishonorable pacts with the regime. A Catholic youth movement cast into the mold of a nationalistic, Teutonic romanticism had no answers for situations such as these. At bottom simplistic, monolithic, and rigidly humorless, it offered at best a gospel that ignored its debt to Abraham, Isaac, and Jacob, to Moses and the prophets, and that excluded the Jews as once the primitive Church had ignored and excluded the Gentiles. The books we read and discussed went well with campfires, guitars, black banners, and the fragrance of wax candles: books by Gertrud von LeFort, Romano Guardini, Werner Bergengruen, Rainer Maria Rilke, Reinhold Schneider. They and others were then, and in some ways have remained, the best that Catholic literature had to offer to a generation growing up amid the cataclysmic upheavals of a new age and struggling for a foothold, for an ideal, a vision, a belief. If ever there had been such a thing as a Holy Roman Empire of the German Nation—with the stress on "Holy," and if ever there was to be a reformation of

German life in Christ, their visions were compelling, their arguments convincing, their imagery arresting.

But there were others who spoke to me as powerfully, as persuasively as they: Thomas and Heinrich Mann, Heinrich Heine, André Gide, Bertolt Brecht, Hermann Hesse, Ernst Jünger—the books in Father's case, my companions in the apartment of my childhood. Their visions, their images, the dreams with which they had nourished, or frightened, or seduced me had not paled when I became a Catholic. For Father there was no longer a conflict between their world and the world of those writers who took faith, Catholic faith, for granted. He had learned to see everything "sub specie aeternitatis"—from the viewpoint of an all-encompassing eternity. I was still young, still searching, but I sensed that, if there was a vision that encompassed the conflicts, the paradoxes, and the contradictions that troubled me, it could not be the vision of a Germany reformed in Christ.

Early in 1936 I once again changed schools. Perhaps Father felt that I should have a Catholic education during my last two years in the gymnasium, an education neither he nor the school in Berlin could give me. Perhaps, too, he sensed my nagging doubts about New Germany and feared that it would alienate me from Catholicism altogether. Perhaps he hoped a Catholic education would provide the environment for a vocation to the priesthood. Yet the moment I walked through the gate of the Catholic boarding school in Opladen, near Cologne, my heart sank: there were again the dim corridors of Potsdam, the common study hall, the common dining room, the locker-room talk, the rules, the line-ups, the headmaster's cane. Yet the Roman collars of our teachers, the cross on the wall of every room, the daily mass, and the prayers before class and meals had an effect: here, I felt, was a community whose life, whose teachings, dared to challenge the regime in power, and I wanted to declare my solidarity. One day I decided to wear the black uniform of New Germany. Alas, I had not counted on the all-pervasive fear among teachers and students loyal to the Church that any ostentation of protest against the Nazi regime, be it ever so symbolic, would be reported to the authorities and bring their wrath upon the school. My classmates seemed to avoid me, and my teachers did not return my smile. I sensed failure. At night, alone in my curtained cubicle in the dormitory, I was jumped and beaten. The next morning I found the uniform, torn and soiled, in the lavatory.

From then on I kept to myself. If Father had hoped that a closed Catholic environment would remove me from the turmoil of the time and help me to come to terms with my own conflicts, he had deceived himself. There was a great restlessness in the school, a kind of passive resistance among the students that showed itself in the frustration of the teachers rather than in open acts of disobedience or rebellion by the students. For the boarders, civilian clothes were the rule, but among the students who lived at home and came only to morning classes and sports, the number of those wearing the uniform of the Hitler Youth increased from semester to semester. They stayed away from mass and ostentatiously remained silent during prayer. The priests were afraid to lay hands on them, and their impertinence infected the boarders.

One day, while I was in town on an errand to Opladen's post office, I stopped to look into a display case of Nazi propaganda material among which were exhibited the pages of *Der Stürmer* (The storm trooper), a viciously anti-Semitic tabloid. A headline running something like "Mass Conversion of Jews to Catholicism" probably had caught my attention. In a long list of Jews who, as the paper would have it, "had become Catholics in an attempt to escape the wrath of the German people," I read Mother's name, together with her address, her place of employment, the dates of her marriage and divorce, and my name and my sister's. In panic I called Mother in Berlin and implored her to go into hiding for a while, but she refused. She neither moved out of her apartment nor did she leave the small firm on the Kurfürstendamm where she worked as a secretary. Quietly protected by her employer and her colleagues, she suffered no repercussions.

Shortly after this incident I returned to Berlin, enrolled in yet another gymnasium, and a few months later, in September 1938, was graduated. I was now nineteen years old, and when the chaplain of the Catholic Students' Home offered me a rent-free room in return for some housekeeping chores, I took a part-time job as a delivery boy and moved out of the apartment of my childhood.

My plans for the future were vague. I knew that in another year I would be drafted for the obligatory six months' stint in the Reichsarbeitsdienst (State Labor Service) to be followed by two years of service in the armed forces. For the moment, I had to sort out my position in Nazi Germany as a half-Jew or, as I was now officially called, "Mischling of the First Degree"—mixed breed or hybrid who had two Jewish grandparents but did not adhere to the Jewish religion. Unlike Jews, whom the Nuremberg Laws had deprived of their German citizenship in 1935, I was still legally a German citizen and not subject to organized harrassment or deportation, but my rights and opportunities were virtually as restricted as those of aliens. To the Nazis, the term *Mischling I* was half a mark of infamy; to others, half a badge of honor. Some of my Catholic comrades were embarrassed when they heard the word from my lips; a few made little effort to hide their contempt or hostility. Before making any definite plans for my future, I felt, I first had to define my role vis à vis the people with whom I might have to live and work, come to terms with a stigma that, by official decree, set me apart from them without threatening to remove me from their midst. As it turned out, a swift sequence of events was about to relieve me of the necessity to make far-reaching decisions.

On Monday, November 7, 1938, a few weeks after my graduation, the third secretary of the German Embassy in Paris was killed by a Polish Jew. I urged Mother to stay away from the office and off the street for a few days, but she would have none of it. The following Wednesday, walking home late in the evening from some meeting, I noticed in the dark sky a faint reddish glow and became aware of the smell of smoke. Approaching the Kurfürstendamm I heard a confused, agitated noise, the crash of splintering glass, and the sound of high-pitched voices harshly distorted by loudspeakers. Immediately, instinctively, I knew what was happening. The moment I turned into the brightly lit avenue, broken glass, glittering like diamond dust, crunched under my feet. Before the devastated Jewish stores, brown-shirted storm troopers, legs spread and arms folded, were staring defiantly at the onlookers that crowded the sidewalks in unbelieving, stunned silence. Storm troopers on trucks, their yells magnified by bullhorns, were racing up and down the avenue. In one of the sidestreets a small synagogue was ablaze, and the smell of smoke was intense. Here and there a cluster of policemen stood idle, watching indifferently. Gripped by a sudden fear for Mother's safety, I headed for her apartment. The street on which she lived was dark, quiet, and empty. Approaching her building, I saw a lone woman sweeping the sidewalk in front of the small tobacco store where I had bought my first cigarettes many years ago. As I passed the store, I recognized old Frau Rosenberg, the owner. The display window was shattered, and in the dark interior I glimpsed what looked like splintered, tangled wood. We nodded at each other, wordlessly. Mother was not at home.

The next morning I went to the small chapel in Charlottenburg where Romano Guardini celebrated mass. There I met Annemarie and together we went to Mother's apartment. She was still in bed and had noticed nothing of what had happened the night before. We implored her to leave the house and live with me or elsewhere for a while. She refused obstinately, as usual, laughing at our fear. But the seriousness of the situation probably had begun to dawn even on her. A few weeks later she visited the offices of the Organization of Jewish Catholics and began to make preparations for her emigration.

Six months later, a couple of months before the war began, Mother's brother, Willi, was in New York; Mother and Aunt Minna were in London, and the Mischpoke was scattered between Shanghai and Copenhagen. Aunt Clara stayed in Hamburg to nurse her mother. Aunt Walli, aloof and taciturn, refused to join the exodus, unshaken in her conviction that Germans would never lay hands on Germans.

In retrospect, I wonder why I did not join the exodus of the Mischpoke. I could have, even though trying to avoid the draft would have amounted to desertion. Father had powerful friends in Switzerland and France (then still a safe place) who would have helped me to escape, and I could have made connections through the Jesuit hierarchy of New Germany. Before the *Kristallnacht*—the Night of the Broken Glass—I had detested the regime as I detested anything uncouth, mindless, and blusterous. Now, having trembled for Mother's safety and witnessed the innate brutality of the masters of my life, I feared them. From now on, the sight of the

Brownshirts and the Blackshirts made my heart pound and the palms of my hands sweat. I felt physically threatened. Yet the thought of leaving Germany never occurred to me. Instead, having been shaken out of a state of indecision and inactivity, I decided to volunteer for military service, to dispatch the six months of Labor Service and the two-year stint in the armed forces as quickly as possible. After that, I expected, I would be able to see my way more clearly. Did I instinctively hope that by submerging myself in the mass of the uniformed, by becoming a component in the sea of faceless bodies, I could hide my identity and escape notice? I was accepted without difficulty. Picking up my military pass, I saw for the first time in black and white, in one of my personal documents, the entry Mischling I. A few days later I was notified to report for duty in the Labor Service on April 1, 1939.

Part Two

. . . .

Preceding page: Richard Kuehn, the author's father, in his room in the priory. A silver cigarette holder, with cigarette, is on the index finger of his left hand.

September 1, 1939

• •

On September 1, 1939, I had been a workman in the State Labor Service for five months. Nothing in my waking up on the morning of that fateful day told me that, at this moment, German troops were beginning to cross the border between Germany and Poland only a few kilometers to the south of our camp. As usual, I opened my eyes a few seconds before six, and as I became conscious of the barracks room I instinctively tensed for the instant when the door would fly open, the work leader on duty would walk in, and yelling "Aufstehen! Aufstehen!" (Get up! Get up!), would pull off as many blankets as he could grasp during the rapid inspection of the bunks. When the door did open and the yell came, I was already reaching for my trunks, careful not to disturb the pile of clothes that formed a perfect rectangle at the foot of my bed. Two minutes later, towel in one hand, toothbrush and toothpaste in the other, I was competing in the wash-up hall against hundreds of half-naked young men for a few seconds' claim to one of the huge, circular stone basins filled with ice-cold ground water. At twenty minutes after six I was dressed in my work outfit of rough white cotton, my bed was made in the symmetry and flatness of a chessboard, and my mess gear was ready for the whistle blast that would call us out for the six-thirty line-up and the trot to the mess hall.

An hour later I began digging in the heavy, moist, reluctant East Prussian soil with a spade whose blade shone like polished silver. We were excavating a drainage ditch that ran the entire length of an airfield, and as far as I could see to either side, workmen methodically, mechanically, gave themselves to the prescribed rhythm of spade work: thrust, push, bear down again, loosen, break, lift, swing—we broke ground and shoveled dirt with the drilled-in precision of soldiers changing guard at a national shrine. And soldiers we were supposed to be. This was our six-month novitiate that was to prepare us for the mental and physical discipline awaiting us, a month hence, in the armed forces. We were trained like soldiers, lived like soldiers, dressed like soldiers, except that our weapon was the spade and our service was out-of-doors manual labor. During the past five months our camp of two hundred workmen had graded roadbeds and railroad beds, helped farmers to harvest their crop, cleaned swamps and forests, and worked in sawmills and quarries.

For some reason, my unit—the twenty-five men with whom I shared a barracks room—had been singled out as ditch-digging specialists from the day we had moved into our first camp in the wooded heartland of Pomerania, south of the Baltic Sea. Here we had excavated drainage ditches for a highway that was to link two towns separated by moraines and dense beech forests. After two months, the project had suddenly been terminated, unfinished, and the camp was moved east to a region of low-lying, marshy plains close to the Polish border. Here we had worked in a deep trench, perhaps two miles long and forever filled with muddy water that reached up to the rim of our hip boots, without having any idea why the trench was there or what we were supposed to accomplish. We never succeeded in either draining it, or deepening it, or shoring up its sides— the shapeless mudhole into which we slithered in the morning was still a shapeless mudhole when we climbed out of it in the evening. A strip of soggy meadow, about a hundred yards wide, separated the trench from a little creek that formed the border between Poland and Germany. Occasionally Polish soldiers, rifles slung over their shoulders, would appear and watch us work, and during breaks we would try to provoke each other with as many obscenities as we could think of in the other's language.

That project, too, had been abandoned after a month, and without forewarning, from one day to the next, we broke camp for an unknown destination. For the first time we sensed that something big was happening when, after a night's train ride, we had arrived in Danzig, where we were loaded on a troopship crowded with workmen from several other camps. So far we had ignored the rumors of war that had filled the newspapers for months; war, after all, had been "imminent" for the past three years, ever since Hitler had sent troops into the Rhineland in 1936. Of considerably greater interest to us was the question of where this voyage on the Baltic Sea would take us. Late in the afternoon of the same day we landed in the nearly seven-hundred-year-old city of Königsberg, the capital of East Prussia, where we camped for a few hours on a picturesque square in the shadow of the monumental medieval palace. At nightfall a caravan of army trucks arrived to take us on the last stretch of this bewildering journey.

This stretch held a surprise. At first we tried to guess where we were headed by the road signs that occasionally appeared in the beams of the truck lights, but since nobody on our vehicle seemed to know much about East Prussia, and the driver ignored our questions, we soon fell silent and gave in to our fatigue. I had been dozing, kept from falling asleep by the wet, bitter night wind that rushed across the open truck and first stung, then slowly paralyzed my face and neck. Suddenly the lights caught a directional sign saying "Gilgenburg," and I was awake and seized by a deep excitement. When we had arrived in Königsberg and I had known that our new camp would be somewhere in East Prussia, I had idly thought about the occasional summer months Annemarie and I had spent as small children in Gilgenburg. But the moment of remembrance had been brief and had lacked color, immediacy, and strength; I was preoccupied with other things than childhood memories. Now Gilgenburg was upon me, a reality on this night, under this sky, only a few miles down this road, and the memory of those summer vacations washed over me like a wave breaking over a beach stroller.

As the truck rumbled through the dark and deserted streets of Gilgenburg I recognized the town square and the familiar shape of the town hall, but I made no attempt to catch a glimpse of the store: I remembered that it had been demolished during a raid on the town's Jewish merchants, in the Kristallnacht the previous year, and that Uncle Markus and his wife and children had vanished shortly thereafter.

We arrived at our destination at dawn and sensed immediately that the rumors of war had more substance than usual. Our new camp turned out to be a vast city of barracks surrounded by a high barbed-wire fence whose gates were guarded by workmen carrying—a strange sight—rifles instead of the usual high-polished spades. Our section of the compound was occupied by workmen from several camps of the Labor Service. Another section was occupied by civilian German workers, and yet another, the largest and completely self-contained with its own mess halls, wash-up barracks, and recreation buildings, by foreign workers—mostly Turks, Arabs, and men from the Baltic states. The camp had been built only a month or so ago, to house the work force for the construction of an airfield. Apparently the work had not progressed quickly enough, because the camp commander, who appeared himself to send us off to our first day on the field, left no doubt in his oration that the Führer expected us to complete the job on schedule. Why the field had to be finished by that date, why it was being built here, or why it was being built at all he never mentioned.

On this September morning, five or six weeks after our arrival, I looked over the crest of my ditch at an airfield that was virtually completed and about whose purpose there was no longer any doubt. Dive bombers, the infamous Stukas, squatted like clumsy black birds at the far end of the field. Their bombs were waiting in the oblong wooden crates stacked up in intervals alongside the two tarred runways. In the center of the field, at the spot where the two runways crossed to form an enormous black X glistening in the morning sun, a group of workers were busy repairing the damage that had been caused the day before by the first plane that had attempted to land on the recently laid asphalt. The plane had appeared in late afternoon as a tiny black dot against the clear sky and immediately triggered the siren that was supposed to warn us of "enemy aircraft." Since no war had been declared yet and we were used to false alarms, and since the ditch in which we were working would, at any case, have offered the best protection against bombs or strafing, we merely dropped our tools, leaned over the edge of the excavation, and watched the machine approach. As it came closer, descending slowly for a landing, we recognized it as a Focke-Wulf transport plane, a plane much bigger and heavier, even when empty, than the dive bombers for which the runways had been built. "That's going to be great fun, fellows," somebody called out with obvious delight. Before anybody could ask what the caller meant, the plane touched down. As the landing wheels skimmed over the asphalt, the plane, as if running into an invisible wall of cotton, lurched first to one side, then to the other, and finally, almost with an air of resignation, lifted its tail end and slowly, gracefully, flipped over on its back. Happily, the pilot survived his dive into the asphalt with but minor injuries.

The announcement that the war had begun came in mid-morning. "Achtung, Achtung, wir bringen Ihnen eine Sondermeldung" ("Attention, attention. We bring you a special announcement"). The voice booming from the four loudspeakers fastened to tall poles at each corner of the field was strangely, painfully incongruous with the peace and stillness of the sparkling morning. While I listened to the long explanation of why Germany had been forced to launch a preventive attack against Polish agitators to safeguard world peace, I kept my eyes on the rows of Stukas, expecting them to begin some action that was in keeping with the urgency of the moment and the purpose of their existence. But nothing happened. The sun continued to make the air dance over the landing strips, and flocks of birds, stirred up by the noise, swept to and fro over the empty field. Listlessly we stood at attention when the national anthem concluded the announcement, and listlessly we picked up our tools and started digging again. My thoughts returned, as they had so often during the past few weeks, to Gilgenburg, which I had not entered again since that night of our arrival in the camp.

The announcement had called to my mind an incident I had long forgotten, but which now seemed ominous: my own war with Poland, a war I had enacted on one of my trips from Berlin to Gilgenburg. East Prussia, although part of Germany, had, as a result of the Treaty of Versailles, been separated from the motherland by a narrow strip of Polish territory which gave the Poles access to the Baltic Sea. A railway line traversed this "corridor," linking the two parts of Germany. The stations within the corridor were patrolled by Polish soldiers, and while the train was halted, the train windows had to be shut and passengers had to clear the aisles and remain in their compartments. On this trip I had worn some kind of children's uniform, with two toy pistols stuck in my belt. At the first stop inside Poland, noticing the soldiers walking slowly up and down the platform, I had jumped up from my seat, pulled down a window before anyone could hold me back, and, aiming my pistols at the soldiers, started yelling, "Bang, bang, bang." The effect on most of the soldiers had been disappointing— they simply ignored me—but one of them had whirled at the sound of my voice and, grinning broadly, aimed his rifle at me. Mother had been terrified and had humiliated me with a public beating, but the considerable commotion I had caused among my fellow travelers had been gratifying.

Now, fourteen or fifteen years later, I was about to put on a real soldier's uniform; all of us carried a draft notice in our pocket. Until this morning the prospect of wearing a soldier's uniform had not displeased me. All other considerations aside, there was something ridiculous about the martial use of a spade and about a uniform that, in spite of all the propaganda, remained in prestige and symbolic strength a second best to the uniform of a soldier. Even the least sophisticated among us had quickly learned, on their first night out, which uniform the girls preferred. But now that a war was on, what could we expect from trading sham uniforms and weapons for real uniforms and weapons? Instinctively we knew that the war was not going to be over in weeks or months, and perhaps not even in two years. Yesterday the draft notice had meant liberation from ridicule, from the drudgery of spade, shovel, and hoe, and, more important for some of us, from the armband emblazoned with the swastika. Now this piece of paper had turned into a tag that linked us irrevocably with the Stukas sitting menacingly on the field, with the ammunition crates, and, as we slowly began to realize, with the grim events that at this moment occurred only a few kilometers to the south of us. All through the past five months we had essentially remained the heterogeneous group of twenty-year-olds we had been when we first met as Labor Service recruits at a collecting

. . . .

station in Berlin, our civilian clothes still reflecting our status in life: un-
skilled laborers, recent graduates from the gymnasium, apprentices of a
craft, bellboys, drifters, clerks, and a few career leaders from the Hitler
Youth movement. Neither the common uniform, nor the common sweat,
nor the commonly felt futility of our life had achieved among us a cohe-
sion that went deeper than a superficial comradeship. The cliques, the few
friendships that had developed had grown out of natural compatibilities in
background and interests, and sometimes out of intense political or ideological convictions. Now the war had suddenly turned our artificial and
temporary association into a fellowship of fate, of a destiny that pointed to
an unknown which we felt vaguely was balanced between life and death.

I sensed all of this as clearly as the men working on either side of
me, but I also knew that, once again, I would be denied a share even in
this fragile fellowship. My own uncertainties, my own doubts were of
longer standing than theirs; I had known since childhood what it means to
face a future marked "No Exit." Here I was, a member of the State Labor
Service, helping to build an airfield for the air force, wearing an armband
with the swastika, expecting to serve, in another month, in an infantry
unit, while Mother and the members of her family either had fled Germany or lived in constant fear for their lives or freedom. Would I have to
die to defend the men who were persecuting them? The announcement of
the invasion of Poland had raised again the old, tortuous questions that
had been dormant for a while, sharpened their edges, and made them more
painful because finding an answer now had become a matter of life and
death. But with whom could I talk? Who could help me to find an answer?
I wanted to break out of the dilemma, the enforced ambivalence, the self-
consciousness that rent me emotionally and stifled the very movements of
my body. I knew that political beliefs did not touch the core of my comrades' lives; few of them had any formed and deep convictions about
anything. They could get into heated arguments, and sometimes into
fistfights, over their views on Hitler and his society, but when it came to a
soccer game, to playing a prank on a comrade, to planning an escape to
town after curfew, these differences were forgotten. I could have thought,
could have felt about the regime what I wanted and still remained one of

them—had I only been able to choose my position freely. But I was officially marked: in their eyes my status, my position, were once and for all defined. To them, whatever I had to say was predetermined by what I had to be, not by who I was.

I thought of Father, for whom the capture of Germany by Hitler had caused no doubts, no dilemmas. On my first leave I had visited him, wearing my Labor Service uniform, and the moment he laid eyes on me he stiffened and his eyes lit up in suppressed rage. "Take that rag off," he hissed, pointing at the armband emblazoned with the swastika. "Take off the whole Goddamned outfit if you want me to talk to you." His outburst was not unexpected. I closed the door behind me, sat down on the sofa, and, while he kept his back turned to me, staring out of the window, talked. "Look," I began, "I will walk out of here if you wish, but that will be the last time you will see me. I know you love me; that I love you, and respect you, goes without saying. You think you know me and understand me. That's true—when it comes to books, religion, ideas, opinions. But what do you know about my life? You sit here in your room, reading and writing, and when you meet people they are of your kind, of your persuasion. You sit here, peacefully waiting out the end of Nazi Germany. You don't have to mingle with people of all kinds about whose views on Hitler or whatever you don't know anything. I do, every day. I have to mingle with them and deal with them. Your identity card shows 'Richard Kühn.' Period. Mine shows 'Heinz Richard Kühn. Mischling Ersten Grades.' Your identity is unsullied. Mine is branded, stamped, marked. Oh yes, I agree with you that Hitler and his ilk are despicable, hateful, evil personified. But you don't have to wear the man's uniform and insignia. I do, and if I refuse I will be shot.

"You were nearly fifty when Hitler came to power. You were born a German, grew up a German, lived as a German in the kind of Germany you loved. That, and your fascination with German history, is what sustains you now. Your opinion, your feelings about Germany and Germans are firmly formed, they are rooted, they will never change. I knew myself to be part of a group of despised or at best tolerated people from the moment I became conscious of myself. I was fourteen when the Nazis took over Germany, and set Germans against Germans. For me, Germany

· ·

is inhabited by Nazis, Germans, and Jews. My love of Germans and Germany I have inherited from you. It has not grown out of my own life, my own experience. It is a love on trust. Sure, there are many Germans I love, as individuals. But that's not the question. Just answer me this. Your favorite expression is, 'When things get rough, you can always fall back on yourself.' I agree—if you have something to fall back on. You, you have built up plenty that will carry you through. You have had time, and opportunities. Tell me, what can I fall back on?"

I did not say much more than this. I spoke quietly, and before I finished he turned away from the window and faced me. For a few moments we continued looking at each other silently. "Let's go and eat," he finally said. We left the house together, I wearing my uniform, and when we came out on the street he put his arm under mine.

As I pursued the melancholy thoughts that the announcement had aroused in me, my eyes fell on Peter and Hans-Joachim, whose heads were visible above the crest of another excavation some distance away. I wondered what they were thinking about the attack on Poland. My friendship with Peter and Hans-Joachim had begun accidentally. One morning, in the first camp, we had been called out from the formation lined up for inspection, and assigned to latrine duty. Cleaning latrines was a brutal business. The pits, which served some two hundred men, were large, and one stood up to one's thighs in excrement and urine. They had to be cleaned out within two hours, and half an hour after completion of the job one had to report to the work leader on duty, in a uniform free of any trace of the work and with buckets and tools sparkling. We started working in silence, but after a while Peter could no longer control himself. "Shit on Hitler," he said, loudly, but not looking up from his work. Hans-Joachim and I glanced at each other in surprise, and then all three of us broke out in laughter. From then on we sought each others' company and tried to spend as much time together as camp life permitted. Our friendship was neither intimate nor even close. It was an unspoken compact of trust that made no demands and required no signs. With Peter, in fact, I had little in common. He was one of those congenitally imperturbable persons who go unnoticed when life is ordinary and routine but to whom one turns for reassurance and support when life is in disarray and precarious. Like me, he had grown up in Berlin, but in an industrial section that was so foreign to me that we couldn't even swap memories about the city in which both of us had spent most of our lives.

Peter was the son of a laborer, and his taste in books, music, and art was pedestrian, but he was alert and inquisitive and had a fine feeling for moral decency. He relished the out-of-doors work, the discipline, and the mentality of camp life and soon earned the respect of the camp leaders for his dexterity with tools and his talent for planning and organizing. The same traits that endeared him to the rank, however, made him unpopular among the file, and although he was competitive and ambitious, I suspected that his unpopularity and his known indifference to the regime kept him from being promoted. He would welcome the war, I thought, as an opportunity to gain the recognition that was being withheld from him.

My friendship with Hans-Joachim stood on a much firmer and mutually acknowledged ground. Hans came from a family of nobility whose members had for generations served Germany as naval officers. His father was an admiral, but Hans neither had any interest in a military career nor did he seem at that time to be emotionally suited for this kind of life. When we had been called out of formation for latrine duty, it was probably because he had provoked a punishment—and Peter and I, fortunately as it turned out, had simply been attached to him because it took three men to do the job in the prescribed time. Hans was the type of man any leader pounces on instinctively: frail, freckled, red-haired, bespectacled, forever out of step during a march, forever unbuttoned at an inspection, forever the last out of bed, forever caught when he broke a rule. He was mostly punished for concealing a book in his work outfit and carrying it to the job site. His passion was the classics, which he read in the original, and the work leaders were probably more envious of his ability to read a book written in a language they could not understand than angry about the infraction of a rule. I knew he would loathe the war, but I could not foresee that he would die as a highly decorated officer in the swamps of Russia.

My ties to Jews were never mentioned among us. On this subject I was not able to muster enough courage or confidence to disclose to them more than everybody else knew, or thought he knew. Only once had I given myself completely into someone's hands. Shortly after we had moved into our second camp, the camp commander had been replaced by a new man. He was unusually young, probably only a few years our senior, and I was immediately attracted to him. Tall, slender, and of graceful bearing, he managed to lend elegance and dignity even to the drab uniform of the Labor Service. Although his manner of giving orders seemed casual, he commanded respect effortlessly, and when he spoke to us, a fine, almost imperceptibly ironic smile never left his lips. While the voice appealed to our love for Führer and Vaterland, and his directives and reprimands bespoke him as a severe disciplinarian, the smile seemed to say, "We are all trapped in this exercise of futility, I as much as you. So let's play the game gracefully and well, without becoming too serious about this nonsense." He was fond of quoting from a wide variety of poems, and after his first appearance in the mess hall one evening during dinner he promptly issued an order to institute a course in table manners, to be given under his personal supervision.

I decided to speak to him, to disclose myself as candidly as I had opened myself to Father a few months ago. He readily agreed to see me. On a Sunday afternoon, when nearly everyone was on town leave and the camp was deserted, I walked to the pine grove that prettily sheltered the leaders' compound and knocked on the door of his barracks. His appearance, when he opened the door, startled me. I had never seen him out of uniform, and for a moment I thought I had knocked at the wrong door. A sleeveless, white silk shirt fell loosely over his wide, dark-blue slacks. He wore sandals, and a pale-blue silk scarf was knotted around his neck. The sitting room to which he pointed me was large, light, and austere. There was a plain wooden desk, bare except for a desk lamp and a book in which he had obviously been reading, and, facing each other across the desk, two straight-back wooden chairs. On a small, half-empty bookcase sat an enormous and complicated-looking radio, and two black, shiny leather trunks were standing upright in a corner. On the wall behind the desk hung a life-size color portrait of Hitler; on the wall opposite a similar portrait of the Reich labor leader. He gestured for me to sit down. He had not said a word since he had opened the door, and now, facing me across the desk, he looked at me without expression, the smile gone. My courage and resolve nearly left me, and for a moment I desperately searched for something to say that could explain my request for this meeting without giving me away. Here was a man who voluntarily devoted his life to a tyranny that victimized my mother, my relatives, my friends, and that contemptuously tolerated my existence, and I was driven to confess to him what normally only torture would have wrought out of me. He could have had me shot. It was madness. It was suicide.

But I finally talked. I don't recall a word of what I said, but I remember distinctly that, in the end, I asked him, "Aren't we both Germans? Don't we wear the same uniform? And if the rumors about war should come true, won't you and I have to fight for the same country?" His eyes, while I rambled on for some twenty minutes, never left mine, and when I ended he remained silent for what seemed to me a long time. Then he got up, and still holding me with his dark, now almost brooding gaze, while I stood instinctively at attention, he said: "I know most of your story. I have read your file. I cannot help you, and I cannot advise you. If you want to become a man you must learn that you are alone. Aloneness is everyone's fate." He dismissed me with a nod, but when I turned, heels clicking, and made for the door, he said, "One moment, please. Before you leave, there is a pair of boots out in the corridor. They got muddy this morning. The polish is in the bottom drawer of the wardrobe. Good evening." Only much later did I remember that neither on my entering his barracks, nor on my leaving his room, had we exchanged the mandatory "Heil Hitler." Shortly after this episode he was transferred to another camp, and, inexplicably, I felt as if I had lost my only friend.

At some time during the morning (or was it noon? or afternoon?) the loudspeakers suddenly began to blare again. The Führer was to address the nation in a few minutes. We scrambled out of the ditch, stacked our spades like rifles, and stretched out on the warm ground, happy about the unexpected break. I had often heard Hitler speak. His speeches were inescapable, whether one sat in a classroom, worked in a coalmine, or lay moribund in a hospital bed. Goebbels had made certain that radios were ubiquitous. Even at home, when one could have chosen solitude, the promise of a kind of masochistic aesthetic thrill compelled one to turn on the radio when Hitler spoke. Here, under the high, azure dome of the East Prussian sky, the loudspeakers that had been installed at the airfield even before the first barracks had gone up, apparently served no other purpose than to be ready for political announcements; I had never heard them until this day.

Hitler's voice, deep, resonant, measured, rolled over the field, through the camp, and across the marshland extending beyond the barbed-wire fence, breaking into funny little echoes on the black rim of the woods on the horizon. I didn't listen to his words. I knew already what he was going to say, and could give myself, without effort of reflection or analysis, to the delicious diversion of this mesmerizing voice. That was the thrill: the voice. Listening to Hitler's voice was like listening to the score of a madman's symphony whose theme one knew by heart, and yet whose movements never failed to excite one to an emotional response. The adagio—didactic, pedantic, schoolmasterly, setting the stage. The andante—the first ripples of impatience, a statement made in as yet controlled fury. The allegro—an accusation or self-justification, the voice still in control of tongue and the thought still in control of voice, but the beat quickening and the tone pitched high in rage. Then nothing but hate and spite, a shrill presto, talk turned into a scream, a scream strangely modulated by a now clearly discernible Austrian dialect. Then, abruptly, silence, a moment of mute linguistic orgasm, and finally the dark, deep, measured tones again, but now raspy, hollowed out by exhaustion, an anticlimactic finale giving the audience the signal for frenzied acclamations.

Today, at this outpost of Germany, there was no acclamation. After the last word, the loudspeakers fell silent; we rose, grabbed our spades and shovels, and climbed back into the ditch. Hitler's voice—curiously, the old thrill had not come, the old magic had not worked. I had been waiting for it, but something in the mix had been lacking. Had it been the absence of a visible audience whose excitement, breathing and palpable, rose in unison with the movements and rhythm of Hitler's speech? Was it that the empty field; the open space; the immovable silent sky; the fierce, angry sun; the smell of ripe, lazy summer had rendered impotent this city voice, these sounds that were at home in assembly halls, factories, bus depots, and beer gardens? Or was it that, between the announcement and Hitler's speech, my thoughts had numbed my capacity for excitement? Whatever it was, this time Hitler's voice had been not much more than noise, disagreeable noise for which I had been compensated with a twenty- or thirty-minute stretch in the shade of a clump of trees.

Punctually at five-thirty the whistle signaled the end of the working day. As usual, we sang as we marched back to the camp—sang with gusto, with a self-denial of our fatigue and cantankerousness that had long become mechanical and habitual. As we marched through the gate we pushed our voices to an end-stretch effort of ringing enthusiasm, proclaiming to the world, as Labor Service regulations had it, happiness over having completed another day's work in the service of Führer and Vaterland. "No audience," somebody said behind me, skillfully blending his voice into the melody of the song. Indeed, there were no listeners. Although other columns of workmen were beginning to fill up our section of barracks, dispersing and getting ready for supper, the rest of the vast camp was deserted. The foreign workers were gone. At this time of the day, the endless alleys between their barracks would throb with the confusion and noise of their laughter, their songs, and their high-pitched arguments in unintelligible languages, and the casual cut and rich color of their clothes which they had exchanged for their work outfits would defy both the nature of the camp and the purpose of the work they had been forced to do. Tonight, the alleys held nothing but dust and chilling silence. We were among ourselves, several hundred men lost in a corner of a camp that just this morning had housed thousands. Sometime between the announcement of the war this morning and our return from the field they had been spirited away, leaving behind nothing but the tracks of truck tires in the dirt.

The war began for us in earnest in the middle of supper. Several siren blasts made us scramble for the exits of the mess hall, hastily fall into formation, and head galloping for the field. The sun had now set, but the air still held a trace of light that softened the contours of buildings and trees and gently pleaded for stillness and peace. In vain. We were running toward what at first sight appeared to be chaos. The airfield, the familiar flat emptiness, had erupted into erratic movements and bizarre shapes, and now, as we approached it, several plane engines simultaneously began to cough. In a few moments, a blizzard of deafening howls and shrieks swept over the field. Now the first bomber began to move down a runway, gathered speed, lifted, and climbed steeply into the dark evening sky. One after another followed. We ran across the field, ducking and jumping between moving and screaming planes that seemed everywhere, and stopped at a huge stack of bomb crates. Someone in an air force uniform climbed on the first layer of the stack and, gesticulating wildly, made us understand that we were to uncrate the bombs. Then he left us to our own devices. Nobody had ever told us how to uncrate bombs, but we learned quickly. Forming a chain from the top to the bottom of the stack, we began to lower the topmost crate to the next lower level until it reached the ground. We were sweating even before we had lifted the first crate—not because of the effort, but for an almost paralyzing fear that the slightest jerk or bump would set off the deadly load that, wrapped in straw, lay silently, threateningly inside. How could we know that the detonator would not be activated until the bomb was hung under the wing of the plane?

By now it had become totally dark. The blackout forbade the use of flashlights or matches, and we worked like blindfolded men trying to maneuver around a precipitous mountainside. The din made it impossible to call out directions or warnings. The air smelled cloyingly of gasoline and burned rubber, and on our tongues was the taste of metal. We were working on the second crate when the air force uniform suddenly materialized among us. It was obvious that the soldier was furious, and although we couldn't understand a word of what he was trying to yell at us, the meaning of his gestures was clear. From here on we simply pried open the hinged lid of a crate, lifted out the bomb and, controlling its glide, roll, and tumble as best we could, let it drop to the ground. The empty crate we kicked over the top. From time to time a small truck, headlights hooded except for a small slit which emitted a bladelike beam, would stop at our stack, another group of workmen would load it with bombs, and the vehicle would drive off into the black chaos.

After a few hours our task was finished. We sat down among the piles of straw and splintered wood, fatigued, numb from the noise, covering the glow from our cigarettes with cupped hands. By now the first planes were returning, and I wondered, idly and incapable of mustering any interest in my own speculation, who or what had been a target or victim of the bombs I had had in my hands. Shortly after midnight we returned to camp. On the way we passed a bomber that had been pulled off the field. A group of air force soldiers were lowering a human form from the open cockpit; another form lay motionless stretched out on the ground, under one of the wings. The troop leader ordered us to a halt and talked for a moment with one of the soldiers, and as we moved on told us that the pilot had been killed by a shrapnel fragment and the gunner severely wounded. We marched through the gate silently, and silently, without the usual bantering, undressed and positioned ourselves next to our bunks. The door opened and we stood at attention; the workleader on duty walked in, uniform spotless and boots shining, took the bed count from the room senior, checked a pair of boots, picked up a spade and, holding it up to the light, carefully inspected its blade, turned, switched off the light, and, saying "Heil Hitler," walked out. The room senior closed the door behind him, and we went to bed. For a few minutes some low conversation went back and forth between the bunks, and then the room fell silent. The noise outside grew louder and more distinct. I tried to concentrate on the words of a prayer, but my soul refused to respond. All through the night, half-asleep with exhaustion, half-awake with a nameless anxiety, I heard the planes roar overhead.

My last month in the Labor Service passed quickly. With the declaration of war on Germany by France and England on the third day after the invasion of Poland, World War II had begun its inexorable course. Rumors about the disposition of our unit changed daily, but nothing happened. A few days after the invasion the Stukas had left, and an eerie silence had fallen over the air field and the vast camp, seeming to belie the veracity of the news of a world in feverish turmoil. We were being kept busy with dismantling empty barracks, with drills that now included instructions in the use of a rifle, and with field exercises that no longer had anything to do with labor but were clearly aimed at preparing us for boot camp. At the end of the month we again were loaded onto trucks, and by the same route that had brought us to East Prussia we returned to a camp in Pomerania, where we were discharged.

Grace Period

. . . .

The corporal standing behind a counter at the military district headquarters in Berlin, where I had gone to report for military service, had a good-natured, work-worn face. His uniform, I thought, did not quite succeed in giving an air of officialdom to this elderly Berliner who probably had not worn a uniform since World War I.

"Name?"

"Heinz Kuehn."

"Wohnort?" I told him I had no place of residence yet, that I had just been discharged from the Labor Service and expected to join the army reserve unit for which I had been drafted.

"Wehrpass?" He leafed through my military pass and looked up. "Mischling of the First Degree, hmmm. Who is the . . . ?" He hesitated.

"The Jewish partner?" I finished for him. "My mother."

"Did she . . . ?" Again he hesitated. There was no one else in the room. Perhaps conscious of an oversize portrait of Hitler that hung behind him on an otherwise bare and windowless wall, his caution got the upper hand over his spontaneous sympathy.

· ·

"Yes," I assured him, "she got away to England just a few days before the war broke out."

"Where is your father?"

"Here in Berlin," I replied.

"Well, we have new directions for people like you," he said. "Your draft has been voided. Just let us know your whereabouts any time you change your address." And he added, not unkindly, "Healthy-looking fellows are either supposed to be wearing a uniform or to be doing something useful for the fatherland."

He scribbled something into my pass and handed it to me. As I took it, he suddenly leaned across the counter, bringing his face close to mine. "Make yourself useful," he said again, in a low voice. "Your papers are on file at Gestapo headquarters, and those brothers are going to keep an eye on you." He dismissed me with a nod. As I reached the street, I opened the pass to read what he had entered. *Nicht zu verwenden,* "not usable," the notation read.

I soon learned that it was not easy for me to be "useful to the fatherland" as long as I also wanted to be useful to myself. Universities were, by law, closed to me. Libraries, publishing houses, radio stations, and art galleries—any kind of cultural and scientific institution— were off limits too. "You know we are in the forefront of the battle for the ideological liberation of the people," their personnel managers would invariably say after taking one look at the word *Mischling* in my military pass. "We can't take chances." "How about the mail room or the stock room, or night-guard duty?" I asked a friend of Father's who owned a small publishing firm. "Heinz," he replied, "even if you swept the floors, you know we would have to send your papers to the Ministry of Culture for clearance. Having you work as a floor sweeper or guard would look to them even more suspicious than having you work as an editor."

I did not feel compelled to be useful. To make what little money I needed to support myself, I spent a few hours a week cataloguing books in the library of the old, cavernous Dominican monastery in Moabit. (The inimitable sarcasm of the Berliners: they had surrounded the home of the Ordo Praedicatorum with streets bearing the names of Protestant reformers or reform movements—Waldenser Strasse, Wiclef Strasse, Zwingli

Strasse.) The work suited me. The library, though in disarray, was extensive, and for the first time in years I could lose myself in the world of books without fear of interruption, without having to cock my inner ear to an expected summons of one kind or another. The monks paid me fairly but otherwise ignored me. They knew me from my gymnasium days when I had occasionally done the same work for them and even lived in the monastery for some time. I think they were disappointed that I had not joined their order after graduation.

Edith had offered me an attic room in her villa, and although I felt uncomfortable that I should be living in her house while Father lived in a furnished room in another part of the city, I enjoyed the villa's quiet elegance and Edith's amiable companionship. The villa had been a farewell gift from her wealthy parents who, because her father was a Jew, had fled Germany shortly after Hitler had come to power, some seven years ago. As small as it was, it was an expensive gift, furnished with exquisite taste. Edith knew how to place an authentic armchair of the Renaissance next to a superb replica of a Louis XVI writing table, and how to juxtapose, on a wall covered with pale yellow silk, an ornately framed copy of Rembrandt's *Man in a Gilt Helmet* with a delicate watercolor by Matisse. Whatever else had gradually driven a wedge between her and Father, it certainly was not incompatibility in refined taste or in appreciation of discreet luxury. No matter how resolutely Father eventually turned his back on *vanitas mundi* (the world's vanity), he never ceased to savor that vanitas as long as it presented itself in meticulous style.

I had visited the villa frequently during the previous seven years, when it had still been a home for Father and Edith and, after their separation, when Father himself had become a visitor. Father loved the place, and he had never fully accepted the fact that it ultimately came to symbolize the defeat of his last attempt to live his life as a husband and father. For this lovely gift, which Edith's parents had hoped would bring happiness and stability to their daughter's marriage, may well have been one of the reasons for its dissolution. Father had never thought of the villa as a nest for himself and Edith, but from the moment it was given to them had tried to persuade Edith to make it a home for Annemarie and me as well. The annulment of his marriage to Mother, and Mother's emigration to England, appeared to have removed the last obstacles to his plan. Edith had converted to Catholicism a few years ago in the hope that she and Father would make their civil marriage sacramentally valid. Yet she had not yielded on the matter of the villa. For her, it was hers and Father's alone, and Father, disappointed and following dictates known only to him, had increasingly withdrawn from her into a life of solitude. He visited the villa often, but rarely stayed there for more than a day or two.

I was seldom at home. Berlin was in a festive mood. The war against Poland was over, and nothing was happening in the west. Germany was waging a *Sitzkrieg,* "a Sit-Down War," as we called it. Nobody was yet concerned about bombs, and people were beginning to make plans for the Christmas–New Year's holidays. I would often lose myself in the throng of shoppers and pleasure seekers crowding the Kurfürstendamm and the Tauentzienstrasse. The wares displayed in the elegant stores were as abundant and as far out of my reach as they had always been, and the aroma of good food that cordoned the restaurants stimulated my imagination and desire as vigorously as in the days when Annemarie and I often had to make do with a daily diet of potato soup and sandwiches. At night the streets were not less crowded and the traffic was even brisker than during the day. People rendered faceless, colorless, and formless in the all-absorbing darkness of the blackout groped and shuffled in throngs from theaters and movie houses to bars and restaurants, and their voices and laughter, strangely disembodied, were carefree and redeemed the blackness.

Sometimes, coming upon the square surrounding the Kaiser Wilhelm Memorial Church, I would stop at the building where Aunt Walli lived and take the tiny elevator to the floor of her apartment. When Aunt Minna and Mother had fled Germany, she had refused to join them. She believed, for reasons of her own, that the Nazis would not touch her, a reckless optimism for which I saw no justification. But it was a time of grace, and in that fall and winter of 1939 she easily persuaded me that the rumors about deportations of Jews to labor camps, and the speculations about the nature of these camps, were but rumors and speculations. We did not know that the deportation of Jews from Vienna had already begun.

I spent many hours of the day, and many more hours of the night, in the company of Stephan. I had met Stephan, a half-Jew like me, shortly after my graduation from the gymnasium, at a retreat in the monastery of my

Dominican friends. The moment I spotted him I was struck by his slender, pensive, melancholic face, whose paleness was accentuated by finely drawn, black eyebrows and long, straight, raven hair. Mephistopheles, I thought. Indeed, by appearance he could have doubled for an Assyrian version of Gustav Gründgens, the famous actor-director who at that time played the role in his casting of *Faust* at the Prussian State Theater. By the end of the retreat we were friends, less, I am sure, because of what we had been able to whisper to each other, than because of what we had instinctively and immediately felt for each other. I was his witness when he was baptized a few weeks later.

Stephan lived alone in his parents' villa in the fashionable diplomats' section of the Tiergarten. His father had been a banker, but whether he or Stephan's mother was the Jewish parent; whether his parents had emigrated, were divorced, or had died, he never disclosed. Every so often he received a substantial check, and then we would roam the intimate cafés, the Weinstuben, and the basement bars on the quiet residential streets off the Kurfürstendamm—not in search of girls, not to get drunk, but to talk, talk, talk, animated, sustained, protected, if you will, by the sweet cadences of a balalaika, discreet light, sparkling crystal, the murmur of anonymous voices, and the unobtrusive attention of tailcoated waiters. Thomas Aquinas, Tolstoy, Thomas à Kempis, Georges Bernanos, Dostoevski, C. S. Lewis, Saint Augustine, Gertrud von LeFort—our spirits soared, flagged, tumbled, soared again, free and secure in a world in which we were at home. Sometimes we would shut ourselves up in the villa for a day, or for days, reading and hardly exchanging a word. The place, done up in Edwardian style and by now showing signs of long neglect, was damp, cold, and gloomy, but we had a fire going in the fireplace, drank wine, smoked Turkish cigarettes, and ignored the events that moved the rest of the world. "La vie est beau et belle," Stephan exclaimed one day, apropos of nothing. I remember the happy outburst probably because of its grammatical absurdity, but its substance expressed our mood precisely.

On December 6, 1939, according to an entry in my workbook, the Theater am Nollendorfplatz hired me as an assistant stagehand. Unlike most of Berlin's theaters, the Theater am Nollendorfplatz, a barnlike structure on the periphery of West Berlin's residential area, possesses no architectural distinction. Its stuccoed façade, resembling that of an over-size movie palace, unsuccessfully pretends to belong to the elegance of West Berlin's generous boulevards; its flanks and stagehouse already merge with the grimy apartment buildings and cheerless streets of the city's harsher sections. Its repertory reflected its ambivalent structural identity: in a city saturated with Europe's finest actors and directors, the Theater am Nollendorfplatz devoted itself to the happy-end operetta. Its playbill that winter announced *Die Fledermaus,* and for the next three months the playfully erotic melodies of Johann Strauss's most enticing work would give a curious quality of enchantment and lightheartedness to realities that became increasingly intolerant of escape and make-believe.

Is it this jarring incongruity that has made these first winter months of the war unforgettable? Or did I preserve the images and feelings intact because they were deeply congenial to the thirst—then keenly felt but never admitted—of a twenty-year-old for romance and adventure? One tune, one song—one snatch of tune or song—of *Die Fledermaus,* and the dust clouds of the stage pit, the smile of a chorus girl, the crystal chandeliers and Persian rugs in Edith's villa, the voice of a landlady, and the vulnerable face of Stephan come to life on the stage of my inner world with an intensity of form and sound and color I experience only in my most vivid dreams.

A few hours after I had been hired by the theater, I moved into a room of my own. It was an impulsive decision, but of the many rooms in which I lived during the war, of the many landladies I had, this room, this land-lady, have remained unforgettable. After forty years, I can still see myself stepping through the stage door, out into an early-December drizzle, walk-ing into a corner tobacco store for a package of cigarettes, and reading the handwritten note on a bulletin board, "Room to let. Gentlemen only." Moments later I rang the bell to Frau Wirtz's apartment.

Frau Wirtz lived in the second rear building, four flights up, of an old, dark, massive tenement on the Nollendorfstrasse, a stone's throw from the theater. "Wipe your shoes," she said, opening the door a crack. Her Berlin dialect was as thick as that of the city's streetcar conductors who, it had often seemed to me, were chosen more for the purity and originality

. . . .

of their "Berlinerisch" than for any of the skills the job required. The hall
was as cold and dark as the staircase, but the air in the sitting room to
which she led me was stifling from the intense heat radiating from a tiled,
ceiling-high stove. The furniture was heavy, black, ornately carved, and
worn—the kind of furniture with which I myself had grown up and which
seemed to be standard issue for the sitting rooms of Berlin's lower middle
class. As soon as my eyes had grown accustomed to the half-light, I was
struck by what at first looked like wallpaper made up of pages of a picture
magazine: every inch of wall, from floor to ceiling, was covered with
scenes from circus life. There were photographs of horses with and without costumed riders; sketches of tigers jumping through flaming rings;
paintings of clowns in innumerable poses and expressions. Other pictures
showed elephants performing various tricks; trapeze artists; dogs dressed
up as ballerinas; and on a canvas covering the space between a couch and
the ceiling, an enormous circus tent framed by miniature flags of German
and foreign towns.

"Are you a student?" Frau Wirtz began the interrogation without ado.
Students were deferred from military service at that time. She stood before
me, short, stocky, white-haired, a cigarette dangling from between her
lips, a wet apron covering her sagging man's belly, while I lay virtually
supine before her, helplessly buried in a deep overstuffed armchair. I explained that I had just been discharged from the Labor Service, and that I
was still waiting for my draft call. "Where do you work?" she wanted to
know. I told her that I had taken a job at the Theater am Nollendorfplatz an
hour ago. With that, her watchful attitude changed suddenly. "Splendid,
splendid, a fellow artist," she exclaimed. She told me that her husband—
"God bless his soul," pointing to a gold-framed, fiercely mustached gen-
tleman in top hat, riding boots and riding jacket, whip in hand—had been
a circus director and that she, until she had broken a hip in a fall from a
horse, had been his star equestrian. Although she preferred more mature
gentlemen as boarders (and would, of course, never take in "skirts"), she
would be proud to rent her nicest room to a fellow artist. The room to
which she took me, down an endless dark corridor, contained a cot, a
wardrobe, a washstand, a small wooden table, a straight wooden chair
painted, inexplicably, red, a small dresser drawer, and a cast-iron potbel-

lied stove. It was tiny, smelled of cold cabbage soup, and, as I discovered the next morning, faced a blank, dirty brick wall, but the bare wooden floor was clean and the crocheted doilies covering every surface of the furniture even gave it a touch of coziness. Over the cot hung a lone framed postcard of Dürer's *Praying Hands*.

This was the first of many similar-looking, similar-smelling rooms in which I was to live for the next four years. A location not of my choosing, furniture that spelled "for boarders," knickknacks that offended my taste—but always, unmistakably, a woman's touch, a sign of gentleness, an expression, no matter how clumsy, of individuality and care that redeemed the lace curtains and the Feuerbach print and blunted the sharp edge of loneliness.

I told Frau Wirtz that I liked the room, paid her a week's rent, and left to pick up my few belongings from the villa. A nice fire was burning in the stove when I returned a few hours later. While I unpacked my two suitcases she lingered, fussing with the bedspread and the curtains. I began to arrange my books on the dresser drawer: three or four volumes of Saint Thomas's *Summa theologiae*, Mann's *Magic Mountain*, Bernanos's *Diary of a Country Priest*, a Greek edition of the New Testament, a volume of Goethe's poems, Sigrid Undset's *Kristin Lavransdatter*—a staple diet that filled a small suitcase and that I had carried with me since early high-school days. Frau Wirtz, scanning the titles, shook her head. "Thomas Mann," she said. "My husband thought he was dirty. But," she added, "I like Undset. She knows life." Lighting another cigarette she assured me again how happy she was to have someone in her home who appreciated the beauty and glory of the performing arts, and left, but a minute later she put her head through the door again. "For you," she announced, "I will throw in the breakfast. I will set a tray for you at seven, and there will be something hot on the stove. And," she added, "if you need breakfast for two, just leave a note on the kitchen table the night before." I knew then that I had found a friend.

If there was beauty and glory in the performing arts and magic in *Die Fledermaus*, I was, for a time, unable to savor whatever ennobling influence the theater may have on the souls of men. The morning shift, to which I had been assigned to learn the skills necessary for the more exacting night-time job, was charged with stage work, but it seemed my task was simply to survive the suffocating omnipresence of dust. We would, for example, dismantle the set for the city jail of the third act and replace it with the set for the first act, the garden and sitting room of Eisenstein's house, while another crew, working on the other half of the revolving stage, repaired the damage done to Prince Orlofsky's ballroom the night before. Towering flats were hoisted, lowered, and turned everywhere, and with every movement the cheap paint covering their canvas seemed to evanesce into a continuous drizzle of invisible flakes. At first the crew tried to teach me how two grips could easily carry even the tallest and heaviest flat, provided they knew how to keep it balanced between them. Their good-natured lessons were futile. Blinded by sweat and seized with irrepressible fits of coughing, I quickly lost control of the heavy weight, causing the flat to crash to the floor and set off an enormous cloud of dust. When, on my second attempt, the flat took with it one of the huge, expensive ballroom chandeliers, I was assigned to the clean-up crew or, as the grips fondly called us, the dust brigade.

From now on I spent my mornings in the subbasement, in an open concrete pit containing the drive work for the revolving stage. Here all the dust stirred up anywhere in the caverns of the stage house eventually settled in ankle-deep layers. After a few minutes of sweeping and shoveling, the brightly lit pit darkened, clothes, faces, and hair took on the color of dirty concrete, and we seemed to have turned into disembodied, shapeless beings roaming silently and aimlessly through a dense fog. My fellow workers, mostly elderly men no longer subject to military service, continuously drank beer while they worked, and more beer during frequent breaks. So did the stagehands working two stories above our heads. The entire morning crew, it seemed, was continually drunk, but never gave one of the usual signs of intoxication. When I arrived in the locker-room at eight in the morning, the men had already emptied several bottles and the noise in the room resembled that of a drinking bout at its zenith. At noon, when the morning shift ended, the men still lingered for a few more rounds, until, long after I myself had left, the cleaning ladies arrived to tidy up dressing rooms, foyer, and auditorium for the night's performance. The artistic life, I had to tell Frau Wirtz, who had eagerly awaited my report about the first morning's experience, is made up mostly of beer, dust, and coughing.

But Frau Direktor, as she liked to be called, had had more experience with dust and beer-drinking grips than I. "Just wait 'til they put you on the night shift," she said. She was right. What in the morning could have been a warehouse or, for that matter, a quarry as far as my job was concerned, in the evening turned into a place of magic, enchantment, and excitement. At six, two hours before the overture would hush and electrify the audience, corridors that had looked lonely, gray, and shabby when I had left them at noon, were now crowded with people intent on some mysterious but important business, and through the open doors of the dressing rooms came the sounds of laughter, high-spirited conversation, and snatches of declamations and songs. The air had been swept clean of dust when the tall door that led from the stage house onto a loading dock had been opened simultaneously with the entrance doors—a simple maneuver that caused a powerful draft of wintry air to surge through the entire building. The stage house was as still and solemn as a cathedral at early-morning mass until, gradually, the muted babble of a crowd gathering behind the heavy velvet curtain would fill even the farthest recesses of the storage galleries. The beer bottles had disappeared from the locker rooms, and the same men who had turned the morning shift into something of a carnival now sat around the tables in quiet conversation or were reading the evening papers, straining for the bell that would call them to their tasks.

When it turned out that I was not any handier with flats at night than in the morning, I was put in charge of properties, a job that gave me responsibility and status and made me an excited though nervous offstage participant in the performance. The basic props for the first two acts had been placed and arranged on the two halves of the stage in the morning when the scenery for these acts was set up, but anything that was fragile, such as the champagne glasses for the ballroom scene, or that was a genuine article and could be stolen, such as pillows, clocks, vases, and similar items, was in my charge, to be set up before the curtain rose or between acts. For most of the evening, however, I had nothing else to do but observe, listen, or give myself to my thoughts and dreams. From my cubicle, surrounded by shelves crammed with the paraphernalia of the art, I had a full view of the stage, the prompter's box, the orchestra pit, and a section of the front rows in the auditorium. I was rarely bored. The orchestra was spirited and precise, the actors played and sang enthusiastically and well, and the audience frequently, at predictable moments, interrupted a rendition with applause. The charming elegance and sparkling rhythm of the melodies, the careful structure and instrumentation of the piece, made it easy for me to forget the blackness outside, Aunt Walli's foolish optimism, Edith's unhappiness, and the uniforms in the audience.

Should I have been more contemptuous about the whole thing? About the actors and actresses, the chorus girls, the musicians, all of whom performed with an abandon as if this night, this performance, were their first, or last, or only chance to bewitch their audience; about the audience—men in black, gray, or brown uniform, or in black tie, women in evening dress and jewels—whose faces were relaxed and open, and whose eyes shone with the intoxication of sentimentality; and, of course, about myself, who sat here for no other reason than to be able to have in my workbook the all-important stamp of a job "essential to the war effort" and who permitted myself to truly enjoy my predicament? If it had been Mozart, or Beethoven, or Verdi with his sense of the tragic, or at the very least Tchaikovsky. Anything that would have been in keeping with the seriousness of the times and my inner world, that would have helped me to keep my feelings and emotions on the same level of veracity on which I tried to keep my reflections. But the King of the Waltz, Vienna of the nineteenth century!

It would have been strange if Eros, with his perfect sense of timing and location, had missed his cue at this moment. My cubicle was a popular spot for the chorus girls, who, because of their strenuous dance routines, suffered more than the other performers from the heat and dust that grew more irritating as the evening wore on. Every so often the pretty, slender, long-legged things, whose faces had lost nearly every mark of individuality under the heavy pancake makeup, would crowd into the tiny room to ask me for a drink of the sparkling soda that I kept in genuine champagne bottles for the ballroom scene. Drinking offstage from these bottles was forbidden, as was any kind of offstage conversation, but how could I have resisted a spicy little conspiracy? How gay they were, how young, how unconcerned! Three, four, or five of them would quickly step into my cubicle, close the door, say a coquettish "Bitte, bitte," hurriedly sip a glass of soda, curtsy or blow me a kiss, cautiously open the door, and having made certain that none of the supervisors was in sight, dart out to make room for the next group. Occasionally some of them would linger, giggling and whispering, or joking with me and mocking my serious-mindedness. They were always in motion, always talking or laughing, always restlessly fluttering about as if in a perpetual warm-up for a dance. Perhaps they were flirtatious—surely they were—but I did not, did not want to pay attention. Surely, they made my blood sing, but the moment the night's illusion was over and I stepped out into the dark, deserted Nollendorfplatz, I sought solace and oblivion elsewhere. There was Stephan and an as yet untried Weinstube on Unter den Linden. There were Father and Edith and spirited conversation in Edith's villa—an island of light and comfort. There were books on my dresser drawer and a decanter with hot toddy on Frau Wirtz's kitchen stove.

One evening, on some errand during the performance, I was climbing one of the innumerable narrow staircases that seemed to perfuse the theater like veins of concrete, when one of the dancers, obviously late for her cue, came hurriedly down, two steps at a time. "Hey," I called as she passed me, "you are all unbuttoned in the back." "Oh, thank you." She made a few helpless gestures and then turned her back to me. "Would you mind?" she asked. She was one of my regular visitors and I liked her because of an air of refinement that set her apart from the other girls. "Delighted, Fräulein Erika," I said. While I fumbled with the tiny hooks, trying to find the loops under layers of frilly stuff, she suddenly said, addressing the wall, "They tell me you are a Jew." I let go of her costume and, not knowing why, put my hands on her shoulders and spun her around. "Nonsense. Idle gossip," I retorted, flustered. For a moment we looked at each other silently. "It makes no difference to me," she said softly. Then she shrugged, freeing herself from my grip. I watched her skip down the steps, reach the bottom of the staircase, and open the door leading to the backstage. "Not the slightest," she called over her shoulder, and slipped through the door.

I remained motionless, my heart pounding painfully against my throat, my thoughts and feelings in an uproar I was unable to control. I didn't think of what she had said. My whole being felt the warm, soft skin of her neck, her arms. My whole being responded to the mellowness, the tenderness of her voice, embraced the lithe, graceful, elusive figure. The feeling of liberation and fulfillment, my longing for surrender, were so intense that tears came to my eyes. Eros, the son of Chaos, smiled and tossed roses in the air.

"Just part of the play," something warned me. "A night-time reality." "If you need breakfast for two . . . ," Frau Wirtz said. "Please," Father's voice replied, evoking with a familiar edge of sarcasm a verse attributed to Luther, "No 'Wine, woman, and song.' " That, I think, should quite well summarize the dialogue I had with my invisible interlocutors as I continued my climb. If conscience had its say, I don't recall its point. At any rate, Eros withdrew, perhaps berating me under his breath for my lack of courage and generosity. Erika continued to visit my clandestine bar, but neither of us mentioned the incident again. I sometimes wondered whether she, too, felt a sudden wave of anguish as we smiled at each other.

Perhaps Eros would have gained the upper hand had I not at that time been preoccupied with a different kind of love. After the performance I would take the subway to Zehlendorf, where Father once again had taken up residence in Edith's villa. Stepping into this house after a walk through faceless, soundless streets, after a ride through the all-pervading darkness of the blacked-out city, was like coming upon an island of light and warmth. Edith detested darkness, and a gloomy day was sufficient to make her turn on the lights in every room, from basement to attic. And craving warmth as much as light, she squandered coal and electricity in vengeful defiance of the restrictions imposed by the regime. But as much as I enjoyed escaping from my cold and dreary room to a comfortable and charming refuge, it was above all else Father's company that drew me to the villa, and I sensed that he desired my company as much as I did his. For the first time in our relationship I met him on his own ground and, as it were, on my own terms. I had grown up and could measure his advice against my experiences and needs, and because of the precariousness of the time and the uncertainty of my fate under the Hitler regime, I was as adrift and footloose as he himself had been for most of his life. Children commonly "discover" their parents only after the children have left the nest and have begun to take their lives into their own hands. I discovered Father in that elegant, secluded villa which, for a brief moment, held all the promises of a home.

The catalyst of that experience was Father's old friend, the writer Hanns Heinz Ewers, whom he had met when they both lived in Paris and who, I believe, had introduced him to Gisela Etzel, Father's first wife. Although Father had sometimes talked about him when I was still small, I had never met him until that winter and I would not see him again afterward. He was a novelist whose mind dwelt in the murky regions of life. Some of his books, with titles such as *The Vampire, The Horror,* and *The Possessed,* enjoyed an enormous popularity and had been in print for decades. A couple of years after Hitler had come to power, Ewers had written a biography of Horst Wessel, a young storm trooper who had been murdered by hoodlums ("Communists" was the official version) and who had composed the lyrics for what after his death became the official marching song of the Nazi party and, after 1933, the second national anthem. Ewers's book—a superficial thriller like all of his novels—was vigorously promoted by the Ministry of Propaganda, and because it was incomparably more palatable than the dross put out by that ministry, soon became better known than even Hitler's *Mein Kampf.*

At that stage of his fame—or notoriety—I finally met the man who, Father had once told me, knew how to handle the devil but was unable to enter a butcher shop because he became ill from the sight of blood and raw meat. From the moment we first shook hands I took a dislike to him. I was also wary of him because of his popularity with the Nazis, but I am sure he would never have entered Edith's house had he been as much as a sympathizer with the regime. Father's attitude toward him reflected a faint irony and sometimes even sarcasm, but no hostility. He seemed to respect Ewers's aggressive atheism and tolerate his intellectual opportunism; it had not been too long since he himself had wrestled with these demons.

I usually arrived at the villa when my three companions were already far along in whatever happened to engage them that night. Sometimes, as if they had waited for my arrival, they immediately drew me into their conversation, but mostly I sat quietly in a comfortable chaise lounge and, sipping a glass of wine, listened to their play of words and wits—just as I had sat, an hour ago, in my backstage cubicle, entranced by the melodies of *Die Fledermaus*. Edith, Father, and Ewers were at ease with one another. Each knew the other intimately, and their closeness was such that a single word, a glance, a gesture revealed as much as a spirited discourse. Edith's warmth, spontaneity, and considerable erotic charm kept the evening from becoming heavy by the sheer weight of masculine sobriety. If she was unhappy about her separation from Father, she knew how to disguise her feelings with the skill and discipline of the true actress. Father, sitting in his favorite chair whose upholstered armrests ended in lion heads finely carved in ebony wood, was relaxed and in high spirits. But it was Ewers's bulky, impeccably tailored presence that conjured up the spirit of the evening. He personified for me Father's past, a time that lay before Father's purification and conversion and that, for want of recollections of my own, I associated with the milieu Gisela had described in her novel, *Is This What Is Called Love?* I immediately thought of that book, which had disturbed me so deeply as a child, the first time I looked into Ewers's eyes and recognized in this man, in his guarded look, all the unlovely features that still, from time to time, broke through Father's words and actions: a violent temper, an unbridled sensuality, a penchant for cynicism, and a slick politeness.

Father, I knew, had long detached himself from that world in which he had been at home in Paris, when Gisela had been his wife and Ewers his friend. But now, observing him in the company of his old friend, animated by wine and spirited talk, I recognized for the first time how radically that world had once been part of his nature: the world of the flesh, as the Hebrew saints would have put it, or, as Father himself would have said, the world of André Gide and of the early Charles Baudelaire. I saw Father as he had been before I knew him, as Mother knew him when she married him, as Edith knew him when she fell in love with him. I saw the man who was at home among the crystal chandeliers, the silken wallpaper, the Persian rugs, the nymphs and fauns.

But I saw something else besides. Ewers and Edith were wholly themselves. Ewers radiated the spirit of his books, a spirit not so much of evil as of an all-too-ready eagerness to question everything that is good, honorable, and beautiful. Edith, hanging on his words as he dazzled us with tales of famous and infamous people he had known, was completely under his spell, while he made no effort to hide his delight in the attention of this charming woman. Father, as obviously as he enjoyed the magic of the hour, held back. He did not challenge his old friend who sometimes ridiculed, sometimes attacked the very things by which Father lived. Father kept a distance which showed itself more in a glance, a gesture, a smile, a silence, than in anything he said. I saw the man I had not known, but I also saw the man I knew: I saw the threshold of his soul, a threshold over which Mother and Edith, or for that matter, Ewers, had never stepped because they were deaf to the language of faith. And I sensed the distance he had traveled in his search for, and finally his fidelity to, a truth whose essence, for him, was surrender—surrender into the hands of God. I cannot describe the experience any better: the exchange that took place between Father and me that winter, in that villa, remained unspoken, unarticulated, and, ultimately, mysterious. What matters is that, when winter had turned into spring, I had learned to understand and accept the man whose own struggle had tragically shattered the lives of the two women who had never ceased to love him.

Shortly after New Year's Stephan was arrested by the Gestapo. I have forgotten the incident that led to his arrest, but when he was released after a couple of months in custody I found him profoundly changed. He seemed to be drinking heavily, and he made no secret of the pleasure he found in embarrassing me with his vividly descriptive tales of his escapades with prostitutes. His delicate features coarsened, giving his face a distinctively Semitic slant it had not had before. He no longer accompanied me to our favorite High Mass in the Saint Hedwig's Cathedral, or to the small basement chapel in the Schlüterstrasse where Romano Guardini celebrated mass for the Catholic student community.

My visits to the villa in Zehlendorf ceased. Edith, abandoning hope that Father and she would ever again live under the same roof, made preparations to emigrate to Switzerland. Father had already completed his own emigration into solitude: he had found refuge and a home in a small Benedictine convent in the countryside south of Berlin. Aunt Walli showed signs of wavering self-confidence. The first Jews were being deported from Germany, and one of her cousins had been among them. Our visits became heavy with foreboding.

Stephan's villa was confiscated by the city, and when his checks ceased coming, he took a job with a machine-building firm. When an office clerk's position became vacant in his department, I decided to join him, hoping that by being near him I could restore our old friendship. I left the Theater am Nollendorfplatz early in March.

Saint Thomas

. . . .

The Sitzkrieg ended in May 1940 with a string of spectacular German victories. German troops invaded Denmark and Norway, occupied Belgium, and broke through the Maginot Line. Many people believed that the war would be over in a matter of months, although their hopes for an early end to the fighting sprang from different expectations. "Now don't you worry any more, Herr Heinz," Frau Wirtz said, offering me a glass of schnapps to celebrate the announcement of the truce between Germany and France. "Now England must make peace or we'll bomb her into the ocean. And once the war is over—by August, I should say—we'll take care of Herr Hitler." By now my landlady knew that I was a half-Jew, and I knew that she was a hard-bitten Communist.

While Berlin was euphoric over the feats of Hitler's armies, I went through a period of deep depression. Unlike Frau Wirtz I feared that an early end of the war would merely serve to consolidate the Nazi regime throughout Europe and that my future life would be determined by the whims of a loathsome power—if I were permitted to live. Yet for the moment I lived, and by all outward appearances it was a life any young man, anywhere, could have lived under nearly normal conditions. The company where Stephan and I worked in the accounting office paid well, and I was soon able to exchange my austere cubbyhole in Frau Wirtz's apartment for a more comfortable room elsewhere. The job was not unbearably tedious, and occasionally Stephan and I left our desks, sneaked into the warehouse, and, hidden by a pile of matériel, played a game of chess, read a book, or simply dozed. We knew that discovery meant a charge of sabotage of the war effort, all the more serious because of our special status, but we were young and reckless, and the sense of danger helped relieve the monotony of the job. I had no concern about food or clothing. The midday meal, served in the company cafeteria, was ample and inexpensive, and for the rest I was always able to buy the sustenance I needed. Meat, butter, and coffee were sometimes in short supply and were to become increasingly scarce as the war continued, but there were always bread, potatoes, vegetables, and margarine.

In time I became a specialist in preparing a wide variety of potato soups, from brothlike liquidity to pastelike density. Often, on a Sunday, my landlady would invite me to dinner, and occasionally, on returning from work, I would find on the table in my room a piece of chocolate, home-baked cookies, or, most precious of all, a piece of fresh fruit. If I was in need of clothing—a suit, a shirt, underwear, or whatever—I could turn to an inexhaustible source of supply, gratis. Since most of my friends and former classmates were serving in the armed forces, their civilian clothes had been retired indefinitely, and I had from their mothers or sisters a standing offer to avail myself of whatever I needed. Mostly, however, it was a landlady who first noticed a pair of trousers frayed at the cuffs, or a shirt torn at the elbow, and who would come to the rescue with a needed garment from a son's or husband's wardrobe.

There was no lack of entertainment either—if I wanted entertainment. Wilhelm Furtwängler conducted at the Berlin Philharmonic, Gustav Gründgens played Mephisto in Goethe's *Faust* at the Prussian State Theater, the baritone Heinrich Schlusnus sang Schubert's *Lieder* at the Singakademie; theater and music continued to flourish, as did cafés, restaurants, nightclubs, and bars. The absence of "Jewish" or "degenerate" contributions to Berlin's cultural life was more debated than felt. Where their absence did create a painfully noticeable vacuum was in film, radio, and the press, which were under the personal control of Joseph Goebbels. Berliners flocked to see Greta Garbo films (which were Hitler's favorite) or purely escapist fare, or American productions such as *I Am a Fugitive from a Chain Gang,* starring Paul Muni, but generally ignored films put out under the direction of the Ministry for Public Enlightenment and Propaganda. I rarely read a newspaper or listened to the radio, except for what I could glean from them for the bare, factual news of the day. My escapes were books (which, banned or not, were readily available from my friends' private libraries); an occasional concert or stage play; a visit with Father, Annemarie, or Edith; and sometimes a date with a girl I had met at the office or at an outing to the beach of Lake Wannsee.

I should have been content, yet lacking a sense of direction and hope for the future, I was unable to acquiesce in an indefinite period of wait-and-see. I became restless. I knew I had no talent for escape into "wine, woman, and song," yet being constantly prodded, teased, and tempted by Stephan, who kept dragging me to nightclubs and introducing me to "girls," there were moments when I could easily have gone his route had it not been for a brief but intensive encounter with the thought and spirit of a medieval saint: Thomas Aquinas. Nothing could have been more incongruous with the spirit, the temper of the summer of 1940, or with my own existence, than logic, clarity, and order—the cosmos of Thomistic thought. "Ad primum sic proceditur . . . Sed contra . . . Respondeo . . . Ad primum dicendum . . ."* The very words seem out of place when they are set down in context with "war" and my memories of Berlin. Gregorian chant was more fitting to the mood of the time than discursive thinking, and for human warmth, for unquestioning *caritas,* for sheer survival as a human being needing to belong, I would soon become more dependent on the Benedictine mode of living than on a system of philosophy—no matter how perennial. Yet Saint Thomas was suited to the grim city: he needed no community, no support, no echo. He was book, intellect, intoxication with methodical, systematic thought. He was available. I studied his *Summa theologiae* at my writing table, in the lunchroom of a

*A standardized form of introducing proposition, argument, and reply in the works of Saint Thomas.

factory, in a bomb shelter, on a park bench. I could enjoy him in solitude or in a crowd of strangers. Above all, he taught me the discipline of critical discernment when I was floundering in a quagmire of sentiments and emotions.

The man who taught me what little I know about the universe of the *philosophia perennis* was Hermann Joseph Schmidt, the student chaplain of the Berlin diocese. I remember him, more than forty years after our paths crossed, as a stout, swarthy man of medium height, whose flashing black eyes and quick, precise movements radiated an immense but tightly controlled inner vitality. He was the kind of person who commands attention in a crowd by sheer force of personality, and whose very existence irritates, indeed accuses, a regimented society: Hejo, as we nicknamed him, wore his Roman collar like a banner. At heart a priest of the big city, he spoke as eloquently about his work in Berlin's hospitals, prisons, and asylums as he spoke about the truth he found in the majestic synthesis of the *Summa theologiae*. In that respect he resembled his famous predecessor, Carl Sonnenschein, whose spirit had been nourished by the cultural and intellectual tradition of Catholic Europe, and who had spent his life attempting to effect radical changes in the social milieu of the metropolis. I remember many things Hejo the thinker and lecturer had said, but I remember the *man* Hejo perhaps most vividly by a remark that revealed the earthier, "streetwise" side of his nature. One evening, as we were walking toward his apartment, I made a remark about a student who seemed sympathetic to the Nazi regime's anti-Semitic policy. "Yes," Hejo replied without hesitation, "he is one of those misfits in Christ whom you would love to kick with such force that your boot becomes stuck in his ass."

Hejo conducted a weekly evening course in Thomistic philosophy—a "Thomas circle," as we called these exercises in merciless logic—in the Catholic Students' Home, an old but dignified four- or five-story building in a quiet residential street near the Tiergarten. The building at Klopstockstrasse 6 used to be Sonnenschein's headquarters. Sonnenschein had died in 1929, and much of his work had been destroyed or severely paralyzed by the Nazi regime. The students with whom he had worked had been a largely homogeneous group, conscious of their privileged status and of the promises of an assured future. Hejo faced a different group across the huge oaken conference table where Sonnenschein, not much more than a decade ago, had given similar courses in an era not yet rent by doubt and fear. Now the privileged status was that of the soldier, the promises of the future were uncertain, and the twenty or thirty young men and women who once a week, for a couple of hours, assembled around that table were less interested in gathering knowledge or in solving social problems than in finding a meaning and a purpose in their time and in their circumstance. Most of them were either students who had been deferred from military service or soldiers in uniform who joined our group during a leave of absence, sporting an Iron Cross or some other war decoration. There was no Nazi around the oak table, I am sure. The lines between the Hitler regime and the Church had already been drawn too sharply for a no-man's land of pure intellectual inquiry and discussion to exist between them.

Yet I sensed that the moral and psychic forces at work among us were mixed and complex. On the surface we were bound by a preference for intellectual work, a sense of being set apart from the rest of the world by faith and by allegiance to the Church, and by the not unpleasant feeling that our participation in something as esoteric and as inimical to the regime as a course in medieval philosophy posed a real, if ever so slight, risk to our personal safety. Underneath this surface, however, we were separated by our individual backgrounds and experiences, by the roles we had to play under a dictatorial rule, and, perhaps most sharply, by the compromises we were willing to make with that dictatorship either out of conviction or to achieve our own ends.

Hejo, too, was acutely aware of these undercurrents and skillfully kept them from disrupting his diligently constructed *schola*. Still, they were apt at any moment to turn the discussion of the most abstract subject into a heated argument over personal and passionately held beliefs. I enjoyed these disputes thoroughly; I knew of no other place in Berlin where groups of people—large or small—still could indulge in debate without having to be on guard. But there would come, inevitably, a moment when a discussion would revive my old doubts and misgivings about the ideology I had gotten to know so well during the years when I wore the black uniform of

New Germany: that peculiar amalgam of German nationalism, romanticism, and Catholic universalism.

When the war broke out, Neudeutschland had ceased to exist as
an organization. The Nazi regime had put an end to the wearing of uniforms and to public appearances by all but its own organizations, and as
more and more men of my age were drafted for military service, even the
weekly group meetings that had been continued behind closed doors,
stopped. But the Neudeutschen continued to exist and to exert their considerable influence among Berlin's closely knit Catholic intelligentsia.
Wherever particular people congregated in Berlin's Catholic circles—to
paraphrase the motto of a well-known brand of cigarettes—there you met
New Germans, and mostly they were in charge of the congregation.

I had been out of touch with the organization for a couple of years,
partly because of my growing disenchantment with its tenets and attitudes,
partly because my friendship with Stephan and my renewed friendship
with Father satisfied my needs for intellectually congenial and stimulating
companionship. But I was not surprised to find my former comrades making up the majority at the Thomas circle. Some of them were now in
uniform and had seen battle; some had married; and others had already
achieved a reputation as brilliant students. Yet as we talked, pursuing the
elusive concepts of being and essence, form and matter, universality and
particularity, it became quickly evident that they still fed their souls and
minds on the images and faded glories of nostalgia, hoping, perhaps, to
find shelter against the bitter wind sweeping in a new and as yet unknown
age. More distressingly, I sensed that their dream was not at all unlike
Hitler's dream of a new Reich, of a reformation of Europe under banners
that were made in Germany. My fellow Catholics understood only too
well in their blood the language of fascism, and while most of them in
their minds and in the way they lived had drawn lines they dared not,
could not, cross, their loyalties often remained divided.

Omnia cohaerent—everything hangs together and interacts: again
and again Hejo returned to the maxim of the Doctor Angelicus. The thrust
of Thomistic thought, he would repeat, coaxing us to think through what-

ever the *questio disputanda* of the evening, is toward unity, toward wholeness; it is intolerant of division. But what were we to make of unity and
wholeness—holiness—in a time whose most persuasive symbols were the
barbed wire and the shattering explosion of a Stuka bomb? "Impossibile
est quod bonum commune civitatis bene se habet nisi cives sint virtuosi, at
minus illi quibus convenit principari,"* Hejo read, leaning back in his
chair and patiently puffing on his pipe in expectation of our first comment.
Yes, we could agree that it is impossible for the common good of the
nation to fare well unless at least those whose job it is to govern are men of
moral integrity. Heinrich Brüning was a man of moral integrity. Yet, was
the *civitas* better off in the Weimar Republic or in the Third Reich? "Non
est probabile quod aliqua communitas ita tota ad malum consentiat quin
aliqui sint dissentientes."** Were we not totally consenting to the pursuit
of evil simply by keeping quiet? Surely those of us who were still alive
and free to walk the street could not be called *dissentientes,* at least not in
the sense of Thomas.

As best he could, Hejo maneuvered his *schola* around the minefields of
issues; he knew it would have been foolish and hopeless to attempt answers or expect solutions where even the mind of a Thomas Aquinas
would have been brought up short by the darkness of an inscrutable mystery. But the word that remained naggingly on my mind and showed me
more clearly than any other disputed question that my world had become
irreconcilable with the world of the New Germans was the word *Jews.*
While I was still wearing the black uniform of the organization, few
among my fellow New Germans paid any attention to the "Jewish question." Perhaps they were too young to bother with things that did not touch
their lives. But on that issue they were not different from their elders,
including our chaplains. Up to 1940, in spite of the regime's vicious anti-
Semitic propaganda and the Kristallnacht of November 9, 1938, most
Germans I met did not believe that the regime had planned anything worse
for the Jews than forcing them to emigrate through harassment and by

* "The common good of the state cannot possibly fare well unless the citizens are virtuous,
at least those whose task it is to govern."
** "It is improbable that a community consents to evil so totally that it lacks dissenters."

starving them out of their livelihoods. Mother had ignored the danger signals until the Night of the Broken Glass. Aunt Walli still ignored them. Even the various decrees by which Jews had to turn in radios, were forbidden to use public transportation, and were forced to work in mines and factories did not persuade many that the Jews were destined for destruction. Those who learned that I was a Mischling were merely annoyed that this information forced them to fit as strange a creature as a half-Jewish Catholic into their familiar world.

But between the spring of 1940, when I joined the Thomas circle, and the summer of 1941, when it ceased to exist, many soldiers returning to Germany had witnessed the mass arrest, deportation, and murder of Jews in foreign countries—too many for anyone around our table to doubt the regime's true intention toward the Jews. "Goodness and being are interchangeable," Hejo explained. "To the extent that something is deficient in the fullness of goodness and being, to that extent it is called evil." While I listened to Hejo expound on the concepts of good and evil, the Evil One of the gospels went about his business with dispatch. I sensed how difficult Hejo's task was. At about that time, typewritten, mimeographed copies of the German translation of C. S. Lewis's *The Screwtape Letters* were circulating among us, fueling our discussions about the Thomistic definition of evil as a lack, an absence, a deficiency. For Hejo, for me, and for some of the others that discussion was anything but academic. Hejo knew very well that his audience could accept the harassment of the Church and the imprisonment or execution of Catholics whose outspoken opposition to the regime menaced the new order of things. In the view of Christian metaphysics, martyrdom was a *bonum,* a good intrinsic to the plan of salvation, and *Religionskriege* (religious wars) were the stuff of modern German history. But persecuting Jews simply because they were Jews was an outrage against German honor, an ugly stain on the shining armor of the knight. Few of us at that time knew of the existence of death camps, but what we knew was enough to cause feelings of guilt and shame, feelings that had either to be acknowledged in humility or covered up by a self-conscious and defensive aggressiveness. "The sun's o'ercast with blood; fair day adieu! Which is the side I must go withal?" Blanch of

Spain asks King John in Shakespeare's drama. For us, the world had become many-sided, and the darkness that spread over the land seemed to
change the very essence of things.

Hejo kept testing and measuring, patiently taking us step by step
from what we saw, heard, and felt to the ultimate source, meaning, and
purpose of existence. "Mr. Raubusch," he would say, addressing a young
man in the black officers' uniform of the Panzer divisions, "in training
your men, have you ever used the word 'courage'? Obviously you have.
Now has it ever occurred to you that there might be an essential link
between courage and humility? That one cannot truly exist without the
other? It hasn't. Well, let's see what Saint Thomas has to say about that
connection in the *Secunda secundae*."* He tried to meet us where we
lived, and after taking us to the dizzying heights of a universe where
everything, from the pebble on the beach to the glory of the Trinity, hangs
together, he would lead us back to our own closed-in microcosm that
suddenly seemed too tight, too dark, too empty. "Miss Heller," he might
challenge one of the women, "you once said that Baudelaire is the most
significant Christian poet of the nineteenth century. We have spent the last
few evenings discussing Saint Thomas's views on 'tristitia'—sadness. For
him, despondent sadness is the root of vindictiveness, of hatred and anger.
Now, did his, if you will, metaphysical dissection of gloom in any way
help you to understand something about *Les fleurs du mal* that eluded
you?"
There was something irresistible, compelling, in a vision where the
abrasive, painful, and sometimes tragic particulars of life showed up simply as deficiencies in a grandiose masterplan. There was something profoundly consoling in a vision where these deficiencies were taken seriously as being peculiar to *homo viator*, "man the traveler," "the vagrant
pilgrim." Here was space in which I could move freely, light by which I
could see, air I could inhale deeply. Sometimes Hejo would close the book
before him, put aside his pipe, and begin to talk about Thomas the man
and the saint, about the time and the life of the Dumb Sicilian Ox. He
liked to dwell on the Dominican's kindness and proverbial courtesy, on his

*The second part of the second book of the *Summa theologiae*.

simple piety, on his equanimity in illness and hardship, and without opening the *Summa* he would quote to us some moving passage that gave a
human form, palpable flesh, and pulsating blood to the awesome figure of
the angelic doctor. Sometimes he would recite a verse or two from one of
Thomas's great hymns, the *Pange lingua* or the *Lauda Sion,* and the room
would become very still as he spoke quietly about a monk who was not
only Christianity's profoundest thinker but also one of its finest lyricists
and greatest mystics. In those moments we sensed, as young as we were,
that Hejo laid bare before us his own soul, and that we were taken into the
intimacy of a friendship whose significance and depth could be fathomed
only with the eyes of faith.

I don't know if these evenings made a difference in the way in which
each of us faced the morning after our discussions: the soldier a bleak
barracks, the student an examination in microbiology, I the tedium of
paper-shuffling in an office. But we were learning to *name* things, and
perhaps in naming them we became less afraid and began to see traces of
meaning and order and purpose emerge from absurdity and chaos. Perhaps
some of us even learned to pray. At any event, the time had passed that
would allow indulgence in idle intellectual wordplay. Whatever influence
Saint Thomas had exerted on the core of our being was about to be tested
severely.

Coincidental with the sessions of the Thomas circle the city experienced its first serious air attacks. I remember well the raid that caused the
eruption in me of that fear that became a permanent affliction, a fear not so
much of death but of unspeakable violence—violence to sight, hearing,
smell, touch, and, yes, taste, the fear of a rape of the senses so brutal and
so complete that not even its monotonous repetition could harden me
against the expected assault. Until that night—sometime in the winter of
1940–1941—the raids, then amounting to only a few bombs dropped hap-
hazardly by reconnaissance planes, had not particularly worried me. I had
rarely bothered to go into the basement when the sirens began to howl,
and sometimes I even watched from an attic window or from a lookout on
the roof the white, spidery fingers of the searchlights explore the silent
vastness of the night sky. That night, I was sitting with some of the mem-

bers of the Thomas circle in the library of the student home in the Klopstockstrasse, talking about the meeting that had just ended. We were in
high spirits, and when the alarm sounded, someone sat down at a piano
and began to play. After a few snatches of a playful melody he suddenly
intoned the *Ode to Joy* from Beethoven's Ninth Symphony, and instantly
we crowded around the piano, arms linked, singing at the top of our voices
Schiller's immortal praise of brotherhood and peace.

I did not hear the sigh of the falling bomb or the sound of the explosion.
I felt a jolt as if the whole building had jumped up, the light went out,
came on again, flickered uncertainly, and then the room was plunged in
darkness. There was a moment of perfect stillness, and then everybody
began coughing at once. The floor rocked again, there was a deafening
crash and the tearing cadence of splintering glass, and then I stood in the
street desperately gulping the night air. The street, dark and empty,
seemed strangely peaceful. I heard the drone of a plane and suddenly, for a
moment, the sharp, dry tack-tack-tack of an antiaircraft gun. We stood in a
cluster on the front lawn, listening and waiting, without speaking. Then I
saw, a few hundred meters down the street, the billow of swirling smoke
rise up into the sky, black against black at first, then turning quickly into a
dirty, ominous red, and then there were only flames, ugly, bright-red
tongues breaking almost simultaneously through the roof of an apartment
building.

I don't know how I got into the house, but now I was standing with a
few others of the group before the front door of an apartment on the top
floor of the burning building. The soft light of small crystal chandeliers,
red carpeting, alabaster railings, a name plate of polished brass. Was it the
discreet elegance that brought us up short? Or the silence? There was not a
sound, no movement. How long we stood there—sheepishly, waiting,
listening—I don't remember. Someone rang the doorbell. Again. And
again. Nothing stirred behind the door. Then I saw the slender trail of
smoke winding along the carpet, and somebody screamed something, and
I felt the door give way, and I thought, My God, we are breaking into
somebody's flat! and I stood in a room brightly lit, panting and motionless, and I did not know what to do. It was a spacious dining room and
I took in every detail of its exquisite decor as if I had to remember it for the

rest of my life: the Persian rugs; a Rubens, a Rembrandt, a Titian in heavy gilded frames; a tall Chinese floor vase; a high cabinet filled with crystals and things of dull silver; armchairs in rococco style; silk pillows; drapes of rich blue velvet covering the entire wall opposite; a smoker's table with an intricate pattern of flowers. The table in the center had been set for two, but the diners had obviously finished their meal in haste, perhaps in a hurry to make the curtain call for the theater. Napkins were carelessly thrown over the plates, red wine shone in tall glasses, there was an open cigar box next to one of the plates, and the Turkish cups on the tray with the silver service were untouched. The chairs were pushed back into the room; a pair of delicate white slippers stood on one of them.

I felt as embarrassed as if I had stumbled on the embrace of lovers. The room—two invisible people—furiously resented my intrusion. Then the drapes fell away, revealing the windows behind them, I heard glass shatter and felt cold air surge through the room which suddenly looked naked. The resentful presence vanished, and I grabbed one of the rococco chairs and made my way to the landing, and now the staircase was full of noise and confusion. People were carrying books and drawers and suitcases and clothes, trying to drag them past heavy furniture that blocked the landings, while others were forcing their way up the stairs. I abandoned my chair somewhere and made my way back to the apartment. There the heat had become intense and ugly black smoke swirled through the rooms. I was nearly blind from sweat and my lungs fought for relief. My companions were throwing things out the window—books, linens, clothing, papers, pillows, rugs. I don't know how long that madness lasted. The last thing I saw of the apartment was the table overturned on its side, and, in the hall, the abandoned smoker's table on which somebody had neatly placed the pair of white slippers.

What had happened did not amount to much: I had been shaken up by an explosion, and I had tried to get people's belongings out of a burning building. Many people all over the world experience this sort of thing in peacetime. Soon I would get to know the real hell of bombing raids. There would be nights, hundreds of nights, when I would listen with numb terror to the interminable whistling of falling bombs, to their sighs and screams, while with every muted cough of an explosion the cellar, pitch dark and utterly silent, would rock gently to and fro like a cradle. There would be nights when, after the "all clear" had sounded, I would open the basement door and start climbing the stairs to my apartment, only to find that stairs, walls, and ceilings ended abruptly in twisted girders and broken beams and jagged wall fragments on some of which the moonlight revealed the pattern of my wallpaper. There would be nights when I would wander for hours through streets framed on either side by solid sheets of flame, buffeted by a roaring storm that seemed to feed on the very stillness of a clear, moonlit night.

Compared with those nights, my first taste of a "raid" had been a trifle. But I sensed that my life, the life of the city, the war, had entered a new and ominous phase. All of us at the Thomas circle knew. As Hejo imperturbably expounded again and again on the interchangeability of being, truth, and goodness, a fine drizzle of plaster dust kept descending on our table from a large crack in the ceiling, covering every surface in the room with a white film. Across the street from where we were gathered, the roof of the building that only a few days before had formed a continuous line against the sky now ended abruptly in jagged stonework. "Thomas Mann," I heard myself say one evening with impatience, "Thomas Mann concludes his *Magic Mountain* with the outbreak of the First World War, which becomes for Hans Castorp a liberation from the oppressive environment of the sanatorium and from the burden of his encyclopedic knowledge. Now, what do you make of . . .?"

And so it went for another few months until, some time in 1941, the Thomas circle ended with Hejo's arrest and deportation to a concentration camp. Many of the young men and some of the women of the circle eventually perished in the war. When I think of them I wonder whether they would have died with a curse on their lips or despair in their hearts had it not been for those evenings illuminated by the light of a thirteenth-century monk. I continued the study of the *Summa theologiae* on my own. The German-Latin edition, a set of several volumes handsomely bound in dark-blue linen, accompanied me from one bombed-out, burned-out room to the next yet intact shelter, until one night these books, too, were buried in the rubble of a collapsed building, together with the rest of my few possessions.

The Priory

∙ ∙

In mid-1939 Father had begun to spend most of his weekends at a small Benedictine convent in the country, some twenty-five miles south of Berlin. Occasionally he lived there for a week at a time, to complete a manuscript or read the galleys for a book. Finally, in the spring of 1940, he took up residence with the sisters. Penniless as usual, he had nothing to offer in the way of contributions or even rent money, but the sisters were exceedingly fond of him and may have accepted in good faith his habitual optimistic predictions that a windfall from the sale of this or that manuscript would soon enable him to pay for his room and board.

I visited him often at his new lodgings. Nothing existed, nothing happened there that should have made a twenty-year-old prefer a weekend among nuns to a weekend in the city, a city that, despite its gradual disintegration, still offered during the first three years of the war numerous opportunities for escape, entertainment, and diversion. Even by traditional Benedictine standards of taste, the sisters of Saint Gertrud lived on the wrong side of the tracks. For Benedictines, beauty speaks eloquently of

God's essence, and therefore they had built their monasteries and convents with a sharp ear for nature's theological language. Where the sisters lived, the creator seemed to have been in a taciturn mood. Some twenty miles northwest of the convent, at the southwestern outskirts of Berlin, Frederick the Great had been closer to the spirit of Benedictine piety than the sisters when he chose Potsdam as the site of his Sans-Souci, the German version of Versailles. There, the Brandenburg march displayed all its charm with sparkling rivers, clear lakes, and lush woods that each weekend, summer and winter, attracted thousands of hikers and campers from the city. Here, in the nation's sandbox, broad tracts of sandy plains and sparsely grown heaths took turns with arid fields, moors, and dense, somber pine woods, and the few farming communities that had stubbornly clung to the barren soil since the days of the "Old Fritz" were poor and sullen.

Yet for the next three years I would put between my life in the city and myself a distance that a bomber could have covered in a five-minute flight, but which, for me, meant a distance between two worlds. After a week in the factory, in the early afternoon of a Saturday, I would take the city railway to the southern outskirts of Berlin, there board a train for an hour-long ride to Sperenberg—a town of which I had never noticed anything more remarkable than a rusty water tower and a couple of windowless warehouses—and then begin the hike that would bring me to the convent gate in about another hour, in time for compline* under normal conditions, in time for a midnight snack if the bombers had been at work.

The moment I left the red-brick railroad depot behind me, the turmoil of the city ebbed away and purer, stronger forces asserted themselves. Four years later, the highway would throb with traffic; five years later, it would be littered with the residues of battle. But now, in the early forties, it was virtually deserted. The stillness soothed my senses, which, in Berlin, were forever on guard against the sudden blast of sirens. The view of the forests on the left and the fields on the right refreshed my eyes, weary from nightly blackouts and the accumulating signs of destruction. Sometimes I would be accompanied by the low, almost casual whistle of artillery shells

*The evening prayer in the Roman Catholic liturgy.

. . . .

seeking some target on the firing range deep in the woods. If the wind was in my face, the pungent odor of dung would tell me that I was approaching Kummersdorf, a string of stunted, dark houses hiding behind weathered fences. Walking through the village I would set off a clamor of barking and yelping that, as I left the place behind, would fade much quicker than the tenacious reminder of the dung heaps I had seen behind every fence. Then the silence of a deep forest would again be my companion until, after another half-hour's walk, I reached my destination: Alexanderdorf, Alexander's Village, a hamlet that had nothing to distinguish it from Kummersdorf except that its name had come to designate the priory itself. "Going to Alexanderdorf" meant, in Berlin, that one was headed for the Priory of Saint Gertrud.

The first time I came upon the high, massive stone wall that, with unmistakable emphasis, closed off the convent grounds against the last houses of the village, I was startled. In a part of Prussia that boasted of its sandy plains and heaths, stone walls were a rare sight. The wings of the heavy wooden gate were swung wide open. From the entrance, a spacious, pebble-strewn pathway lined with trees led straight to a manor. On the left was a frog pond shaded by weeping willows and, occupying almost the entire north side of the grounds, a high-roofed timbered barn. On the right were vegetable plots, a large flower garden, and a modest vineyard. A spacious stable, tool sheds, and a cluster of greenhouses bounded the estate to the south.

The manor, which housed the convent proper, was as much out of character here as was the stone wall. "The castle," as the local farmers still called it, had once been the seat of the counts of Schwerin, an old and distinguished family of Junkers, the landed Prussian aristocracy. From here they had governed a vast estate the northernmost boundary of which had reached the outskirts of Berlin. "The castle" still spoke of their power and wealth, their arrogance and Prussian heaviness of spirit. A ponderous tower of cut granite stone jutted out from the center of the two-story building. Fluted clay shingles covered the steep roof. High, arched windows framed by beams of weathered oak looked out on a large flowerbed set into what had once been the basin for a fountain, and clusters of majestic old fir trees gave an air of restrained elegance to the no-nonsense structure.

A small, one-story wing with separate entrance was attached to either side of the building. One served as a guesthouse; the other furnished a modest room each for Father and two Benedictine monks. Behind the building, enclosed by a high wire fence, stretched a park of oak and maple trees, clumps of tangled bushes, and tall pines. Impenetrable to sunlight and carpeted with a deep layer of pine needles, it offered the sisters an occasional escape when the summer heat in their cells became too stifling. Father Ludger sometimes amused himself here hunting squirrels with an air gun. Only when the war began to close in on this forlorn stretch of land did we learn that a park like this can offer unexpected advantages.

In Berlin, the feverish tempo of the workday only glossed over a spreading mood of impotence. At Saint Gertrud's, the drive of the day's tasks was toward building up, creating, harmonizing, cultivating. At a time when some of the largest and most famous Benedictine abbeys in Germany had been confiscated by the Gestapo and their monks expelled, and nothing was farther from the mind of a German abbot than to establish a new monastery or convent, Saint Gertrud's became the youngest foundation of Europe's oldest monastic order. Most of the twenty-two sisters had been nurses working in one of the Catholic hospitals in Berlin. As so many young Catholics of that time, they had become attracted to the liturgical movement that, under the guidance of the Benedictines, fostered authenticity in cult, an understanding of the original meaning of rites, and lay participation in the mass and other modes of worship. Soon they had committed themselves to the daily praying of the liturgical hours and to the practice of Gregorian chant.

In the summer of 1934, when Hitler's blood purge of his opponents gave Berliners their first taste of the open brutality of the new regime, they purchased "the castle" and its grounds and founded a Benedictine community. They turned part of one of the barns into a bakery that furnished parishes throughout Berlin with altar breads; grew flowers that they sold to cemeteries; made liturgical vestments; and opened up a kindergarten for the local farm families. Eventually, they converted one of the wings of the manor and part of a stable into a guesthouse. Meter by meter they mixed the sandy soil with fertilizer and good ground to raise vegetables for their own kitchen. For milk, eggs, and an occasional meat dish they kept a few cows, chickens, and some pigs. They did away with the traditional division in Benedictine convents between choir and lay sisters: all of them did the daily chores, all of them studied and practiced the liturgical forms of worship, and all of them followed the bell calling the community to prayer. Here the Benedictine motto, *Ora et labora* (Pray and work) was lived without any concession to culturally and historically conditioned forms.

What the priory offered to Father was, foremost, a *routine*—an ordered, disciplined regularity of tasks, a framework for time, and a purpose for every hour, every day, and every week. To him, I am sure, submission to this routine was liberation from a lifelong struggle to order his life toward a purpose that for most other men consisted of caring for a family or of serving a profession. At fifty-five he submerged himself into the monastic routine with a fervor that would have suited a novice still aglow with the certainty of having been called. But unlike many a novice, he remained completely believable. A mystic all his life, he now surrendered his thoughts, his feelings, and his time to the norms and dictates of an exacting style of adoration that freed him from the uncertainties and dangers of a hermit's piety. For the rest, nobody would have noticed any change in him, and even those of his relatives and friends who themselves were nonbelievers but had long accepted his "Catholic bias" saw nothing particularly eccentric in his finally choosing a convent as his living quarters.

His first three years in the priory—the first three years of the war— were among the happiest of his life. His days were filled with praying, studying, and writing, and with taking long walks through the heathlands and pine forests surrounding the priory. His genuine affection for simple people made him popular among the farmers and villagers of the vicinity. His friends looked up to him as the example of one who had successfully reconciled in his mode of life the impulses toward a monastic piety with the cultivation of a refined yet unmistakably worldly humanism. His social life was busier than ever. For the guests of the priory a visit with Herr Kühn soon became one of Saint Gertrud's attractions, and on weekends his modest room, as he good-naturedly complained, bore more resemblance to a pigeon loft than to a monastic hideaway. He was at home, he belonged, and, perhaps most important, for the first time in his life he was free of financial worries. For the first time in his life, too, he was free of the continuous demands on his time and money by those for whom he felt himself responsible, if not before the world, then certainly and deeply before God. Edith was in Switzerland and about to emigrate to the United States. Mother was in London, and Annemarie and I lived and worked in Berlin. Even his considerable need for cigarettes was taken care of: when the rationing of tobacco began, his friends at the priory supplied him so generously with coupons that he could satisfy his three-packs-a-day habit until tobacco became altogether unavailable.

I soon became dependent on my weekend escapes to the priory. For the first time in my life I saw Father with some regularity, although we rarely spent much time together alone. There was the discipline of the liturgical hours that called us to the little chapel four or five times a day. There were other weekend visitors claiming Father's time; there were his manuscript, his magnificent stamp collection—a hobby he had pursued since boyhood—my fatigue, and my desire to spend a few quiet hours with a book. Sometimes we would play a game of chess in his tiny room, where I sat in an overstuffed chair, facing him across his desk. Sometimes we would take a long walk through the flowering heath or through the somber wood, singing the psalms of one of the liturgical hours or discussing a book. Often, after lunch or dinner, we would join other guests in impromptu conversations. As brief as these moments were, we cherished each other's company without once admitting, perhaps not even to ourselves, that these moments were precious and sustained us.

I still take pleasure, after more than forty years, in remembering an incident that, small and insignificant in itself, shed more light on our growing intimacy during those few short years than any other experience or exchange at that time. One summer evening Father had accompanied me, as he was fond of doing occasionally, on my long hike back to the Sperenberg railroad station, where I was to catch the train for Berlin. Waiting for the train, which was late, we had seated ourselves outside the station house on a bench from which we had a full view of the spacious town square before us. It was still light, and the square, shimmering in the hot air, was deserted. We had been engaged in conversation when Father suddenly stopped talking in mid-sentence. Following the direction of his gaze I observed a woman who had appeared at the far right of the station building and, having crossed the tracks, had begun to walk diagonally across the square, her back toward us. Small of waist and broad of hips, her gait was leisurely, a flimsy red dress clinging to her ample figure. We had followed her with our eyes for what seemed to me an inordinately long time, when Father broke the heavy silence with a sigh. "She has one of those rear-ends," he said, "that positively extend an invitation to be goosed, don't you think?" I laughed, not quite knowing whether I should be amused or shocked. I had never heard Father talk loosely about women; off-color remarks just didn't fit my image of him. "Yes," I finally managed to reply, "I agree." And, suddenly delighted with this rare moment of man-to-man talk, I added, "Well, it seems the nunnery hasn't damaged your Old Adam too badly." It was his turn to laugh.

There were other things besides the enjoyment of my closeness to Father that drew me to the priory at every opportunity, even though the increasing frequency and intensity of the air raids on Berlin began to make any kind of travel difficult, tedious, and risky. For the first time in my life I felt the magnetism and quiet power of the liturgical life of the Church, of the solemn rhythm of psalms, hymns, litanies, and prayers. My introduction to the forms of Benedictine piety was all but spectacular; in fact, to anyone lacking an inner disposition for the language of the sacred hours, the sisters' celebrations would have appeared anemic. "Deus, in adjutorium meum intende," the prioress would intone, and the nuns in the choirstalls behind us would fall in, "Domine, ad adjuvandum me festina."* Their voices were cool, restrained. The small pipe organ suffered from hypoxia. Father, standing or sitting next to me, would discreetly clear his throat after the fourth or fifth strophe of the first psalm and begin to sing to himself at about an octave lower than the rest of us, and a shade off-key. The handful of guests who had come to the service trailed Father's

---

*"God, come to my assistance. Lord, make haste to help me." Opening of the hours for daily liturgical devotion.

bass haltingly and self-consciously. Lauds, prime, tierce, vespers, compline:** the same even voices, the same rhythm and tonality, the breathless organ, the fragrance of incense, Father oblivious of his environment and at one with prayer and song.

Soon I knew the psalms, the antiphons, and hymns by heart. Sometimes, in a bomb shelter in Berlin, my lips would instinctively form the words of the *De profundis,* or, in happier moments, I would hum, behind my desk in the factory or in my bleak lodging, the lovely melody of the *Ave Regina caelorum,* the *Magnificat,* the *Nunc dimittis servum tuum.* The few hours I spent on an occasional Sunday in this chapel left a resonance that carried me, perhaps without my knowing it, through many fearful days and sleepless nights in the grim city.

I rarely exchanged more than a few words with any of the sisters. Their presence was glimpsed and felt rather than encountered, but their unobtrusive ubiquity permeated the grounds with an air of lighthearted serenity which, had it been lacking, would have robbed Saint Gertrud's of the unique and irresistible attraction it held for me. The least visible of the sisters was the one who had created the community and whose personality shaped its style and character until she died in 1975: the prioress. In physique and composure, Mother Justina could have served as a model for a female counterpart to Saint Thomas Aquinas. When I first met her (although one didn't really meet her; one came into her presence), I was stunned by her massive, motionless form. Yet my feeling of discomfort, almost of helplessness before this intensity of black cloth, vanished the moment I became conscious of the broad face framed by the white lining of her veil. An inner tranquillity seemed to make the plain, in themselves uninteresting features translucent, so that I had the sensation of viewing a wide sunny valley from the top of a mountain. The clear gray eyes held my own steadily and attentively. There was no hint in her expression that this serenity masked, as nuns' faces sometimes do, a spirit of resignation or conscious withdrawal. Her bearing expressed, unmistakably, a barrier and a distance, but she broke quickly into a smile, and she could be lively and witty in conversation. Yet I never could quite shake the awareness of a

**The hours for daily liturgical devotion.

boundless energy and an uncompromising will that lay poised behind the barrier and the distance. I once observed a Russian soldier approach her, shouting and gesticulating. As he stepped close to her, his voice fell, his arms dropped to his sides, and he stood almost at attention before she had opened her mouth.

During the five years the priory was part of my life, I got to know only one sister well: Sister Eucharis, the portress. She was then perhaps in her late twenties, of medium height, pleasantly chubby (as far as her habit permitted such observations), and fine-featured. Although she gave the impression of a somewhat eager breathlessness, I judged her to be shy by nature. At times she seemed completely withdrawn, and then her dark mood would fall like a shadow over the guests at the dinner table: the spirit of the priory was not accustomed to darkness. I did not believe she would last long as portress, but when I saw her again after a separation of more than thirty years, she still served the community in the same capacity. Over the years, she became Father's closest friend. She never quite learned the ways of a nun. There remained about her an air of independence, a sparkle of unselfconscious femininity, that neither her religious garb nor a posture acquired in years of self-discipline could hide. We knew that we were fond of each other, and therefore we kept a friendly but firm distance. In time, she became Father's constant companion, his true *fille d'alliance*. Their friendship, embedded, as it were, in the salutary strictness of the religious life, and quietly supported by her superiors and coreligionists, was real and intimate, and it lasted until Father died. No other sister was more unlike Mother Justina, but to me and to Father and the other guests, both were equally expressive of the spirit of Saint Gertrud's.

Since the late thirties, when the sisters were finally able to store provisions for more than a few days' meals, they had taken in guests. A two-story modern guesthouse was built back to back with one of the barns, and when this house quickly proved too small, the sisters converted one of the wings of the manor and parts of the stables for the same purpose. Saint Gertrud's had none of the features that usually attract visitors to Germany's famous Benedictine abbeys: the irresistible combination of authentic architecture, inspiring scenery, flawless performance of Gregorian chant, and rich meals. Here, the architecture was colorless, the scenery was devoid of thrills, the chanting was correct but a little too ethereal to cause gooseflesh, the meals were simple, and flies were everywhere. But the spirit of the place was genuine—artless, serene, open, of a springlike flavor—and until the air raids paralyzed and eventually put an end to rail transportation, guests came to the priory not only from Berlin but from all corners of Germany.

When I began to visit Father, I first kept to myself, partly because of fatigue but mainly because the wariness I needed for survival in the city had become habitual. Besides, what did I have in common with people attracted to a community of women? Yet as I met and got to know some of the regular guests, I found myself more and more drawn into their inner world. On a typical weekend, summer or winter, I would join some ten or fifteen guests for the day's meals in the manor's dining room. This room, with its oaken, scrolled, stiff furniture, had remained virtually unchanged from the days of the previous owners, except that the monumental portraits of Prussian officers and gentlewomen had been replaced with equally dark, heavy-framed scenes from the lives of Jesus and Saint Benedict. Although the sisters did their best to lighten the room's heaviness with sprigs of green and flowers and flippantly airy lace curtains, the stern spirit of Prussia continued to lurk in the dark corners. We dubbed it the *Preussenzimmer,* "the Room of the Prussians." It was not the kind of room that stimulated conversation; besides, the priory was not the kind of place where meals meant table talk. Guests were not exempt from the schedule by which the sisters lived. The bell would call us for lunch or dinner; three minutes later a couple of novices would serve the soup; and after another twenty minutes, when the bell called the sisters to their next task, the table would be quickly cleared and covered again with a heavy cloth of dark-red velvet.

Yet during these few minutes the alliances were formed that set the pattern and marked the character of the social life at Saint Gertrud's. Because we were dispersed in four or five different buildings, the meals gave us the opportunity to size each other up, assess each others' intellectual compatibility, and, most important, quickly judge by the usual leading questions and comments a new arrival's political reliability. For every new

Rosa and Richard Kuehn, the author's parents, shortly after their marriage in Switzerland.

Heinz Kuehn with his sister, Annemarie.

Heinz Kuehn at boarding school in Potsdam, about 1930–1931. Such caps were worn by gymnasium pupils to distinguish them from those not attending an institution of higher education.

Annemarie and Heinz Kuehn in the Berlin apartment.

Aunt Walli, who died in transport to a
concentration camp.

Aunt Minna.

Heinz and Rosa Kuehn in the
summer of 1932.

Rosa Kuehn, shortly before her emigration
to England in 1939.

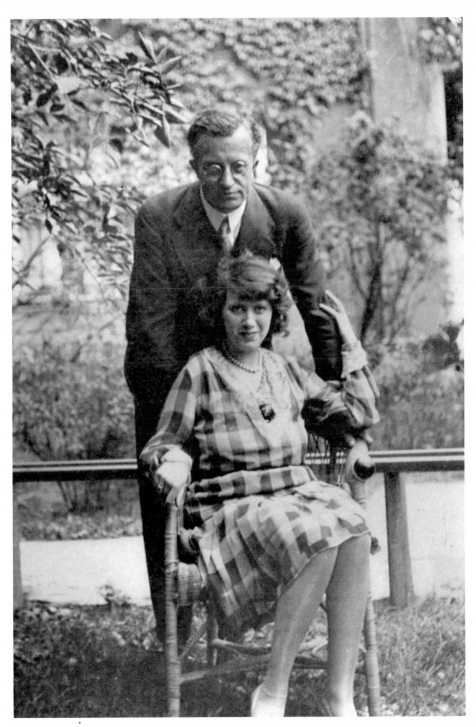

Richard Kuehn with his third wife, actress Edith Freudenheim.

Page from Heinz Kuehn's *Wehrpass* (military pass) showing the entry *Mischl I—Mischling,* or mixed breed, of the First Degree.

A page from the military pass, documenting Heinz Kuehn's changes of residence during the war.

Heinz Kuehn in the drill uniform of
the State Labor Service.

Heinz Kuehn digging a ditch while
in the State Labor Service.

Barracks life in the State Labor Service. Heinz Kuehn is seated in the
foreground, far right. Peter Schmidt, Heinz's future brother-in-law, is standing,
far left.

Cover of *Arbeitsbuch* (workbook).

Page from Heinz Kuehn's workbook, documenting some of his places of employment during the Nazi regime.

Cover of *Kennkarte* (identity card).

Heinz Kuehn's identity card.

The main building of the Priory of Saint Gertrud.

Mother Justina, O.S.B., prioress of
the Priory of Saint Gertrud.

Richard Kuehn with
Sister Eucharis, his *fille
d'alliance,* in his room
in the priory.

Richard and Heinz Kuehn taking a stroll on the grounds of the priory during
wartime.

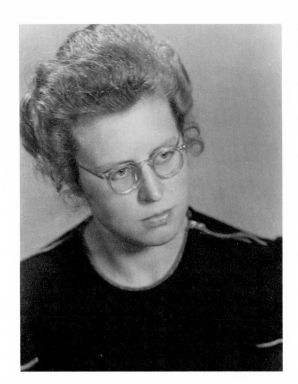

Annemarie, the author's sister, during the war.

Heinz Kuehn, about 1941–1942.

Heinz Kuehn during a quiet moment between air raids, Berlin, about 1942–1943.

A U S W E I S

OdN

Der Inhaber dieses Ausweises ist Mitglied des Berliner Verbandes der Opfer der Nürnberger Gesetze. Alle Dienststellen der alliierten Besatzungsmächte und alle deutschen Dienststellen und Behörden werden gebeten, den Inhaber dieses Ausweises in seinen Angelegenheiten zu unterstützen.

Предъявитель сего удостоверения является членом Берлинского Союза Жертв Нюрнбергских законов. Просьба ко всем учреждениям Союзных властей и немецким учреждениям и властям оказывать пред. явителю сего удостоверения во всех его делах поддержку.

The bearer of this certificate is a member of the Berlin „Association of the Victims of the Nürnberg Laws". All branches of the Allied Forces of Occupation and all German Offices and Authorities are requested to lend their assistance to the proprietor of this certificate in settling his affairs.

Le porteur de ce certificat est membre de l'Association des „Victimes des Lois de Nuremberg" à Berlin. Toutes les autorités des Forces Alliées d'Occupation et tous les bureaux et autorités allemands sont priés d'assister le porteur de ce certificat à régler ses affaires.

MAGISTRAT VON GROSS-BERLIN

Ausweis

für Verfolgte

der nationalsozialistischen

Sondergesetzgebung

№ 3750

HAUPTAUSSCHUSS OPFER DES FASCHISMUS

Opposite: top, Membership pass, Berlin Association of the Victims of the Nuremberg Laws. In the Third Reich, these laws defined the status of Jews; *bottom,* Identity card for persons persecuted by the special National Socialist legislation. Issued by the Central Office of Victims of Fascism.

Heinz Kuehn, about 1946.

Regina, at the time of her courtship with Heinz Kuehn, about 1947.

Regina and Heinz Kuehn with four of their six children, Milwaukee, 1953.

Angelika and Birgitta Kuehn with neighbors on the steps of the house where the Kuehns lived in Milwaukee during their first year in America.

arrival was a potential threat—not a threat in the usual sense of disrupting the congeniality of a group whose members are comfortable in each others' presence, but a threat to the political safety of each guest and to the very existence of the priory.

Under these conditions, the priory left little room for casual acquaintanceships. The people who came there already had a strong common bond in the interests that led them to this unique community. When, in addition, they were compatible as persons, intimate friendships quickly developed. In spite of my youth and a way of life that had nothing in common with theirs, Father's friends accepted me as readily as I was drawn to them. The coterie that formed in the summer of 1940 and lasted until the bombs became ubiquitous consisted mainly of three women and, besides Father and myself, a dentist in whose apartment in Berlin Father had lived on and off before settling in the priory. The doctor had a flourishing practice in a fashionable Berlin district, but people who met him for the first time and did not know his profession usually guessed him to be a professor of philosophy, a monk in civilian clothes, or an artist specializing in iconology. He could have done more than adequately for any one of these. By temperament a pessimist and melancholic, he appeared to be sinister and aloof, an impression fortified by his dark complexion; blueblack slick hair; a seemingly lipless, unsmiling face whose cheeks shone forever with a bluish tint; and deep-set, watchful black eyes.

In Berlin, I met him occasionally at the Thomas circle or at one or another of the many clandestine discussion groups and study clubs that formed something of an intellectual underground movement. Here at the priory he enriched our conversations with his profound knowledge of the Christian mystics, Russian art and literature, and the history of the liturgy. About fifteen years my senior, he had married the previous year, and his wife occasionally joined him on his visits to Alexanderdorf. She was extremely shy, and although for the last two years of the war she lived in a cottage near the priory to escape the raids on Berlin, we never got to know her well. Eventually I learned that her father, who had been a prominent industrialist, had suffered some terrible fate at the hands of the Nazis and that her family had been virtually wiped out. The nature or circumstances of the calamity she never disclosed to me, although I am sure that she had told the story to Father, who seemed to be the only person she liked and trusted.

The three women, who shared an apartment in Münster, the capital of Westphalia, were Ida Marie Soltmann, who directed a vocational school for girls; Anni Borgas, who was a photographer; and their roommate, a kindly, motherly woman of whose presence at our conversations we were aware only because of the soft, rhythmic clatter that accompanied her needlework. I was especially attracted to Ida Marie, a petite woman in her forties whose slender, delicately boned face under a crown of magnificent blond hair was illuminated by large gray eyes that seemed forever to glitter in an expression of good-natured irony. One of the first women in Germany ever to be admitted to a university, she was well known in the circles of her profession and among Germany's Christian intelligentsia for her administrative talent, her success as a counselor and educator, and her skill at repartee. Her husband had been killed in the First World War, and in her younger years she had been an ardent campaigner for the cause of Marxism; what kind of connections had kept her out of a concentration camp we could only surmise. Like Father a convert to Catholicism, she had a thorough knowledge of theology and Scripture and shared Father's preoccupation with French literature and history. Their compatibility and fondness for each other were so obvious that their friends never gave up hope altogether that they would eventually marry, even though "Frau Doktor" (as we called her) occasionally protested in mock horror that she had no intention of becoming "Mrs. Kühn number four."

Anni Borgas, the youngest of the trio, was tall, lanky, and quick and resolute in her movements. Everything about her was light and airy, from the blond hair, which she wore cropped, and the light-blue eyes in her elegant face, to her long, delicate, restless hands. Her photographer's world was one of images of the past—she was known throughout Germany for her superb photographs of medieval churches, castles, fountains, monasteries. She was fascinated by faces, particularly the faces of medieval people. In her photographs, weathered stone became warm and pliable, and the empty eyes of emperors, saints, housewives, children, and soldiers glowed with a life that seemed to feed on an inner, hidden source of light. When the rest of us had moved for too long in the world of ideas, she would begin to squirm and, finally, break in at the first opening we gave her to remind us that faces are more reliable clues to character, personality, and the mood of an era than reputation or writings.

These were the people whose company I sought whenever I had an opportunity to leave the city, whose inner world I wanted to make my own, whose ideas and visions I needed to endure a life none of them had ever experienced, none of them could have a part in. Typically, on a summer evening the six of us would sit after compline around the small iron table under one of the old fir trees that stood in front of the manor like nature's monuments to the priory's more masculine days. The sky would still be luminous, the air sweet and cool. Perhaps it would be one of those exquisite evenings for which Berliners serenade their "sandbox," the nickname they had given to Berlin's environs. The house and the grounds would be perfectly quiet. The compline marked the beginning of *silentium strictum* for the sisters, a strict silence that would be lifted again only after breakfast the next morning. At some moment during our conversation, Sister Eucharis would appear in the doorway, quickly walk around the flowerbed to our table, and with a wordless smile hand me a package wrapped in newspaper. She would nod in reply to my "Danke schön" and disappear again in the house. She knew I would have to start out for the Sperenberg depot in a few hours, to catch the midnight train to Berlin; the package contained my customary sandwiches for the journey.

Instinctively the voices of my companions would be hushed as they engaged in that great and elegant European art which my own generation was no longer able to enjoy nor, indeed, cared much about: the art of conversation. As I listened to them I sensed in their words, their ideas and visions, something I would not experience myself until much later: the sustaining power and the vitalizing energy of knowledge, culture, and tradition. In age, they and I were far apart, but they had grown up reading the same classics as I, studying the same languages, getting the same slant on German and world history, sitting patiently through the same seminars on Goethe's *Faust* and Kant's *Kritik der reinen Vernunft* (*Critique of Pure Reason*). Then each of them had to measure and test, in his own way, insights acquired from books or lectures against the experience of the First World War and the political and intellectual upheavals in its wake. Their education and early environment had supported them, at least in their formative years, in a quiet acceptance of basic Christian tenets, but all of them had gone as adults through long periods in which they emotionally and intellectually either severely questioned Christianity or rejected it out of hand. Yet the old synthesis of knowledge, faith, and tradition, so methodically presented in school and at the university, and often less than wholeheartedly accepted, had proven capable of living and developing. For Father, the synthesis included Jean-Paul Marat as well as Saint Augustine. For Ida Marie, it included Marx and Engels as well as Henri Bremond. For our dentist-philosopher, it included Saint Hildegard von Bingen, whose advice on matters of health he preferred to that of his own physician, as well as Dostoevski. And Anni, our photographer, could launch into a dissertation on the theology of art as easily from a mosaic of a Byzantine saint as from a portrait of Heinrich Himmler.

Heinrich Himmler—that was the symbol for the new stage on which they acted out the fascinating play of their ideas and convictions and tested them for substance, authenticity, and persuasiveness. I was their audience, intended or, mostly, unintended. They knew their play was good; what they played were variations on their theme in an attempt to capture the Zeitgeist. I was the wanderer between both worlds, the world of an isolated Benedictine convent and the world of the German capital drunk with *Kriegslust,* the Germanic lust for battle. In another three years there would be only one world, and the exigencies of survival would govern the life of the priory as mercilessly as they governed the life of the city. By 1944 there would be no more guests, no more conversations, and the sisters would have become wise in the ways of war. Yet by then I would have reached my own synthesis, another beneficiary of Europe's indestructible gifts. In the meantime, my testing ground lay in Berlin.

Technical Progress

. . . .

"**C**ongratulations," Father said when I told him that I had found a job with a company manufacturing ballbearings for tanks, planes, and submarines. "Now you can support the war in the Company for Technical Progress [the name of the firm], and I will support it in the nunnery." Father was ironic as usual, but, as jobs went under the circumstances, I did not fare badly. From my lodgings in West Berlin I could reach the cluster of bleak concrete buildings in the suburb of Tempelhof in half an hour by city railroad. My schedule was comfortable: on weekdays I punched in at the gate at seven, punched out at five. On Saturdays I left at two. I rarely worked on Sundays. Most important, the job was considered "essential to the war effort" and therefore gave me some sense of security in view of the never-ceasing rumors that half-Jews would be rounded up and sent to special labor camps at one of the fronts. If there was anything uncomfortable about the job—at a time when the uncomfortable quickly became the norm—it was the location of the plant next to the Sarotti chocolate works. There were days when the sweet vapors enveloped me the moment I stepped off the train, choked off the fragrance of flowers and fruit trees abounding in the lovingly tended garden plots along the way, corrupted the taste of my cigarettes and my lunch, and lingered in the subconscious of my deprived taste buds when I came home. Next to the flat, cold smell of long-dead buildings, the fragrance of a bar of chocolate is, for me, the most poignant odoriferous reminder of the war.

I had joined the Company for Technical Progress in mid-1941, when the firm where Stephan and I had worked together had been dissolved, and I continued to work there until mid-1944. Most of the men and women who were then a part of my working day have merged with the faces and voices I have encountered since in many other offices and under different circumstances. Only two stand out in sharper silhouette among the ten or twelve with whom I shared a cheerless office for three years. I remember Herr Lehmann, a tall, slender, gray-haired man with the bearing of a Prussian officer of the old school because he had refined the Berliner's knack for epigrammatic comments to an art and because he used this gift liberally to express his profound contempt for an order of things that forced him to conceal his true feelings. When he was angry or excited, he forgot his usual clipped High German and, belying the image of the dignified disciplinarian, fell into the dialect that revealed him as a true child of the city's tenements. Fräulein Rink, a plump spinster with a determined limp and bright, inquisitive eyes behind enormous horn-rimmed glasses, remains unforgettable simply because her quietly attentive kindness made the mindlessness and abrasiveness of the day bearable. I knew nothing about their private lives nor about the inner sources from which they drew an inexhaustible patience, but they showed the strength and detachment of those who have managed to rise above the relentless grind of the everyday world, and in their presence I felt comfortable and, inexplicably, secure.

The Company for Technical Progress had a vital function in my life during those three years: it made me get up in the morning with a purpose, it filled my working days with tasks, it provided some sort of continuum in a time of dissolution, and after nights of fear, terror, and chaos, it forced me to return, morning after morning, to a measure of daytime sanity, of daytime ordinariness, to the reassuring demands of the familiar and predictable. My contribution to the war effort must have been negligible. As an office clerk my main duties were to open incoming mail, assign it to the proper person for handling, check the accuracy of invoices and ledgers, answer the telephone, and serve as an all-round errand boy.

My coworkers quickly realized that my interests and talents lay elsewhere and that I belonged to the endangered species of those for whom Nazi legislation dictated the way of making a living. Even if they had not known that I was a half-Jew, it was easy for them to guess why I worked for the firm. Young and healthy, and manifestly lacking any special skills, I should have been wearing a uniform. In fact, on the street, in public places, on the subway or city railroad, my appearance was so conspicuous that I was frequently stopped by the Security Police to show my workbook and military pass, which served as my identity papers. My colleagues treated me with understanding and sympathy and, just like each of my successive landladies, accorded me small favors. Often a secretary or shopworker would seat himself next to my desk and, opening the conversation with a tale of some calamity, confide in me his innermost thoughts about the Nazis. My feelings about their kindnesses and confidences were mixed. Being the confidant of people of whose lives and motives I knew virtually nothing put me at risk, and their favors, as much as they gratified me, seemed like the kind of public sympathy a man invites whom people know to be doomed by an inexorable fate.

Yet even outside my immediate environment I encountered no hostility among those who knew of or guessed at my Jewishness. In the plant and in the offices, known Nazis were, by tacit agreement, isolated with a superciliousness that smacked of conspiracy and could easily have been interpreted as treason. We greeted each other with "Morjen" and "Wiedasehn" (Berlin dialect for "Guten Morgen" and "Auf Wiedersehen"), and when a "Heil Hitler" became unavoidable, the salute resembled the gesture with which one brushes a fly off his forehead, and the words became indistinct in a sudden fit of coughing. Political jokes abounded and were told openly. We rarely talked about the fighting on the various fronts. Once a week we were led in shifts to the cafeteria to view a documentary film or newsreel about the war, but when, by the end of 1942, no propaganda film could any longer conceal that the war had taken a bad turn for the Germans, "Goebbels' fairy tales," as we dubbed these productions, were dropped.

Outside the company, my life in those years had no center of unity. It was a period, ushered in by that first air raid at the time of the Thomas circle, that for me and for countless others belongs to the waste material of the stuff of which one's life is made, the extraordinary, obscenely fascinating, unforgettable waste material called war. After more than thirty years, my hands still tremble a bit, my throat and my chest still tighten, and I become aware of my heartbeat when I think of air raids or when I hear the wail of a siren. I still dream of raids. Curiously, the one experience of the war that had the least effect on how, today, I feel, or think, or interact with others has taken a permanent hold of my body and my subconscious mind. There are many things in my German past I do not want to forget but remember only with difficulty. The bombs I could easily dismiss from memory, but my poor body won't let me forget them. In that sense they are part of who I am today, part of my German legacy.

The experience can be quantified. According to the 1959 edition of the *Encyclopaedia Britannica,* from the first British air raid on August 25, 1940, until the last American air raid on April 20, 1945, Berlin was blasted with 76,652 tons of explosives and incendiary bombs. During the last two years of the war alone, the British bomber command and the U.S. Eighth Air Force made a combined total of 1,000 bomber raids on the city. Berlin was the most-bombed city of the war.

The raids inverted my life—not figuratively, not symbolically, not subtly, but radically. The day became marginal, the night central. Nightfall now signaled danger. The moment the sun went down my body mobilized its guards. My throat tightened ever so slightly. I began to swallow more frequently than usual. My heartbeat accelerated, my chest contracted almost imperceptibly, and I became aware of something like a knot in the pit of my stomach. The grip of my hands seemed to be less firm, and my steps were curiously uncertain. All my senses, all my nerves, all my feelings seemed to be located in my ears. Whether I read or talked with someone; whether I listened to music on the radio or played chess with a friend—my real self had stepped out of the small circle of light, out of the boundary of a deceptive peace, a fragile serenity. It had penetrated the tightly drawn curtains and the deep shadows of the room and roamed the vast, stony, threatening blackness above the sculptured rooftops, straining for that sudden undulating scream that would explode the empty blackness and shatter the indifferent loneliness of the deserted streets. That wail of terror that suddenly filled the waiting night with purpose!

Would the raids have afflicted me less severely if I had had a job, an occupation, a responsibility, that engaged me wholly? A moot question. Different people reacted differently to the bombs. Father suffered terribly, from the moment the alarm sounded until the "all clear" was given, even when the hours passed uneventfully. Stephan, as sensitive, as nervous a person as I have ever known, seemed indifferent to the danger even when the basement rocked under the impact of explosions. Annemarie never lost her composure; it was difficult to tell what she felt. I remember a young soldier on leave, decorated with the Knight's Cross, who began to cry when the first detonations shook the shelter, while his wife, holding their daughter on her lap, calmly braided the child's golden hair. At the office, some people talked incessantly about the raids, others never did. Some never sought shelter, others, when darkness set in, took their suitcase and sleeping bag and moved into the basement for the duration of the night.

Waiting for the alarm became no less exhausting than suffering through the raid, even though I occasionally managed to ignore my body's nagging. After dinner, I would go to a movie or lecture, or visit a friend, and sometimes I would even spend a whole night on the sidewalk in front of a theater, wrapped in a blanket against the chill, waiting with hundreds of others in the total darkness of the blackout for the morning hour when the box office would open. If a raid interrupted our vigil, we scattered into nearby shelters, but after the "all clear" everybody, by gentlemen's agreement, moved again into the spot he had occupied before the alarm was sounded. The pulse of Berlin's nightlife still beat strong during those years, and unless they were damaged beyond repair, theaters, music halls, and movie houses continued their performances almost until the Russians began to shell the city.

As the bombs churned up not only the streets of the city but the very fabric of its life, keeping up appearances of normalcy at all costs became increasingly important. It mattered a great deal to Goebbels to keep the theaters open. It mattered a great deal to me that I brushed my teeth, shaved, and polished my shoes before I set out to work, even though I might have spent another sleepless night in a basement filled knee-high with water, or the roof of the house I was leaving was still in flames. It did matter to me that I forced myself to offer a seat to a lady in the over-crowded city railroad even though I was sick with fatigue. Forms and habits were protective in an unaccountable manner, and people clung to them instinctively and with a tenacity which, under the abnormal conditions under which we lived, seemed occasionally ludicrous.

One night my landlady, a countess in her eighties, had invited her daughter, a couple of friends, and me to a dinner party. She had just served the soup when the alarm sounded. We went into the bunker she had had built in the backyard of her villa. There followed one of the worst nights of bombing I ever experienced, made all the worse because the narrow concrete cubicle buried six or seven feet in the ground and covered with a mound of dirt, offered virtually no protection against the tremors of the tortured earth, while the air ducts magnified the hellish din of explosions, collapsing structures, and antiaircraft guns stationed in the Tiergarten nearby. After the "all clear" we went back into the house, to find the dining room a shambles of clumps of plaster, fragments of glass and wood, and splintered furniture. Without saying a word, the old lady began to sweep the floor. My first impulse had been to run out into the street and help wherever help may have been needed, but there was something in the face, in the bearing of the frail figure that made me and the others follow her example. When the room had been restored to a semblance of order, she covered the table with a fresh cloth, set it again, lit a couple of candles, and served us the rest of the meal that miraculously had remained intact in the pots. Only after the dessert, when I opened the door to my room on the second floor and stared at a gaping hole where a few hours ago a stained glass window had graced a small bay, did I discover that an entire wall of the house had collapsed.

If there is anything with which I can credit the bombings, it is that they fostered my propensity for solitude. Most people stayed at home at night because they dreaded being trapped in a strange shelter, not knowing what happened to their apartment and belongings, without the support of familiar faces and voices. For me the curtailment of nightlife turned into a boon. Books, the perennial and universal survival ration, kept my spirits alive. I read more during those years than at any other time. I have a shelf-full of books that survived the destruction of the various rooms in which I had lived because I kept them in the suitcase I carried with me into the shelter: Etienne Gilson's *Saint Augustine;* Gilson's *Saint Bonaventura;* Antonin Sertillanges's *Saint Thomas Aquinas;* Blaise Pascal's *Pensées;* a volume of letters by Saint Francis Xavier; Paul Fechter's *History of German Literature;* Wilhelm Windelband's *Textbook of the History of Philosophy.* Heavy stuff, but I read every one of these books, from cover to cover, between 1941 and 1944. I read others too—Georges Bernanos, for example, and Thomas Mann and Sigrid Undset, and I became fond of the works of American novelists such as Jack London, Sinclair Lewis, Theodore Dreiser, Ernest Hemingway, and William Faulkner. I remember these books more clearly than anything I have read since. My body's nervous alertness seemed to sharpen my mind's perception, in spite of the nagging anxiety that made my senses roam the silent darkness outside.

Yet it was not all books that filled my evenings. I continued having an occasional rendezvous with a girl, and once or twice I even thought I was in love. But these romantic affairs were short-lived. The times were inimical to courtships. The virtual certainty that an evening at the theater or a movie, or in a bar, would terminate in a public bomb shelter did not foster intimacy. Meeting your partner in your own quarters was still, as a rule, unacceptable in those days, and even if one or another of my landladies would have condoned my being visited by a lady during the day, only the most exceptional landlady, such as my star equestrian, Frau Wirtz, would have opened her door to a lady visitor after nightfall. Of course, love, or the flesh, would have found ways to overcome these obstacles had a romance been uppermost in my mind. But my mind was starved for other things, things proper to the mind, my mind, things a day of mindless work in a factory could not provide. I had no patience for the charming, titillating tedium of courtship or conquest. Vice versa, the ladies quickly sensed, I am sure, that my thoughts and desires were not wholly preoccupied with their person.

I also began writing a diary, and for the first and only time in my life I kept up a regular correspondence. My partner was my cousin Klaus, the son of one of Father's sisters in whose house I had often lived as a boy. In those years I had looked up to Klaus, who was eight or ten years older than I, more as an uncle than a peer; we had seldom met and had had little in common. He had just completed his studies of art history when he was drafted and immediately sent to the Russian front. For Christmas 1941 I had sent him a few books, and from then on we wrote to each other at least once a month until he was killed a few weeks before the end of the war when the truck on which he tried to escape the advancing Russians rode over a land mine.

When I reread the stack of his correspondence recently I was struck by the similarity of our condition regardless of the total dissimilarity of our environment: mine a relatively comfortable furnished room where I wrote by the light of a chandelier, on a table whose crocheted tablecloth was pushed back to make a hard surface, listening to the silence; his a snow-covered mudhole somewhere in the Russian steppe where he wrote by the thin beam of a flashlight or the flicker of a candle end, supporting the writing pad on his knees, listening to the distant Russian guns. I was a Christian, Klaus an agnostic, but because both of us were conscious of the presence of death, we asked of each other how we should live. Some excerpts from his hastily penciled notes:

January 18, 1942: "What I have experienced here in Russia, where I have been since the first day of the offensive, is not conducive to making one talk. You understand? . . . In the meantime, here as everywhere, patience must be our watchword. Even a Russian winter is bound to pass." March 12, 1942: "I was delighted with the choice of the books you sent me—your own books! What joy, what consolation to be able to read for two whole days! This will help in the days ahead, for now I must mount my sled and leave your books behind. We are pressing forward, and much is bound to happen. . . . When will all of this ever end? We won't come home for a long time." May 4, 1942: "I shouldn't have asked you for certain reports. . . . I understand perfectly that there are certain things in our condition that you are as unable to write about as I. The longer I am 'out here' the less I am inclined to comment on my experiences. These things demand distance; one is glad if, under their immediate impact, one can master them interiorly. Patience! You and I must keep our own inner life intact—that's already much." June 14, 1942: "We are caught in vicious guerilla warfare against partisans and scattered troups. . . . It is good for me out here to learn about the difficulties at home, and the compromises you must make. . . . But here as there, it is fundamentally a question of inner freedom. More and more I find that, in a time of faltering convictions and doubtful values, only one thing counts: to keep your heart alert and awake. . . . We can gain nothing but the riches of the heart. (At the risk of sounding pompous: here, in the depth of the woods, in the swamp, not knowing what the next hour will bring, I can permit myself to say it once, deliberately, as a deep inner experience: the riches of the heart)." August 8, 1942: "I need all my strength to preserve my inner integrity." December 15, 1942: "Just a quick greeting for Christmas. . . . I am sitting by the light of a candle end—at three in the afternoon; no time or chance for reading or writing, only the flight into the world of my thoughts remains. Perhaps thus I can celebrate Christmas most authentically! . . . The watchword, Heinz, is still: Patience and perseverance, above all in matters of heart and soul." June 1, 1943: "Merely a sign of life between two missions. . . . Deep forest, and endless morass, and wet tents. . . .here today, there tomorrow, always on the move. It can happen that one detests all words, and sometimes happiness is simply that one has no time for brooding." October 26, 1943: "My leave was a period of grace in spite of all the confusion of the time. . . . I managed to blot out everything else—to pretend nothing else existed—and thus these days became a pure source of strength. . . . When I returned to the front I learned that my unit had been wiped out; only a few comrades survived. In which world do I live?" November 21, 1943: "You thoroughly misunderstood my remark about 'blotting out everything.' Out of context it contradicts everything I believe. What I meant—in reference to my short leave—was that there must once be a silence (which must be neither escape nor distraction), when what is otherwise dormant can grow again— seeds pushing up for light! Out of the seeds grows new readiness—it is not a dead but a vivifying, creative silence I mean. There is nothing that would absolve us from the inner duty to face the things of this life with vigilance and humility."

And so we struggled, each in his own way, in a time of faltering convictions and doubtful values, for the possession of our inner self, trying to share what mattered to us most: the things of the heart and the soul. There were few others during these years with whom I could talk of the riches of the heart or the joys of the mind, and often months went by when there was none. Annemarie had married Peter, my former comrade in the Labor Service who had become my friend when he had bared himself to me with the words, "Shit on Hitler!" Because Annemarie was a half-Jew, and marriages between Aryans and non-Aryans were forbidden by law, the wedding had taken place secretly. The couple lived in a small apartment nearby, but when Peter was home on leave they were understandably cautious about inviting company, and when Peter was away on the front the threat of raids kept Annemarie and me as much apart as they kept us from visiting others. Stephan, too, was now married, but trying to reach the part of the city in which he and his wife lived meant that I would almost certainly be trapped en route by an air raid. Besides, he had now become completely uninterested in the books and ideas that once had sent our discussions soaring, and his bitter mockery of my beliefs made our rare meetings increasingly painful. Even my occasional visits with Father in the priory had become heavy and lusterless because of the raids. Often the train, trapped by a raid, remained motionless on the tracks for hours, and when I finally entered Father's small, peaceful room late on a Saturday night, the tensions of the week lifted from my shoulders, and the mere anticipation of a night deliciously free from the threat of sirens and explosions drowned me suddenly in an ocean of fatigue. During most of the weekends I spent in Alexanderdorf I did no more than sleep, eat, and attend a couple of services, while the books I had brought along remained unopened and the chessboard on Father's bookshelf untouched. Happiness, as Klaus had come to learn, at times simply meant the inability to think.

The Company for Technical Progress never had been a place where the riches of the heart were a topic of conversation, but Herr Lehmann's caustic wit, Fräulein Rink's placid disposition, and the quiet sympathy of my fellow workers for my precarious situation had made the drab office something of a refuge: the work, the people, the conversations, the order of the day, even the meals in the cafeteria—all had been pleasantly and effortlessly predictable. Now the increasingly frequent air raids, often lasting throughout the night, gradually took their toll. Fatigue led to irritability, irritability to moroseness, moroseness to clashes. The raids became the main topic of conversation: Which district, which street, which building had been hit? Who was missing at work? Why had there been a raid in the first place, since it had been raining? What was the matter with the radio that had still talked about a bomber squadron approaching Magdeburg when the bombs were already falling on Berlin?

Yet as the nightly raids became routine, even the bombs ceased to be a subject of conversation. The senses became numb from continuous overstimulation, and small things—a few grams of genuine coffee, a parcel with silk stockings from Paris, a pocket knife retrieved from among the rubble of a collapsed basement—assumed momentous significance. The respite from our preoccupation with these dreadful banalities was, as Klaus had called his time of leave, an unexpected grace. One morning, as I was walking through the plant on my way to my office, I was startled by a new sound that rose above the noise of tools and engines and set off dancing echoes of hope and lightheartedness: French! The voices of the young Frenchmen were like a challenge: fresh, uninhibited, melodious; they struck me like rain falling on parched ground, like a cool breeze on a sultry evening, a patch of blue breaking through a steely sky. What had we lost? Jean-Pierre. Marcel. Jacques. Simon. Claude. Their eyes shone with mockery and undisguised pride, their politeness was tantamount to arrogance. They whistled, they laughed, and sometimes they sang.

In the weeks that followed, other slave laborers joined the French: Poles, Lithuanians, Czechs, Yugoslavs. By the end of 1942, German had become in the shops just one other sound in the polyphony of languages. For some of us, the presence of the captives became a release. I soon became fluent in conversational French. Herr Lehmann used his lunch break to play chess with a young Lithuanian and to teach him Berlin dialect. Fräulein Rink, whose family stemmed from Poland, began to study Polish under the tutelage of one of the workers from that country, and one day I observed in a corner of the cafeteria a plant foreman, a known Nazi, engrossed in a Russian grammar.

Yet the mood toward the foreigners was by no means universally congenial. French esprit and Slavic melancholy did not always mix well with Prussian discipline and seriousness of purpose. The Germans resented the indifference with which the foreigners went about their work and were suspicious of the meaning of words they did not understand. The tensions sometimes erupted into fistfights. Yet while Germans and slave laborers mingled, however uneasily, under the coercion of a common task, under the threat of common extinction they kept apart. What perverse human instinct was at work here? In the bomb shelter, trembling with fear for their lives, the French huddled with the French, the Germans with Germans, the Poles with Poles, the Lithuanians with Lithuanians. "J'ai peur" (I am afraid), somebody whispered into the perfect stillness of the gently rocking concrete shell. "Ja, ich habe auch Angst" (Yes, I too am afraid), somebody else shot back, indignantly.

One November morning in 1942, when the Russian counteroffensive at Stalingrad was in progress, Herr Lehmann pinned a large map to the wall of the office. Brown pins marked the German movements, red pins the Russian movements, and white pins the movements of the Allies. It was an act of open defiance, but nobody told him to take the map down. For a few months we entertained ourselves with moving the pins around every morning and after each newscast, and arguing about their position, but by spring 1943 the reports from all fronts had become so uniformly disheartening that few among us were still interested in news or maps. Although the pace of work hardly slackened, a mood of listlessness settled over the place that affected even the foreign workers. Jokes disappeared from the vocabulary of political gossip. Fräulein Rink put away her *History of Poland,* and Herr Lehmann his chessboard. The Nazis in the plant became more aggressive. Posters appeared with ugly words: *court-martial, sabotage, summary execution.* The plant guards—elderly, retired workers who did large favors in return for cigars or a bottle of schnapps—were replaced with young men in smart uniforms, sporting revolvers and shiny boots.

In January 1943 the daytime bombings of German targets by the U.S. Eighth Air Force began, and although another year would pass before the first American bombs would fall on Berlin, the sirens now sent us into the shelter at any hour of the day, whenever American bombers approached a target in northern or central Germany. The nightly raids by the British also quickened noticeably. The plant began to disintegrate. Windows that had been shattered by explosions had at first been replaced with panes, and roofs that had been blown off had been replaced with shingles. Now windows were boarded up, and roofs remained uncovered. Heavy beams shored up the cracked ceiling of our office, which, dimly lit by naked light bulbs, became indistinguishable from a bomb shelter. When the roof above us was destroyed by an incendiary bomb, we moved in with the occupants of the floor below, leaving Herr Lehmann's map to the mercy of wind, rain, and sun.

In the fall of 1942 I had made another effort to get Aunt Walli out of Germany. I knew her time was running out. In Hamburg, Grandmother Riese, the lady whose long hair I had loved to comb when I was little, had died, and the day after the funeral Aunt Clara, her constant companion and nurse, had been deported to an unknown destination. Walli was distraught about the death of her mother and the disappearance of her youngest sister, but all attempts Father and I made to persuade her to go underground had been in vain. The nuns in Alexanderdorf had offered her a hiding place, and even Aunt Lene, Father's youngest sister, had finally overcome her husband's reluctance and had invited her to take refuge in her villa in Düsseldorf. But Walli had turned a deaf ear to our pleas. "Look," she said quietly, "I am not going to endanger the lives of other people, and, besides, I just can't face the prospect of having to spend the rest of the war in the confinement of a basement or attic. Here people are nice to me and," pointing to the yellow patch sewn to her blouse, "the Star hasn't made any trouble for me. I have my apartment, I have a niche in the air-raid shelter, the grocer pampers me, and the work in the factory is all right. I am much better off than Rosa and Minna in London. And if they send me to a labor camp—so what? At least I'll be safe from the bombs. My husband was a captain and received the Iron Cross for bravery in World War I. The Nazis wouldn't dare lay hands on me. They know by now that they may lose the war and have to account for their actions."

My last effort to save Walli came about by happenstance. During an air raid, alone with the old countess in her little pillbox, I had become voluble from sheer anxiety, talking freely into the darkness about my life, my concern for Aunt Walli, about Father and Annemarie, about the priory, and whatever else moved me in those days. The darkness did not respond, but a few weeks later, after I had already moved out of the heavily damaged villa, I received a telephone call one night that proved that my monologue had penetrated the din of explosions and antiaircraft guns. "This is Frau Solf," the voice said. "A mutual friend has told me about your aunt. I should be pleased if you would care to join me for tea some evening." We agreed on a date and she explained to me that her apartment could be easily recognized even in the darkness of the blackout by a life-size wooden statue of an Indian chief standing outside the entrance door.

Thus, for a few months, I became a member of the Solf Circle, one of the small, individual groups that made up the network of conspiracy against Hitler. Frau Solf's husband, Wilhelm, had once been colonial minister under Kaiser Wilhelm II, and during the Weimar Republic had become one of the leaders in the fight against the incipient Nazi party. After his death, his widow and her daughter, Countess Ballestrem, continued his fight, drawing into their circle members of the Prussian nobility and other leading figures of the Weimar Republic, and devoting themselves mainly to helping Jews escape from Germany. A Gestapo spy infiltrated the Solf Circle at a tea party given on September 10, 1943, in the home of one of the conspirators, and most of its members were executed. Frau Solf and her daughter, however, survived the war. During their trial in Berlin, which was held on February 3, 1945, during an air raid, a bomb killed the presiding judge, the fiendish Roland Freisler, and destroyed the court room and their dossiers. They were released from prison by a fluke a few days before Berlin fell to the Russians.

I learned about the fate of the circle only long after the war. During the months I belonged to it, nothing at our meetings had the air of a conspiracy whose members were conscious of the deadly game they played. Sometimes we were a group of five or six, sometimes a dozen or more people came. The "Herr Doktor" and the "von" of the nobility dominated the way they addressed each other, and several times we were joined by men whose names, faces, and rank I knew from newspapers and newsreels, but who, in Frau Solf's sitting room, looked strangely humble in their ill-fitting civilian clothes. The sitting room was comfortable in spite of its enormous size and almost overwhelming sumptuousness. Dominated by an aquarium that occupied the length and height of an entire wall and in which tropical fish of all colors, shapes, and sizes flitted gracefully through a soft bluish glow that had lost any resemblance to water, the room casually harmonized priceless art objects from every continent of the globe: black-lacquered cupboards from Japan with hand-woven Gobelins from Turkey, enormous silver samovars from Russia with delicate Chinese vases, intricately carved screens from Mexico with Persian rugs and pillows, African masks with wall hangings from India. While Frau Solf and her daughter served tea and home-baked cookies, we talked quietly about art and history, about music and books, about anything except the war, but the moment we put down our teacups and seated ourselves around a large coffee table of polished ebony, harsher realities broke the spell of an elegant soirée. Reports on the latest escapes. Why had this one failed? How much money was available for the next batch of counterfeit identity cards? Assignments: who was going to be responsible for the escape of whom? It was all quite businesslike, but no papers, no files or notebooks, appeared. The shiny tabletop remained bare except for silver ashtrays and a minutely detailed military map showing the frontier between Germany and Switzerland.

On New Year's Day, 1943, I rode the cage elevator to Aunt Walli's apartment, rang the bell, and, barely waiting until she had locked the door behind me, began talking about her escape. I was resolved to break down her resistance this time, because I knew through the Solf Circle that Berlin was to be declared *Judenfrei* (free of Jews) by the end of April. I told her that I had made arrangements for her to travel to Innsbruck, that she would be contacted there by one of our local collaborators, that he would escort her to a village at the foot of the Alps, that she would meet a guide there who would take her to the Swiss frontier, and that our Swiss contact had been notified to expect her. Once in Switzerland she could be helped by Father's friends or Edith to join her brother in New York, or Mother and Aunt Minna in London. She listened to me quietly, and when I had finished she shook her head. "I will not go," she said simply. I pleaded with her, shouted at her in my frustration and anger, and when she persisted with her familiar arguments about the inviolability of German life and the exaggerated rumors about concentration camps, I finally, in despair, told her about the imminent roundup. It was in vain. For the first time I sensed that she was disturbed and afraid, but I also recognized in the end that her beliefs—as foolish and illusory as they were—were ultimately unassailable because they constituted the very fiber of her proud personality. Although she had tears in her eyes, her voice was firm and gentle when I left.

The letter that contained the instructions for her transport to a labor camp came a couple of weeks later. It talked about the kind and quantity of warm outfits she had to pack, about requirements of personal hygiene and the preservation of health during the transport and under barrack conditions, and it even included some sentences about the frame of mind that would turn a temporary hardship into an honorable service to the German people and the war effort. Walli was taciturn but calm when I arrived late in the evening at her apartment to accompany her to the collecting point, a synagogue somewhere in West Berlin. Silently we walked the few blocks to a streetcar stop, our steps echoing in the deserted streets. Silently we waited in the cold darkness. The passengers occupying the dimly lit compartment of the car looked up briefly when we entered, then looked away. I noticed several suitcases in the aisle. Nobody talked, nobody whispered. The conductor appeared, collected our fare, and disappeared again behind the thick curtain separating the compartment from the platform. At every stop a few more people climbed aboard, carrying suitcases or bundles tied together with rope. Opposite us a young woman held a baby on her lap, and when the child suddenly let out a sharp cry, she opened a button of her coat and pressed the tightly wrapped little bundle against her chest. The suckling sounds fell into the stillness like tiny explosions.

When the conductor announced our stop, everybody rose and began talking at once, but outside the voices died as if swallowed up by the cavernous night. As we approached the synagogue, more and more people set down their suitcases, and small groups formed at the foot of the stairs leading to the entrance. Now there were voices, here and there intermingled with sobs, and from somewhere laughter cut sharply through the night. I too put down Walli's suitcase, but when she made as if to embrace me, I shook my head and took her by the arm. Together we mounted the steps and pushed through a high and heavy door that closed silently behind us, and then we stood motionless in a dark emptiness until I made out faint reflections in polished stone and metal that pointed to a source of light. Our steps reverberated through unseen vaulted spaces as we walked toward that door through which I could now hear the confused murmur of a multitude. I yanked the handle and was stunned by a blaze of light. At my feet stretched what seemed an enormous circular pit sloping down to an arena crowded with hundreds of people. Sitting, standing, kneeling, milling, or stretched out on the floor, they were in great agitation, and their voices, pierced by shouts and laughter and the wailing of infants, rose up to me like the muted noise of a carnival crowd heard from the top gondola of a Ferris wheel. As I scanned the scene my eyes fell on a figure standing, opposite me, at the far end of the nearly empty bleachers that circled the arena. It was a young woman, and the moment I saw her I became oblivious of the crowd and the noise, oblivious of time and space. She stood alone, both arms raised in a gesture of beckoning or greeting, her head thrown back in a shout of joy I could not hear, her raven hair cascading over her light raincoat, her face radiant, no, jubilant, her large dark eyes brimming with mirth. The Pride of Judah! The thought struck me with such force that tears came to my eyes. I turned to Walli, but she was gone from my side.

Of the rest of that night I remember nothing.

By mid-1943 my belongings had been reduced to two suitcases filled mostly with books, and my furnished room to a cot and a washstand behind a wooden partition in a small grocery store whose owner, a kindhearted spinster, had offered me this corner when my own room, two floors above the store, had burned out. When, during the Christmas season that year, the store, too, was literally pulverized by a direct hit and my landlady killed in the raid, I decided to move into the priory in Alexanderdorf. The sisters put some furniture into a vacant storage room in one of the barns, and for a few months I tried to commute between a small village in the country and my place of work in a city under siege. It was, of course, an impossible arrangement. Commuting became an end in itself. I slept in trains immobilized for hours in total darkness, oblivious to the smells and sounds and undulations of an amorphous mass of human flesh that kept me propped up by its sheer density. I rode into the city stretched out on the roof of a railroad car or flattened against its side, seeking a precarious foothold on some protrusion and gripping something in desperate determination not to be catapulted onto the roadbed at the next jolt. I rose before dawn, when the sky over Berlin was still convulsed by the incandescence of battle, and I would walk through the silent forest toward the priory long after nightfall, when the sky above me was already reverberating from the roar of the approaching bomber formations. When, in March 1944, American bombers began their daytime attacks on Berlin, I would often arrive at the factory only to crawl into the bomb shelter before I had opened the first file.

Life was reduced to the exigencies of survival. The bombs not only ground the eloquent faces of streets into the desolate sameness of rubble and ruins but also leveled the organic contrasts by which the rhythm and patterns of human life are shaped. Women wore men's trousers, replaced hats with scarfs, and pinned up their hair. Men let their hair grow and no longer shaved regularly, and those working at a desk had, in appearance, become interchangeable with those standing at the assembly line. A fine, gritty layer of soot, ashes, and plaster covered floors, desks, filing cabinets, and machines. I no longer perceived a distinction between home and office, between working life and personal life, nor, for that matter, between night and day or between freedom and necessity. At times, only the fragrance of chocolate, stubbornly asserting itself against the acrid smell of burned-out buildings, against the taste of ashes, reminded me of the forms and colors and tastes of a life that now seemed to belong only to the world of books and dreams.

Yet leaving the city, leaving my job, would have been tantamount to desertion or treason unless I could have proved to the authorities that I had found in the country a job considered "essential to the war effort." But if such jobs had been available in the country, thousands, tens of thousands, of Berliners would long ago have left the disintegrating city. I don't recall by what stroke of fortune, or what kind of manipulation, I did find that job, but in May 1944 the owner of a sawmill in Kummersdorf, the village that lay halfway between Alexanderdorf and the Sperenberg railroad station, offered to employ me as office manager. The catch, in my eyes, was negligible: I had to tutor his son in French, German, and Latin composition. The military authorities and the Gestapo, to both of whom I had to apply for a transfer, knew nothing about the poor boy whom my new employer hoped to push through the gymnasium with my help, but they considered a sawmill sufficiently essential to the war effort to affix the all-important stamp of approval to my workbook and military pass. According to these entries, I joined the construction firm of Bernhard Lau and Sons on May 1, 1944. Five weeks later, the Allies landed in Normandy.

Part Three

....

Preceding page: Regina Kuehn, the author's wife, with Angelika and Birgitta, the Kuehns' German-born daughters, on the quay in Genoa the day before their embarkation for America, November 1951.

Bells
and Guns

· ·

In the summer of 1944 the Priory of Saint Gertrud was an island of serenity, almost of peace. In the fields and gardens, in stables and barns, in the bakery and chapel, the sisters went about their business with the same quiet smile on their lips, the same detached gentleness in their eyes that had made me fond of the community the first time I had visited it some five years previously. In the morning their chanting, floating through the open chapel windows and giving life and hope to the breaking day, accompanied me for a stretch as I walked along the highway to the sawmill, and when I approached the grounds again, late in the afternoon, their voices—clear, sweet, and solemn—would reassure me that life, their life, was still intact. Twenty-five miles to the north, in the city, there was the taste of ashes and the smell of death, the sight of naked roofs and shattered windows, of empty shells of buildings and of churned-up streets. Here the sky was high and merry; the heath was in blue and golden bloom; the air was scented with the sweet fragrance of pine, birch, beech, and jasmin; the woods resounded with the song of birds; and the fields, wide and still under the sun, were pregnant with the joy of harvest.

In my room in the barn, fresh flowers graced table and windowsill like a restatement of long-forgotten innocence, and the very sight of Father sitting at his desk in his smoke-filled study, imperturbably turning the pages of a book or writing his daily quota of manuscript, brought back a sense of order, tranquillity, and purpose. Here, the riches of the heart were still the center around which the day's tasks were ordered.

I relished my job as one would relish an undeserved and unexpected vacation: some paperwork in the wooden shed that served as office; an occasional inspection and inventory of the piles of planed beams, planks, and boards that drenched the yard with the intoxicating honey-fragrance of their sap; a trek by horse-drawn wagon deep into the forest to measure the allotment for the next fell; a visit to the lumber shop, where the screeching of the electric saws and the blinding spray of sawdust evoked the panic of the air raids. The two or three hours I spent at the kitchen table in my employer's house, trying to explain to a wide-eyed fifteen-year-old the purpose of the Latin gerund, the trickery and beauty of French irregular verbs, or the stylistic finesse of Goethe's *Faust,* proved more taxing than the day's simple chores. The boy, I realized after our first lesson, should have been in my shoes, helping his father, and leaving the intellectual rigors of a German gymnasium to minds of finer tuning. Still, we quickly became friends, and sometimes I wonder what may have become of him.

The peace was, of course, illusory, the serenity not more than a fleeting surge of well-being; the nascent sense of order and purpose died almost the moment it had gained a precarious foothold in my consciousness. The signs of war were visibly and audibly manifest, pointing ominously to the day when the embattled city would draw this privileged spot into the vortex of its destruction. In the priory, the guest rooms were no longer occupied by guests who had come to the community to participate in the liturgy and refresh themselves in the atmosphere of Benedictine piety, but by women and children who had left the city to find refuge from the relentless bombing raids. Annemarie, who had had no sign of life from Peter since he had been sent to the Russian front many months ago, and who was pregnant, was among them. Dr. Zahn, the dentist in whose apartment Father had lived for years before moving into the convent, had built a modest frame house for his wife and small son in a wooded grove on the edge of Alexanderdorf. Other families had followed his example and a whole colony of *Bombenflüchtlinge* (refugees from the bombs) had sprung up around the priory. Hearing the laughter of children and the squeals of infants on grounds and in rooms once distinguished from ordinary space chiefly by silence was perhaps a curious but here nevertheless dramatic sign of the presence of war.

Across from the priory, along the edge of the woods, a small camp had been built for prisoners of war. The four or five crude wooden barracks housed Yugoslav officers. Another camp had gone up on a field adjoining the sawmill. Here, with their wives and children, lived the French slave laborers who worked in the mill and on some of the farms. The Yugoslavs, who were guarded after a fashion by a handful of old men from the village and suffered virtually no restrictions, were frequent guests at the priory and in the houses of the bomb refugees. The French, on the other hand, among whom I felt comfortable and who treated me as if I were one of their comrades, firmly kept their distance.

Still, it was the kind of lazy summer—remote, deliberate, benign—that could have made one forget the war, that even dulled the cutting edge of the terror of the bombs. Neither the priory nor the villages in the vicinity had sirens. During the day my employer's wife would keep the radio going to listen to the Early Warning System that reported the movements of enemy aircraft over German and German-occupied territory, and when it appeared that Berlin was going to be the target and that the approach would be made from the south, she would call out through the kitchen window, "The bombers are coming!" and the pace of work would slacken and, at the sound of the first faint hum of a plane or the sight of the first silvery speck high in the cloudless sky, come to a halt. Like ringside spectators, necks craned, we would watch the slow, deliberate course of the perfectly V-shaped formations in which each tiny bomber was clearly discernible, until the air gradually became saturated with a deep roar and windows began to rattle. Then, even before the vapor trails had dissolved into drifting clouds, I would feel—not hear—the first detonations: not more than a sudden slight pressure on the inner ear, a brief flutter in the air as if a huge invisible bird had streaked past, close-by.

At night a telephone call from a military base in the area would alert the mayor of Alexanderdorf, who in turn would sound a large cow bell mounted on the roof of his house. If the bell went unheard in the priory, the roar of the planes would wake us, or, more correctly, everybody except me. Because whether the bell was heard or, as often happened, not rung at all, I was already awake. I don't know what triggered in me the alert that made me suddenly sit up in bed, gripped by the throat-tightening certitude that a raid was imminent. The window of my room faced north, where, beyond the flatland of fields, heath, and woods lay the city, but whether the window was open or closed, whether the direction of the wind was favorable or not, it would have been impossible for me to hear the sirens of Berlin or of any of the towns nearby. I simply knew, and although still groggy from sleep and barely conscious of my surroundings, I would mechanically set out on my prearranged route of door-pounding: the families in the guesthouse; the families in the barn across the yard; Father, the two monks, and the guests in the convent building—everyone except the sisters, who as yet refused to be disturbed. "Alarm!, Alarm!" I would call through the door, and the response from within would come quickly except for Father Ludger's, whose near-deafness required that I hammer on his door with my shoe.

Moments later, most of the men and some of the women would assemble at the edge of the park, waiting for the awesome spectacle that was about to unfold on the northern horizon. There were no shelters on the grounds of the priory, and the only basement—in the convent building— was *clausura:* off limits to the laity. Still, in the summer of 1944 I felt no compulsion to seek shelter: leaning against a tree, the carpet of pine needles soft under my feet, I knew, I felt with intense distress what others, friends whom I loved, were suffering at this moment under the sky that now began to explode in the north, but for the first time in years I had lost the feeling that those planes droning overhead were seeking *me,* that those bombs that made the ground on which I stood shudder were meant for *me.* An illusory peace, a brittle safety, yet a peace of sorts and a vast relief.

The breathing spell lasted throughout the summer and early fall, while momentous events happened elsewhere. Early in July 1944 the Russians advanced into Lithuania and Latvia; on July 20 a plot to assassinate

Hitler failed, and in its wake many of Nazi Germany's most prominent figures either committed suicide or were executed; on August 26 General De Gaulle entered Paris, and a month later the Allies invaded Germany from the west. I knew that our community lived on borrowed time, but the reprieve from what we sensed to be the inevitable catastrophe was sweet and precious. Sheltered for the moment from the brunt of the assaults on Berlin, and having as intellectual companions men and women who understood the language of faith and convictions, I began to settle down in a routine that I hoped would become permanent once the war was out of the way. Guided by Father Bonaventura, who was an expert on scholasticism, I took up again my long-neglected systematic study of the *Summa theologiae,* and whenever I could I joined the nuns in the celebration of the liturgical hours. "Deus, in adjutorium meum intende. Domine, ad adjuvandum me festina." Lauds, matins, vespers, compline: one always returned to the sacred hours that blunted the shock of whatever had happened and forced the soul to submit its restless, confused images to a grander design, a larger vision.

Once, during a daytime raid, an American fighter plane that had flown protective cover for the Liberators crashed in the woods nearby, and I joined the search party that immediately set out to find the wreckage. We found the plane in a sunlit clearing carpeted with daisies and humming with bees. The front end of the fuselage was still intact, but the canopy was missing. The pilot, still strapped in his seat, was dead. He wore no headgear, and his blond hair stirred in the breeze. His eyes were closed and his face was calm. When the cart arrived that was to take the body to the village for burial, I indicated that I wished to return on foot. When the others had left I rummaged once again through compartments whose contents the men had taken with them; examined the instrument panel, the seats, and other parts of the fuselage, trying to figure out the meaning of the various signs and instructions in the cockpit; and then began to search the woods for other parts of the wreckage. I was fascinated by the realization that only hours ago the things I held in my hands and touched had been handled by the "enemy," had rested on the soil that had become Mother's home. When I found in the underbrush a submachine gun and some cartridge clips I wrapped them in my windbreaker and returned to

. . . .

the priory. I shoved the bundle into a corner of my closet and, hearing the bell announce vespers, went to the chapel for the service. I thought of the shattered plane, of the young face that had looked so serene in death, of my mother, of an enemy who had suddenly become palpably, over-whelmingly real, and then my ears caught the voice of the prioress, "Fidelium animae per misericordiam Dei requiescant in pace,"* and my soul responded and grew still, and I prayed for peace for a young man who had become my friend when he died in a patch of daisies, the sun on his face.

If faith supported by the discipline of a religious community gave me a feeling of trust in the permanency of the things I cherished, the lives of others were kept intact by the enormous strength and tenacity of the normal and familiar in a disintegrating world. Or perhaps my employer was simply foolish when, in October, he sent me on a journey to a town somewhere on the eastern border of German-occupied Poland to deliver a bid for a construction job that was not even to begin for another year. As soon as the train had crossed the Oder River I saw the full extent of that absurdity: everywhere men, women, and children, sometimes joined by soldiers, were digging trenches, erecting barricades, unrolling barbed wire, and working on what I learned later were encampments for heavy artillery. In Alexanderdorf, the air was pregnant with foreboding. Here, some sixty miles farther east, the land was already being readied for bat-tle. When I saw children wielding shovels in pouring rain, I suddenly felt ashamed of my life in the priory, and I thought with distaste of my endless discussions with Father about the re-emergence, after the war, of a Chris-tian Europe.

On the return trip I found myself in Potsdam with a few hours to spare before a train was to leave for the last leg of my journey, and on the spur of the moment I decided to visit the boarding school I had left eleven years ago when it had been turned into a training school for the Nazi elite. I had been fourteen then; I was now twenty-five, and in this interval the Third

*By the mercy of God, may the souls of the faithful rest in peace.

Reich had risen and waned. The gate to the grounds was open, and nobody challenged me from the guardhouse. Uneasy because I knew I was
trespassing in one of the citadels of nazism, I walked rapidly toward a side
entrance to the main building. But nobody was in sight. The vast school-
yard, flanked on one side by the *Turnhalle* (gymnasium) and on the other
by the dining hall, was deserted. I had a glimpse of the athletic field where
our day had begun at six with running, jumping, and obstacle racing, and I
remembered that behind the trees lay the hospital where I had been confined for the first month of my freshman year because Annemarie was ill
with some infectious childhood disease and where I had been initiated into
the vulgarities and mindless cruelties of a boys' boarding school.

The building was as silent and dead as the grounds. My steps echoing
loudly in the endless, gloomy corridor, I quickly traversed the wing that
had housed the upperclassmen and that had been off-limits for me, crossed
the spacious hall that formed the center part of the building and whose
walls of polished stone gleamed in the light flooding through high windows, and entered another gloomy corridor where I had been at home for
three miserable years. Here I knew every door, every staircase, every
crack in the linoleum, every one of the faded museum prints that lined the
wall in heavy, ornate frames, and I tried to evoke, without success, the
names and faces of the hundred boys who had occupied the rooms behind
these doors and with whom I had lined up in this corridor for meals and
bedtime roll call. Nothing had changed, and yet, in the oppressive silence,
everything looked foreign. Here was the room I had shared with ten others
during my last year in school. Here, next to the window, was my old desk;
this desk, I remembered, had belonged to Hans, this one to Gerhard. The
desks were bare and dusty, the wardrobes behind them empty, the two
windows dull. This door had led to the suite of one of my teachers, and I
remembered the small bedroom where he used to cane me mercilessly.
Again I tried to evoke feelings, voices, images, but the voices I heard, the
faces I saw, remained distant, indistinct. I could not muster the excitement
that would have made me climb the staircase to the dormitory or turn the
corner for the dining room where, fourteen years ago, I had heard, over
the radio, Hitler's voice for the first time.

I turned back, and as I approached the central hall again I heard the sound of a piano. One of the common rooms, I now remembered, whose high doors of polished wood led into the hall, had been the music room and had held a grand piano. The music came from behind that door, and now, as I walked toward it, I also heard voices and laughter. I stood in the entrance before I had even decided to enter, and a voice called out, "Achtung!" and I was face to face with seven or eight young men standing at attention in a sun-drenched room that had fallen silent. Off in a corner, next to the piano, stood a girl; it was she who had apparently been playing. They all wore brown uniforms in the manner of the Hitler Youth, but of a more elegant cut, and they were all unusually tall and slender, and very blond. I must have said something that put them at ease because I remember that we exchanged a few words and that they explained to me why the school was deserted. I have forgotten what they said because I was enthralled by their extraordinary good looks, by the freshness of their youth and their sparkling eyes, and preoccupied with the effort to keep up the role of a person in authority which their behavior had forced on me. Or perhaps I was simply stunned by a scene that did not fit—did not fit at all—into the images my experience had formed of Nazi Germany: the piano did not fit, the blond beauty of the girl did not, the intelligent, lively, fresh faces of the boys did not, nor, for that matter, did the role into which I was cast vis-à-vis a group of brown uniforms, a role that merited another "Achtung!" when I turned to leave. A perfect set-up for a propaganda picture, but being spontaneous and real, it had denied me the contempt, the hate such pictures used to arouse in me. For a moment I had wished to be one of them.

I was about to walk past the guardhouse when I noticed that someone was watching me through its open window. On an impulse I stopped. "Hello," I said, looking up into an old man's face. "I used to go to school here." The face disappeared from the window and now I recognized the man who stood in the door as one of the groundkeepers who had already been white-haired when I was a freshman. "Ja," he said, "I saw you come in and you looked familiar. Let's see, you are about twenty-five, twenty-six, so you must have graduated about thirty-eight." I told him I had indeed graduated in 1938 but that I had left the school in 1933. "I see," he

said. "Well, things have changed since thirty-three." I asked him if he
knew what had happened to my old teachers, and he told me that some of
them had left the school the same year I had left, when it had been turned
into a National Political Training Institute, and that most of the others had
been drafted at some time during the war. "Wasn't Bolle your headmaster?" I nodded and suddenly I heard Bolle's voice and saw him storm
into the classroom and rant about the goddamned Brownshirts and Hitler
the lunatic and the ruin of Germany while we sat in awed silence until
some boys began to snicker because we had never seen Bolle lose his
temper and the man stopped shouting and just stood there holding us with
his eyes and we sat in stony silence for forty-five minutes not daring to
move or cough until the bell rang and he dismissed us with a gesture.
"Bolle was killed." And he added the names of four or five of my teachers
and named the battles in which they had died. "What about my graduating
class?" I asked, mentioning a few names to trigger his memory. The old
man fished a pipe out of his pocket and began to fill it. "As I said, things
have changed since thirty-three. There were forty who graduated in thirty-
eight. All of them went into officers' training right afterward. Most of
them were killed, some injured, some captured. I know of only three who
are still with their troops. Anyone in particular you want to know about?"
I shook my head and left.

        Shortly after I returned from my trip to the east, the first bombs
exploded on the grounds of the priory.
    The night raid had begun as usual. Father, Annemarie, and I were
standing with a few others at the edge of the park, watching the first
slender beams of the searchlights probe the darkness in the north. Then the
hum of a plane broke the tense stillness of the night, the searchlights
multiplied, crisscrossing each other in an erratic search for an elusive
object, and then the darkness ignited, releasing tiny drops of fire that
gradually formed gigantic incandescent triangles. As the "Christmas
trees"—as we called these flares dropped by the pathfinder planes to de-
marcate target areas for the bombers—slowly drifted to earth, we heard
the deep, steady roar of the first formation approaching the city. Now the
planes were overhead, and their reverberations grew louder, more intense,

. . . .

almost palpable. Suddenly the monotone was broken by sounds we had
not heard before: by an engine being accelerated to a shriek, by the dry
cough of a machine gun, and then, unmistakably, by the undulating
scream of a plane hurtling to earth. The formations were being attacked by
German fighter planes. There was another burst of machine-gun fire, and
simultaneously I heard, for the first time in five months, the familiar sound
again: the whistling of a falling bomb—much louder, sharper, than in the
basements of the city. "To the trench!" I yelled. The trench had been built
a few days earlier by a group of some twenty or thirty infantrymen who
had appeared one afternoon at the priory and requested quarters. Nobody
knew why they had come to Alexanderdorf. The sisters had turned one of
the barns over to them, and in front of it the soldiers had dug a deep trench
to serve as cover during the air raids.

"Welcome," a voice said out of the darkness as I slid into the excavation. "Come one, come all, and thrill to the greatest show on earth. Satisfaction guaranteed or your money back!" But this was not the moment for
banter. A series of explosions, in staccato fashion, shook the ground, and
the speaker and I threw ourselves in the mud, our arms butting against
each other as we cradled our heads. Above us a battle was now raging.
The air was convulsed with the pitched screams and deep moans of planes
rapidly descending and ascending, with gunfire, and with the interminable
whistle and wail of falling bombs. "You know how to pray?" the voice
said suddenly as another detonation rocked the trench, covering us with a
shower of debris. I lifted my head and looked in the face of the young
lieutenant who was in command of the soldiers. In the naked light of the
flares his face looked stark white and lifeless, as on an overexposed pho-
tograph. "Vater unser," I began. Together we slowly recited the Lord's
Prayer, but when I began the Hail Mary he remained silent. I finished the
prayer and again we joined in the Our Father. When the racket subsided
we got up and, leaning against the side of the trench, waited for the night
to return to darkness and silence. Then we shook hands wordlessly and
returned to our quarters.

After that night Alexanderdorf became familiar with bombs. For some
reason resistance had stiffened around Berlin, and the attackers, unable to

reach their target, would drop their bombs wherever they were turned back, to lighten their load for the return flight. The battle of that night had left numerous gigantic craters in the fields and woods surrounding the priory, but except for a few shingles blown off here and there, the buildings had remained undamaged. Still, the sisters, who had waited out the terror in their cells, had been so shaken by the experience that they decided to have a bunker dug in the park, in back of the convent building. Some eight feet deep, its walls shored up by heavy planks, its ceiling of logs supported by heavy beams that carried the weight of a mound of sand and gravel ten feet high, the Chapel of Our Lady of the Roots, as we dubbed the structure, contained a row of crude benches on either side, a small altar, and a tabernacle into which the Blessed Sacrament was placed when a raid threatened. During the raid a couple of candles were lit on the altar, and the sisters chanted as many of the next day's canonical hours as their enforced confinement allowed—prudently gaining time for some extra sleep the next morning. Father and I joined them a few times, but when I found him one day digging a hole underneath an oak tree in the park, I knew that we had both sensed that our presence in the extended underground clausura had not been welcome. The hole covered us up to the shoulders provided we crawled in feet first and pressed tightly against each other, and in this position, resting our arms on a hundred-year-old gigantic root, we would now spend endless hours for the next six months.

For Father, seeking protection against the bombs was a quiet admission that the reality of war had come home to him. As long as the raids and air battles had been confined to the city, he had managed to keep up an attitude about the war that was almost offensively blasé: for him Germany had lost the war from the day it began, and, as he frequently protested, he was above paying any attention to Germany's death throes. Sometimes, when we stood at the edge of the priory's park and watched the awesome spectacle of a night raid unfold over the northern horizon, he would, oblivious of me and the other guests, whistle to himself the tune of "God Save the King." Now he no longer whistled. The death throes had seized that tiny portion of the German colossus where he had hoped to ride out the catastrophe in equanimity, and he was afraid. Fear, the common denominator of life in the city to the north, had now begun to strike at the substance of our privileged existence in the priory.

The soldiers departed a few weeks after the night of the air battle. After that night the lieutenant had begun to seek me out and we found pleasure in each other's company. Werner was of my age and had been a student of philosophy under Martin Heidegger. He had fought in Yugoslavia and Romania, countries that were now in the hands of the Soviets, and had spent some time in a hospital in Germany, but he either did not tell me or I have forgotten what had brought him and a handful of his men to Alexanderdorf. Well read and well bred, he had about him a quality of purity and innocence that was touching, but our conversations were far from comfortable. As so many of my contemporaries who loathed the Nazis but had grown up without firm beliefs and without a unifying vision of the world that could carry them through a time of faltering convictions and doubtful values, as Klaus had once put it, Werner had concocted for himself an ideology that served at bottom only as a justification for his own torn, searching mind. I had not read much of Ernst Jünger, the former World War I officer who at that time apotheosized passionate commitment to war and work as the fulfillment of a heroic existence, but I was familiar with the works of Werner's other favorite writer, Oswald Spengler, and did indeed keep in my suitcase a copy of his *The Decline of the West,* profusely annotated with sarcastic comments in Father's hand. "You are trying to harmonize the mutually exclusive, and you know yourself that's impossible," I told him. "You accept Jünger's devotion to work and reject his glorification of war. You believe in the decline of the West, but you reject Spengler's prophecy of universal vulgarism under the aegis of Caesarism. Why the devil don't you start reading some decent Christian authors? You prayed once, remember?"

It was our last evening before his departure for the eastern front, and I had dared to be more frank than I used to be. We were sitting near the window in my room, without light, smoking and watching the Christmas trees that seemed to hang motionless over the distant city. Since the approach of the bombers had not occurred over our area, we had not bothered to seek shelter. "Look, Heinz," he said after a long silence, "I'll read the books you gave me, and I'll try to pray. In the meantime, you pray for me." At dawn the next morning he came into my room, dressed in field uniform and carrying his officer's coat and full-dress uniform over his arm. "Here, keep these," he said, throwing the clothes on my bed. "I won't need them for a while, but I may come back soon. And take this too." He handed me his officer's sword and embraced me. Then he turned and left. I hung up the uniform in my closet and put the sword with the American gun. I would not see Werner again, but I would soon have a most unpleasant occasion to remember our farewell.

With the cold wind, the rain, and the early twilight came the *Ostflüchtlinge* (the refugees from the east). Once before, in early summer, refugees had come through Alexanderdorf: Lithuanians, Latvians, and Estonians, whose countries had then been penetrated by the Russians, but the flow of cars and wagons had soon subsided. Now they came in a tidal wave from East Prussia and the territories east of the Oder, fleeing before the Russian armies. They clogged the highway with carts, carriages, and covered wagons. They filled schoolrooms, town halls, warehouses, barns, and stables. They asked for food, medicine, milk for their babies, fodder for their animals. Some came with nothing but what they wore on their bodies and carried on their backs, others came with caravans of wagons hauling furniture, machinery, household goods. Some offered diamonds for food, others stole or begged. Some died in the priory, a few committed suicide, many were ill. All brought tales of plunder, rape, arson, terror. We spread straw on the threshing floor of the barn where I lived, and when I left my room early in the morning I had to make my way gingerly among bodies that snored, moaned, and whimpered in their restless sleep.

Father Bonaventura and Father Ludger, wearing overcoats over their vestments, said mass in the park, in the barns, in the yard. During raids the women and children huddled in the trench the soldiers had dug, while the men sought cover under the trees. The sisters nursed the sick, mended clothes, and made journeys to the neighboring towns and villages to beg for food and medicine. Their provisions had long ago run out, and now we lived from meal to meal without knowing when the next meal would be served. Annemarie, herself near her time, cared for pregnant women and for infants who had lost their parents. Father became invisible; he kept to his room, sad and bewildered, and talked of the exodus that would radically change the demographic pattern of Europe for generations. As the gray multitude pressed on—cold, wet, and hungry—the highway again became quiet and empty, the park and yard appeared strangely deserted, and in the barn only the straw on the floor reminded me of the treks that for weeks had turned the priory into a disorderly camp.

On Christmas Eve, villagers mingled in my barn with the guests of the priory, bomb refugees from Berlin, French laborers, and Yugoslav officers for a simple celebration. There was a pine tree illuminated with candles; there were candles on tables and jugs with red wine taken from the provisions of the sacristy. The mood was quiet and relaxed, except for a few minutes when we waited in tense silence for the drone of a plane to fade. Before the French departed, Jean-Pierre, the foreman, called me over to their group and unceremoniously handed me a block of wood the size of two hands and shaped in the form of a Gothic window. The block showed in relief a Madonna with hands joined in prayer, and the engraved inscription "Souvenir d'un captif."

Shortly after the Christmas holidays Annemarie returned to Berlin to await the birth of her child. Besides having greater confidence in the medical services available in the city, she wanted to be with her friends when her time came, and both reasons proved stronger than her fear of the bombs. The previous summer, in expectation of the baby with whom she could no longer have lived in the priory, the men from the village had built for her a small house of prefabricated wood, on the heath in back of the park. During her absence I dug a bomb shelter next to the house—a hole in the ground, covered with a mound of sand and gravel and shored up by some beams and planks. To be able to reach the house via a shortcut through the park, I cut a hole in the wire fence separating the park from the heath, and although the sisters patiently and pointedly mended the fence several times, the shortcut became for everybody the established route to the House on the Heath. When Annemarie moved in with her baby daughter late in January, I began to spend my evenings with her, trying to make up for the absence of Peter, whom Annemarie believed to be on the Russian front and from whom she had had no word for months.

We usually finished our evenings in the little bunker; the child had been born during an air raid, and for the first four months of her life she would spend the better part of her nights underground.

I had known since about Christmas that I could expect to be drafted soon for the Volkssturm (People's Army), a kind of local militia that had been established on Hitler's orders late in 1944 to serve as the last line of defense. It was obligatory for all men between sixteen and sixty who had not been called up for military duty and were not significantly disabled. I faced a grim choice. Joining the poorly trained, poorly armed Volkssturm would almost certainly have meant death or captivity, but my chances of surviving the war as a deserter would have been even slimmer at a time when young, healthy-looking men wearing civilian clothes were suspect under any circumstances. Mother Justina, the prioress, and Father urged me to go into hiding and offered their help. It was late January, the Russians had overrun East Prussia and taken Warsaw and were now advancing toward the Oder. In the west, the last German effort to drive the Allies from German soil had collapsed in the Battle of the Bulge, and we expected the war to end in a matter of weeks. I was still wavering when, early in February, the letter came that ordered me to report to an army barracks near Zossen, some seven miles northeast of Alexanderdorf. I went. Without knowing it I had made my decision.

Barracks life is governed by rumors, and the Volkssturm was no exception. The first thing I heard when I joined some hundred other men in an otherwise deserted mess hall was that we had been picked to defend the headquarters of the German General Staff that either had just moved to Zossen or was about to move there, and where from now on the Führer himself would take command of the *Ostfront*. I learned after the war that Zossen had indeed housed the headquarters of the Armed Forces High Command and Hitler's command post and that it had contained sprawling underground installations that served as the communications center for all German armies throughout Europe. We did not know these facts at the time, but they were known by enemy intelligence and accounted for the increasingly heavy concentration of bombing raids and the stiff German resistance in our area that had puzzled us during the last months of the war. But as we marched in a column along a wintry highway to our post—white-haired farmers with gnarled faces and bent backs side by side with boys too young to sprout a beard; some of us wearing trench coats, others World War I army jackets; some of us carrying leather suitcases, others knapsacks, or boxes tied with rope—we must have looked like prisoners being marched to a concentration camp rather than a task force charged with defending the Führer's central command post. After a few hours we ended up in a little village and took quarters in a barn attached to the village inn.

In the following weeks—with the barroom of the inn as our command post, the barn as our barracks, its straw-covered floor as our bunks, and a dozen or so shoulder-deep holes we had dug the night of our arrival as our bomb shelters—we were, as our company commander had put it, "hammered into a fighting unit on which the Führer could look with pride." Our commander was a gray-haired World War I veteran who wore a captain's uniform that had long become much too tight for him, and whose sad, intelligent eyes behind rimless glasses belied his fierce words. He did not have much material to hammer into anything. Our job consisted of digging trenches across the highway where it entered and where it left the village and across some feeder roads in the vicinity, deep and wide enough to serve as traps for enemy tanks, and excavating the frozen ground in strategic places in fields and woods from where one could fire bazookas at tanks trying to detour the traps. After a few days of this kind of work our clothes were torn and our shoes tattered, and a good number of the men were lying in the barn with various ailments or injuries or had had to be sent home. Occasionally a black touring car would drive up to a construction site, a group of SS officers would alight and silently, with grim faces, inspect our work and disappear again. At night we would congregate in the barroom, drinking watery beer and listening glumly to the news, and whoever could borrow a bicycle in the village would slip away to spend a few hours at home.

One day a shipment of assorted firearms arrived—a few bazookas, and rifles and submachine guns made in Czechoslovakia, Russia, Italy, and other occupied countries—and after the veterans among us had figured out how to use them we spent the mornings with firearm drills. We had received neither blanks nor live ammunition, but the first time I pressed myself against the side of a trench, aiming my useless Czech rifle at an imaginary line of Russian soldiers advancing through the snow-covered field that stretched before me, I was flushed with an intense elation when I realized that I was holding in my hands a weapon with which I could defend myself. That piece of cold, dead metal, I thought later when I was lying on my bundle of straw, trying to explain to myself a moment of exuberance that had surprised and, at first, shocked me, that piece of dead metal had, as useless as it was without a bullet, restored to me a sense of self-worth, a feeling of freedom and self-reliance after years of utter defenselessness. I think at that moment I lost forever any faith in pacifism.

In the night of February 13–14 the massive bombing raids began that devastated Dresden, one of Europe's most beautiful cities, some seventy miles to the south of our post. When I was awakened that night by the sound of a distant siren, I listened for a few minutes for the familiar hum of approaching planes but, hearing nothing but the snoring of my comrades, dozed off again. Suddenly I was fully awake. I knew something was happening out there, in the night, that the darkness and silence were hiding something big and terrible that made my heart pound. Now others stirred, and little islands of light sprang up in the darkness where the men had switched on their flashlights, and voices rose, confused and bewildered. And then I felt the first tremor—no, not a tremor, not even a quiver, perhaps not more than an infinitesimal spasm of the earth—but my body, like Pavlov's dog, reacted before my mind grasped the significance of the signal, and I ran outside and jumped into the nearest hole. Black silence enclosed me, and for a few moments I could hear nothing but my breathing and the beating of my heart. As my eyes grew accustomed to the darkness I became aware of a curious flicker that could have been quite near or quite far, and then the very air seemed to turn faintly luminous and I could make out the stony flatness of a black field beneath a black sky. Now an ominous glow rose from the horizon where I had first noticed the flicker, and I heard the ever so gentle roll of drums and felt the familiar flutter and the brief pressure on my inner ear.

"My guess is that Dresden is catching it," a voice said above me, and I looked up at a pair of hip boots above which I could make out nothing but the tiny glow of a cigarette. "Kill your cigarette, you damned fool," I snapped. The glow disappeared and the boots slid down. It was the captain. "Sorry, sir," I said, trying to execute a salute in an enclosure that put us knee to knee and chin to chin. There was no reply. We managed to twist away from each other, and for a long time we stood silently side by side, listening and watching.

"War is terrible," the captain said suddenly.

"Ja, Herr Hauptmann," I echoed, "Krieg ist furchtbar." I was immediately on my guard. Did he want to bait me, or did he speak his mind?

"Those people are being slaughtered for a lost cause," he broke out vehemently when another roll of the drums had faded. "*We* know the war is lost, the Nazis know the war is lost, and still the killing goes on."

"Whom do you expect us to fight here, the Russians or the Americans?" I asked, trying, not very skillfully, to evade his point.

"*We* are not going to fight anybody," he remarked. "Even if they send us Waffen SS (armed SS) for support. They told me in Zossen they would, and you know as well as I what that means. A Russian bullet in your heart or a German bullet in your neck."

He went on to tell me that he had been a teacher of German literature at a gymnasium in Zossen, that he had joined the Nazi party soon after Hitler had come to power, but that he had quickly become disenchanted with the Nazi regime. When the war broke out he had retired. He had planned to move to Innsbruck to complete a book on Goethe's theories of color when he had been drafted for the Volkssturm. As he talked, I remained taciturn, sensing that he did not expect a reply or equal confidences on my part. When it had become still for a while and we heard the drone of distant planes, he observed, "They are going home. Let's hope it's over for now." He offered me a cigarette and lit mine and his. "Turkish," he said. "Compliments of the SS. They have everything in Zossen." We waited for another ten or fifteen minutes, and when my body told me that it no longer felt threatened, I saluted, climbed out of the hole, and stretched out my hand to hoist him up. Together we walked to the inn where he had a room, and when we had reached the door he turned and seized me by the arm. He made as if to say something, but he only shook his head, muttered "Good night," and quickly stepped over the threshold.

The next morning, during the work line-up, the captain announced that from now on I would be responsible for supplies and be relieved of all other duties. There followed what I remember as a curious interlude of tranquillity, a period of dreamlike quality during which I even took up, almost mechanically, some of my old habits of reading, studying, and meditating. I spent many hours at a table in the spacious but deserted dining room, sitting by the window with a textbook on scholastic philosophy and luxuriating in the warmth of the spring sun that flooded the handsome room. Usually the only sound I heard was the buzz of an early fly, but occasionally I would be startled by a sharp explosion that made the window rattle. My comrades were target-practicing with the bazookas. Ammunition had finally arrived, but most of the bullets did not fit our rifles and every other bazooka grenade was a dud. Sometimes I would go to the barroom and, having made certain that nothing stirred in the house or yard, tune the radio to the BBC. The penalty for listening to the BBC was summary execution, but the risk from my outfit was minimal: news from the BBC was conversational currency among us and was as openly discussed and compared with German radio news as if the British sender had been just another legitimate source of information.

Once or twice a week I bicycled to a nearby town to requisition food and other supplies from an SS office, and when the supply truck arrived I would check off the items and store them. The SS man with whom I dealt was a jovial, fatherly fellow who spoke with a cigar between his teeth, knew the sisters, and called me "Herr Doktor," and who would often send me on my way with a few bars of chocolate, a few grams of real coffee, or a package of cigarettes. Once he put a case with ten or twelve bottles of fine French cognac on my carrier. "Here," he said, "take this before the Russians get it." And he added, "And drink it, but I am afraid you will have to polish off a bottle a day." I hid the treasure in the cellar of the inn, intending to break it out on a special occasion, but in the end the Russians got it anyhow.

As openly as we discussed the BBC news we talked about our plans to desert when the Russians—or, for that matter, possibly the Americans— closed in on us. I carried in my pocket a sketch I had drawn with the help of comrades who knew the area and who had described to me how to avoid open spaces and highways and reach Alexanderdorf via backwoods, hedgerows, wagon trails, and creeks. I don't know if I would have deserted in earnest or, for that matter, if any of us could have escaped the Russian tank forces that on the final days of the battle for Berlin would overrun the area between Zossen and the outskirts of Berlin in a matter of hours. Things took a different turn for me, unplanned.

One night I woke up with excruciating abdominal pains, and by morning I was delirious with fever. The captain had me carried into one of the guest rooms of the inn where I could lie in a bed and began telephoning hospitals in the vicinity. He merely learned that all hospitals had been evacuated, together with physicians and nurses. The pain and fever subsided after a couple of days, and by the last week of March I had gained sufficient strength to mount a bicycle and pedal to the priory for what I thought would be a week of convalescence. I never saw the captain or any of my fellow *Volkssturmler* again.

At the priory it was business as usual as we waited for the arrival of the Russians who now stood at the Oder, less than fifty miles away. The sisters praised God in the chapel or in their bunker, baked hosts, and planted vegetables and flowers. Father was deskbound in his study, puffing a pipe stuffed with dried and pulverized leaves of nettles or roses and imperturbably penning page after page of a manuscript that was to contain his edited and annotated version of a nineteenth-century history of Christianity. Annemarie nursed her baby and helped the sisters run a kindergarten for the children of bomb refugees and villagers, while I, wrapped in a blanket, lay on a lawn chair in the sun, dozing and wondering whether I should return to the Volkssturm or go into hiding until the Russians came. Although the air raids now were a round-the-clock condition of life and explosions of bombs shook the priory frequently, the fine spring weather cast over the land a gentle spell that belied the stories of the refugees of murder and rape and plunder and arson. Occasionally troops in trucks or on foot, armored cars, or a tank or two would move past the priory, or a black limousine flying a staff flag would drive into the yard and some SS or army officers would join us in the dining room for lunch or dinner. On these occasions we would attempt to learn something about the situation on the fronts and the purpose of the troop movements, but it was evident that the officers were as confused as the troops we watched moving in opposite directions along the highway.

I had thus spent about two weeks when one of my comrades came to the priory with a message from the captain that I should report to the post within three days unless a physician certified that I was still unfit for duty. That same day I decided to return to the inn. In the dark hours of the morning of my planned departure I was awakened by a low, steady, muted rumble, a sound my body could not identify. My watch showed four. I got up and stepped outside. The rumble, which had grown louder and more distinct, did not come from the direction of Berlin but from the east. To have a better view of the eastern horizon I walked across the yard and through the park to a spot where it bordered the heath. My eyes had grown accustomed to the darkness, and I could make out the contours of Anne-marie's house some hundred yards out on the heath and beyond it the rooftops of Kummersdorf, but the sky above the black ridge of the distant woods was dark, empty, and silent. "Artillery," Father's voice said behind me. "Must be a hell of a barrage. The only time I heard anything like it was at Verdun." "Russian or German?" I asked, but I did not expect him to answer. After about a half-hour, during which we remained silent, the rumbling ceased abruptly and the world grew quiet again. "That's it," Father said. "My guess is that this was meant to soften up our troops, and the Russians will now be attempting to cross the Oder. If they succeed they could be at our doorsteps in a few hours." As we walked through the park back to the priory, he turned to me. "Don't leave just yet," he said, and there was pleading in his voice. "Let's listen to the morning news and then you can decide."

The news that morning—Monday, April 16—reported heavy fighting all along the Oder, with the heaviest concentration on Küstrin, fifty miles directly east of Berlin. "The push on Berlin is on," Father remarked. For the next four days we waited. I was now a deserter but I made no attempt to hide. I wrapped the American submachine gun, the ammunition, and my diary in oilcloth and buried the package under an apple tree in the garden behind the guesthouse, but aside from that neither I nor the sisters or anybody else made any particular preparations for the unimaginable

. . . .

horror that the refugees had said lay ahead of us. The highway, our barom-
eter for what agitated the world beyond our enclave, had again become
quiet and deserted, as if it, too, lay in waiting. Once a group of soldiers
appeared in the yard, and I was astonished at their youth; some of them
could not have been older than fourteen or fifteen, and with their fresh
faces and dapper uniforms they looked like a troupe of actors about to give
an open-air performance. They set up a machine gun in the park and
another one at the edge of the wood across from the priory and began
digging a latrine, but after a few hours they packed their gear again and
moved on toward Berlin. The rumbling that had alarmed my body with its
unfamiliarity had become continuous: in daytime an endless freight train
pounding in the distance, at night a growling thunder accompanied by
sheet lightning. Occasionally the rattle of a machine gun would suddenly
echo through the woods, and the nearness of the sound would startle us.

On the morning of the fifth day after the radio had reported the Russian
assault on the Oder front, I had gone to lauds and attended mass, and
when I was leaving the convent a sister called to me through the kitchen
window. "Something for your sister's baby," she said, placing a saucepan
wrapped in a towel on the windowsill. Taking my usual shortcut to reach
Annemarie's house I had just crawled through the hole in the fence and
was about to straighten up again when I heard the earsplitting scream of an
approaching plane. A number of things happened simultaneously: I threw
myself to the ground; I saw the plane, which was heading straight toward
me at the level of the treetops; I heard the sharp whistle of a falling bomb
and waited with bated breath for the sound of an explosion that did not
come. A moment later I stood in Annemarie's kitchen as another plane
screeched overhead. "The Russians are here!" I yelled, running into the
bedroom and lifting the baby out of her crib. "Into the bunker!" Annemarie, who had been standing at the stove stirring something in a pot,
seemed to pay no attention. She not so much as glanced at me as I pushed
past her with the baby in my arms, but continued to stir the pot, and when,
after what seemed an eternity, she took her place next to me in the dark
hole she quietly began to feed the child its pap while the roar of planes
following each other in quick succession caused our little shelter to vibrate
so violently that I feared it would collapse. The ruckus ceased abruptly,

and we crawled out into the brilliant sunshine. I was about to return to the priory when I remembered something. "Happy birthday!" I said, and seeing Annemarie's blank look I added, "April 20. A birthday present for the Führer. Special delivery from Stalin."

Early in the afternoon of the same day, when the sun was still high in the sky, I stood in the shade of a tree outside the wall closing off the priory grounds against the highway and saw the tank come up from between the last houses of Alexanderdorf. The colossus whose clanking had brought me running to the gate was moving slowly, almost hesitatingly; it stalked the road like an unearthly insect, its giant black cylindric tentacle sniffing the air. I pressed myself against the trunk of the tree as the ground began to tremble with its approach. Instinctively I knew that this was not a German tank. And then something—perhaps a picture or a newsreel suddenly remembered—made me exclaim under my breath, "The Americans! My God, an American tank!" I wanted to shout and had to restrain an impulse to run toward the mass of jingling, churning metal that was about to grind past me.

Suddenly the tank halted directly in front of me, and I spotted the five-pointed red star and beneath it, running the length of the turret, some crudely painted Cyrillic letters. The gun turned slowly toward the priory, the hatch of the turret opened, and a head appeared, encapsulated in a black leather hood with earflaps. The soldier, shading his eyes, looked intently at the manor housing the convent, while the long barrel of the gun remained fixed in the direction of his gaze. After a few seconds the head disappeared in the turret, the hatch closed, the gun turned and lined itself up with the highway ahead, and the monster let out a belch and rumbled on, filling the air with the stench of kerosene. I watched it until it rounded a curve and disappeared in a grove of trees, and then I walked slowly across the courtyard, back to the priory, as the bell began to ring for supper.

V-E Day

. . . .

"**T**e Deum laudamus," the prioress intoned, and the sisters fell in, "te Deum confitemur," their voices clear and smooth. Father discreetly cleared his throat. The pipe organ began to wheeze, covering up the self-conscious voices of the handful of men and women who had come to vespers.

This morning someone from the village had brought the message to the priory that Germany had surrendered to the Allied forces. That was the reason for the Te Deum. The news had spread quickly among our small community—the sisters, the refugees, the wounded and dying in the barns and stables, the Yugoslav officers, the French laborers. But nobody had seemed impressed. On my way to the chapel I had met Sister Michaela, the gardener. "Now the Russians will go on a rampage," she had said. Perhaps being late for the service and breaking the rule of silence were, after all, signs of unusual excitement for a nun as proper and closed-mouthed as Sister Michaela. For Father, I knew, the announcement of Germany's capitulation would be less interesting than an announcement of the next distribution of tobacco rations. For him, the war had ended in

Germany's collapse and mutilation the day it began. Looking at him side-
ways as he gave masculine firmness and substance to the old hymn of
victory and praise, I sensed that he was oblivious to the occasion for the
song and to his environment.

For the men and boys whom we had dragged out of the woods and
picked up from the highway after the fighting in our area had ceased, the
news would be meaningless: they knew that if they did not die they would
soon end up in a Russian prisoner-of-war camp deep in the interior of the
Soviet Union. The nuns, I speculated, would long for nothing more than
to be able to return to their accustomed ways, to be relieved of the burden
of caring and praying for a population of hapless strangers who had turned
the convent into a campground. For Annemarie—would she now hope
again for Peter's return from the Russian front, or would she find some
peace if she knew with certainty that he had died? Only the French and
Yugoslavs would be jubilant about the prospect of returning home. But
would the Russians let them depart?

"Deus, cuius misericordiae non est numerus," the prioress began to
pray in conclusion of the Ambrosian Hymn. I waited until the nuns had
filed out of the choir; Father Ludger, showing no trace of his eighty years,
had briskly stepped into the sacristy, and the last person of the little congregation to leave had dipped his hand into the holy-water font and closed
the door behind him. I felt a need, almost a moral obligation, to be alone,
to comprehend and to articulate to myself what it meant that the war had
come to an end. I had been fourteen when Hitler had come to power,
twenty when the war began. I was now twenty-six and had come out of six
years of war alive and unscathed. I had not died in France or Russia
because the regime had considered me unworthy of serving in the armed
forces. The bombs had spared me in Berlin and here, and because of an
attack of appendicitis I had escaped death or imprisonment as a soldier of
the Volkssturm.

And what had saved me during the past three weeks? A few hours after I
had seen the first Russian tank appear between the houses of Alexanderdorf, the convent grounds had swarmed with Russian soldiers, and my
life, or my freedom, had been in jeopardy ever since. Curiously, I reflected, I had felt no fear from the moment a Mongol in a black, high-

necked blouse had kicked open the door to Father's study, had grinned at us without bothering to raise his automatic weapon, and, saying, "Deutschland kaputt," had with one sweeping motion plucked the heirloom watch from Father's desk. The soldiers that had come and gone had been disciplined, almost businesslike. At the convent gate they had posted a wooden sign with the word *Convent* painted on it in Cyrillic letters, and although some incidents of arson, plunder, rape, and murder had occurred in the neighboring villages, the priory and its occupants had been spared the horrors of which the refugees had warned us.

Only once had I been certain that I had forfeited my life. On the second or third day after Russian troops occupied the area, a battle erupted in the woods across the highway. Until then, we had heard only occasional machine-gun fire, but now the tanks that had been quietly squatting in the field behind the priory and on the heath near Annemarie's house joined mortars and cannons stationed elsewhere in a constant barrage of some target nearby. Shortly after the firing began, a truck packed with Russian soldiers drove into the convent yard, the soldiers leaped down and, submachine guns on the ready, fanned out and began to search the grounds. Father and I were standing in front of the manor, watching the men go from house to house, from barn to barn, when suddenly five or six of them ran toward us and surrounded us. Prodding us with their guns, they marched us to a clearing in the park where we joined the two monks and a group of other men who had been seized by the soldiers. One of the Russians, a blue-eyed youngster in khaki uniform and fur cap, stepped up to us and began a tirade in Russian. We did not understand anything, except the two words "Deutscher Offizier," which he shouted again and again, pointing menacingly at each of us in turn as he spit out these words. It was obvious that he suspected one of us of being a German officer. But how could we explain to him that none of us was a soldier? As we remained silent, he called out a command to his comrades, and three of them positioned themselves opposite us, some twenty feet away. Behind the trees of the park a tank gun was at this moment firing rapidly, and the earsplitting din rent the air, but as the soldiers leveled their submachine guns at us it had seemed suddenly as if a curtain of silence was being drawn around our group.

What had I thought? Had I prayed? Above all, what had made the
soldiers lower their weapons, walk away from us, climb on their truck and
drive off, leaving us standing there stunned by our sudden reprieve? I tried
in vain to evoke the feelings of that moment, but as in the remembrance of
a dream, when images crowd each other, I saw again the empty spot
where, a second ago, the soldiers had stood, pointing their weapons at us;
saw myself walk across the yard and enter the barn; saw myself open a
door and stare at the devastation that had been my room. Among my
clothes that had been ripped out of the closet I had found the officer's
uniform that Werner had left with me on the morning he said farewell.

There had been other threats to my life—interrogations and moments
when I felt the cold metal of the muzzle of a gun in my nape or behind my
ear—but I had felt no fear. The real horror of these past three weeks had
been the bloodbath among the German unit that was trapped in the woods
and had been the target of the guns. After the guns had fallen silent the
Russians had called in bombers. For five, six, seven hours the ground
under our feet had trembled, incessantly, the windows had rattled, and the
very air had been convulsed in agony as bomber after bomber, swooping
down on the priory, screeching, had skimmed the treetops of the park, had
released its load somewhere across the highway, and again climbed
steeply into the sky. We knew what was happening in the woods, less than
two miles from us. We knew, also, that this unit that was being wiped out
had never wanted to fight—that they were fresh recruits forced by their SS
officers to attempt to break through the Russian lines. The sisters had
assembled to pray for the victims of the massacre, but when I stepped into
the chapel to join them for a few minutes, I heard no chant, no prayer,
only someone's soft weeping. For me, for them, it had been the worst
bombing of the war.

After the bombers had done their work we went with horse-drawn wagons into the forest to haul out the dead and dying. There were only dead
and dying—some two hundred, most of them younger than I and many
mere boys. The farmers took the dead, and whatever parts of a human
form we found, to the village for burial. The wounded and dying filled the
barns and stables of the priory and the now-deserted camp that had housed
the Yugoslav officers. For days and nights on end we comforted the

wounded as best we could, without a doctor, without medical supplies of any kind, without food, and we prayed with the dying until they closed their eyes. Once in a while Russian soldiers had walked through the rows of maimed and moaning men, searching each one for the tattoo mark of the SS, and whoever bore the mark had been dragged off.

I thought of Father. Throughout these last months of the war, throughout these days and nights of chaos, violence, and death that forged nuns, guests, and refugees into a community whose sole aim was to survive from hour to hour, Father had kept to his room—writing. At moments, I had hated him for his seeming callousness and indifference, but now, in this moment of contemplative silence, I suddenly realized that this was the only way in which *he* could survive. He could not have tended to the wounded and dying in the barns; he could not have kept vigil with the women, to help protect them against assault from Russian and German soldiers, or from plundering refugees. He had seemed impervious to Annemarie's grieving for her husband, whom she believed killed or imprisoned in Russia. His fear—which was the terror of the body in the face of annihilation, a terror that made his hands tremble as he wrote—became bearable and found relief through the only discipline he knew: the discipline of writing.

I began to understand that in his writing during these months he tried to express his hope for the kind of Germany, indeed for the kind of Europe, he expected to emerge from the ruins of the war. For him, the war had always been the radical purge that had to precede the restoration of Europe on the foundation of a Christian humanism. He fervently believed in that restoration; it was the only thing that had mattered about the war. Of course, like every one of us, he was singularly prepared to die in the holocaust that laid waste the Europe he had known, but in him the fear of death was so much more poignant because, unlike most of us, he had a deep and unshakeable faith in Germany's survival and Europe's transformation. I thought of the manuscript on which he had been working when the first Russian soldier entered his room. It had contained his labor on a condensation and revision of the *History of the Religion of Jesus Christ,* a fifteen-volume work by Count Friedrich Leopold von Stolberg, one of the many prominent German poets and historians of the romantic era who had converted to Catholicism. It was the kind of book, Father believed, that was needed for an intellectual reorientation of the Germans and that people, starved for truth and spiritual direction after twelve years of Nazi oppression, would turn to after the war. Would it ever find a publisher? I wondered.

I thought of the men who were still lying in the barns, the dying and those near recovery, and wondered again what would be the fate of the survivors. Why had I not been killed? Why had I not been taken prisoner? Aunt Walli, Aunt Clara, I felt with certainty, had not survived the concentration camp. Hejo, who had taught me that logic, order, and meaning ruled the cosmos? I knew he had ended up in Dachau—perhaps, I thought, Saint Thomas had protected him. The stillness in the chapel became oppressive. I must have dozed off, because I woke with a start at the sound of an approaching tank. The floor of the chapel shook as the monster passed nearby with the din of a thousand empty oil drums being rolled over cobblestones. Abruptly, the racket ceased. That would be Sergej, I concluded, and he has missed his appointment. Sergej was a *Lebenskünstler,* "an artist at living." Every so often, just before vespers, he would drive his "Stalin III" to the back door of the kitchen, politely ask for a glass of milk or water, and then eat his supper while sitting on top of the turret and listening to the sisters' chanting as it drifted through the open windows of the chapel. Yes, I thought, something like order, a resemblance of a daily routine had already begun to assert itself against the chaos.

What *had* ended? Twenty-six years of my life. Had it been a period of grace? Of passive endurance? Of merely shameful waste? Or had it been a period of mixed blessings? What *had* begun? It was no use. The chapel was quiet and empty. Father Ludger, who, as was his habit, had lingered for a few moments before the altar, had left long ago. In spite of the open windows, the air still held a trace of the smell of burnt sugar; incense clings. The windows are intact, I observed idly, and there are no large cracks in the walls or ceiling. The building had taken the near-misses of American, British, and Russian explosives with good-natured defiance. Bombs. Had Mother and Aunt Minna survived the bombings of London? I had had no word from them for three years. How had Stephan and his wife fared in the battle for Berlin? I must return to Berlin, I thought, now that the war has ended. Yes, now I could begin something, could make decisions on my own because something had once and for all ended.

All of a sudden I was seized by a surge of relief, almost joy: the *bombings* had ended. Until this moment I had not realized that for two weeks, since the massacre in the woods, I had not heard the roar of planes, the whistle of bombs, had not felt the shudder of the tortured ground. Five years of bombings had come to an end. Tonight, tomorrow night, each night thereafter, I would stretch out on my bunk, on a bed, without having to cock an inner ear to the menacing silence of the night. There would be no alarm, no sirens, no bombs. Not tonight, I thought. Never again. I would plan my departure for Berlin. And someday I would rise to the enormous implications of a turning point in history, would begin something, do something. Not today. At the moment, nothing mattered but the sweet promise of the gift of sleep.

Interregnum

. . . .

I arrived in Berlin on a sunny day in June, on a bicycle that the sisters had somehow kept from being stolen or requisitioned, with all of my possessions except my books strapped to its carrier. On my way through one of the southern suburbs I stopped at a villa that belonged to the family of one of Annemarie's former classmates, finding her and her parents engaged in watering the flowers and vegetables in their little garden. Since the city's water system was shut down, they had to fetch the water in buckets and cans from a nearby canal. They invited me to spend the night with them, and when I returned to the garden gate to unload my belongings, the bicycle had disappeared. Thus, stripped of everything I didn't carry on my body that day, I began my new life.

When I look back at those six years that I spent in Berlin after the war, several thoughts leap to mind that probably reflect the true significance of this period in my life more accurately than anything else that may be anecdotally more interesting or historically more important. The first, still filling me with incredulity and wonder, is that the Nazis and all their works had vanished so utterly, as totally as if they had never existed. Only the ruins of their monuments spoke of their glory and their fall, but in the city of 1945 these ruins could just as well have been the remains of an ancient civilization, having no significance beyond that usually accorded to museum pieces. Of those who built these structures and who worshiped there—not a trace.

Another thought that strikes me is how quickly the basic processes and relationships of normal, civilized living asserted themselves against the ghastly backdrop of destruction and decay, and under extreme physical and mental hardships that daily, for years, claimed their victims among the old, the ill, and the very young. Granted, my life, now favored in as many ways as it had been disfavored under the Nazi regime, was in that period incomparably different from the life of all too many who had survived the Third Reich and the war but had been wounded in mind, heart, or body beyond recovery. Yet by the time I left Germany in 1951, most people in Berlin, no matter under which occupying power they lived, had managed to achieve a standard of living that was at least tolerable and often quite satisfactory.

The last observation is rather a question for which I have no answer. The six years of reconstruction, which were historically and for me personally of momentous import, evoke in my memory a feebler echo and weaker colors, and seem to be of leaner content, than the six years of the war that had left a record of universal destruction and that I had endured, to all appearances, passively. Between 1945 and 1951, the foundations were laid for a new world. The atomic bomb became mankind's apocalyptic symbol. Churchill coined the phrase *Iron Curtain,* and Bernard Baruch the phrase *Cold War.* The United Nations came into being and the State of Israel was proclaimed. The Communists conquered China, and Germany was divided into a German Federal Republic and a German Democratic Republic. I myself achieved, to all appearances, more during this time than in any other period of my life. Yet the war, to me, had been a life intensely and fully lived; what followed were years of my life. Why this should be so I don't know.

I began my own rehabilitation by engaging a talent I thought I possessed but had, up to now, never put to the test: the talent to write.

When I had told Father that I was leaving the priory to begin a new life in Berlin, he had asked me what I intended to do there, and on my vague reply that I wanted to become a writer, he had suggested that I write a book about angels. "I think we have finally learned to take demons seriously," he had added, "and people should be receptive to a book on the angels. Besides, it would fill a lacuna in contemporary Catholic literature." The idea immediately appealed to me: my mind was starved, and the subject would require considerable reading and research in theology, philosophy, psychology, history, art, and imaginative literature—fields each of which I would have liked to study at a university had I not been penniless. But libraries were accessible, private libraries that had survived the bombings, and above all the magnificent State Library of Berlin that, along with the Humboldt University, the Russians had opened again almost as soon as the smoke of battle had cleared from the streets.

That I *did* write the book; that it *was* published two and a half years after Father had suggested the theme; that it was acclaimed by scholars and ordinary readers alike; and that it became a standard work in this genre of literature—each of these accomplishments still, more than forty years after the war, impresses me as a small miracle. The subject that in the rarefied atmosphere of a secluded convent had struck me as natural and eminently reasonable appeared utterly incongruous if not preposterous in the city whose ruins were stalked by the demons of hunger, cold, sickness, despair, and suicide. Like everybody else of Berlin's four million inhabitants, I needed shelter in a city more than half of whose dwellings had been leveled by bombs and fire; I needed food at a time when people fought over a slice of bread to the death; and I needed money to pay for food and shelter when barter and the black market were, if not the only, then certainly the most readily available sources of cash. For months I did not dare to mention to even my most intimate friends that I was working on a book, let alone a book that dealt with angels.

The job that sustained me for the work of writing should have dissuaded me even more persuasively from immersing myself in a subject that was dear to the heart of Plato, Aristotle, Saint Augustine, and Raphael. The Saint Gertrud Hospital in the district of Wilmersdorf hired me as a handyman, and on the first morning I reported to work, a sister led me without ado into the basement, opening the door to a room lit dimly by a naked bulb and filled from wall to wall, from floor to ceiling, with enormous piles of what appeared to be pieces of dirty clothing, wafting a sickeningly sweetish smell that took my breath away. "These are the uniforms of our patients," she explained matter-of-factly. "Most of them are dead and the few who aren't won't need them anymore. I want you to sort out the pieces that are in good enough condition to be refashioned. The stuff that's too badly soiled or torn we'll burn." And so I began my first peacetime job: salvaging for the living what was salvageable from the grisly legacy of the dead. One by one I picked up and examined the uniforms of the men who had died on the threshold between war and peace: the gray uniforms of the infantry, the dove-blue uniforms of the air force, the black uniforms of the tank divisions and of Hitler's palace guard, the SS. Many were faded and frayed, testimonials to years of soldiering; some seemed new, as if only recently issued; almost all of them showed black stains of dried blood here and there. Where the blood had soaked large areas of either jacket or trousers, the piece had stiffened to the hardness of a board. Those I assigned to bins that the maintenance men would cart during the night to the incinerator. Sometimes I found attached to a jacket a silver eagle worn by officers above the right breast pocket; or an Iron Cross of the first or second class. Once a Knight's Cross, the Third Reich's highest decoration for bravery, fell out of a pocket. These insignia I kept, to exchange them later on the black market for food or cigarettes.

After a couple of weeks, when I had finished my task, I was put in charge of fetching food, medicaments, and supplies from the various centers from which the Russians distributed these things among Berlin's hospitals. It was a pleasant assignment. My vehicle of transport was a horse and wagon, and obtaining food and medicine depended on my skill at being in the right place at the right time and at negotiating persuasively with the Russian or German in charge. I quickly became the favored son of the sister supervising the kitchen, who spoiled me with such delicacies as baked bread, margarine, and marmalade, or an occasional meat dish. Another sister, the pharmacist, kept me supplied with Russian *makhorka* tobacco, which with the aid of newspaper I turned into cigarettes. Traversing large areas of the city with my wagon, I realized for the first time the extent of its destruction. Whole districts had been turned into boulder fields out of which windowless, blackened, serrated façades rose like enormous, lonely stalagmites. Once-proud and elegant boulevards now twisted as narrow paths through hills and mountains of rubble, and when it happened that their course led over the top of one of those elevations, I would sometimes halt the horse and scan my field of vision to orient myself by familiar landmarks. All along these routes groups of women were busy collecting bricks, knocking off the mortar with a hammer, and setting them up in neat piles for future use as building material. For the better part of the six years I lived in postwar Berlin, the endless ping-ping of these hammers seemed to be the predominant sound in the city.

Toward the summer, when the days turned hot, out of a ruin or a field of rubble a slender, undulating, black column would sometimes rise high into the blue sky—flies, millions of flies drawn to and seemingly held motionless above a poisoned water reservoir or cadavers hidden in the debris. There were zones of sight and zones of smell. Wasteland changed suddenly into districts where intact houses, with their windows sparkling in the sun, paraded fiery geraniums and roses on their balconies, and as suddenly as destruction alternated with wholeness did the stench of decomposition that I knew so well from my days in the basement of the hospital turn into the less sickening but throat-constricting odor of cold ashes and seared matter. I encountered surprisingly few Russian soldiers on these trips; they tended to keep to their quarters and let the Berliners take care of the business of the city. In contrast, when the Allies moved into Berlin in the fall, French, British, and American soldiers were much in evidence in their respective sectors, demonstrating to the Berliners that their city was, after all, the victors' domain.

I had begun to do research for my book from the day I had found the job in the hospital, and the sisters had given me shelter in what used to be the patients' solarium and now served as a storage room. But the sounds, sights, and smells of a large hospital where patients and cadavers often were stored together in corridors and staircases made it difficult to achieve a modicum of privacy even at night. When the solarium began to attract ambulatory patients who wanted to sun themselves or simply sought an escape from the stench and commotion in their rooms, I moved into a furnished room in a nearby apartment building, sacrificing the cook's and the pharmacist's favors to the need for solitude. My landlady, a young woman who was waiting for the return of her husband from the Russian front, matter-of-factly included me in her motherly concerns for her four or five small children. We lived on potatoes she managed to scrounge from farmers during day-long forays into the country and on whatever rations were available, and while we were always hungry we were rarely famished. When the Allies arrived, the district where I lived and worked was included in the American sector and I was able to get in touch with Mother in London. Her occasional package with British chocolate and American cigarettes considerably strengthened our bargaining position on the black market and in the potato fields and bought for me the freedom from concerns for physical survival I needed to devote the evenings to my manuscript.

As preposterous as such a thought may have seemed in Berlin in 1945, and especially in the grim winter of 1945–1946, the tone, the mood, of the city was that of a quiet, resolute optimism, of a purposeful assertiveness that had always characterized the Berliners and that had given way to bitterness and cynical despair only during the last year of the war, when it seemed that Hitler intended to make this once-magnificent capital the pyre on which he and his gods were to be consumed. Although the Russians, anticipating the entry of the Allies, stripped the city of any machinery, materials, and industrial equipment that had remained usable, from entire factories to sewing machines, they did encourage and support the restoration of what is essential to the normal functioning of a metropolis. Within months the water system had been purified and clean water, though rationed, was available in amounts sufficient for survival. Soon we were able to replace candles with electric light for a few hours each evening and to listen to radio broadcasts as long as the electrical current kept flowing. As tunnels, stations, bridges, and other structures were repaired or replaced, the city railroad and subway networks, both dependent on electricity, were gradually returned to service. Throughout the day the city reverberated from the detonations of dynamite charges that leveled dangerously unstable ruins or cleared the way for building projects, and at night we were often jolted by the detonation of a bomb that had remained buried in the ground unexploded, and suddenly, unexplainably, went off.

For years our thoughts had been preoccupied with, indeed often fed on the prospect of death, and our senses had become numb from the daily, relentless onslaught of images and sounds of destruction. Now the tiny flame of hope that had been kept flickering in the violent gusts of cynical resignation, fear, and despair gathered nourishment and strength from the sounds and images of reconstruction, and our thoughts began to feed on the prospect of life. "Who was killed?" was probably the most frequently asked question of the war years. Now the question was, "Who has survived?" Mother and Aunt Minna, I learned, had survived the German raids on London, the first making a living as a private nurse, the other as a housekeeper. My friend Stephan and his wife had survived the last year of the war and the Russian assault on the city and now lived in the suburb of Zehlendorf. I visited them often. Stephan, too, had turned to writing and was about to publish a book, an autobiographical account of his erotic adventures during the time of the air raids that had devastated Hamburg, where he had lived for a few years of the war. Effervescent and eccentric as ever, he told me he had sworn off his Catholic past, considered himself an atheist, and thought I should marry his wife's sister, a dark, sensuous beauty, who would cure me of my Catholic complexes. Hejo, the priest who had introduced me to the world of Saint Thomas, had survived the Dachau concentration camp and had settled in Cologne. Peter, my brother-in-law, had returned from the war, suddenly appearing one day in the yard of the priory, where Annemarie was still living with their infant daughter. Peter quickly became involved in the activities of the newly established Christian Democratic Union, Konrad Adenauer's party, an engagement that turned into a career and eventually led him and his family to West Germany.

The past, of course, lingered and churned underneath and intruded into the new structures of life that were slowly forming. When, early in 1946, I had finished the first few chapters of my book, the small but regular advances on future royalties that I received from the publisher who had accepted the book, combined with whatever the precious content of Mother's occasional parcels from London would fetch on the black market, enabled me to quit my job at the hospital and live by my own wits. I decided that now the time had come to satisfy a desire I had had since boyhood: learning how to play the piano. *My* life, I probably felt, was on the mend, beautifully on the mend; all I had to do was retrieve as quickly as I could what for so long had been denied me.

My teacher, a fragile, white-haired lady who had, she told me, once counted among her pupils the ladies of the court of the Kaiser, delightedly accepted an occasional bar of chocolate or a tin of corned beef as payment, exchanging them for briquets to feed the tiny potbellied stove that stood next to her piano and whose flue pipe unceremoniously crossed the entire length of the room midway between floor and ceiling, ending in a crudely fashioned hole in the wall. She permitted me to practice on another piano that stood in a small, otherwise bare room which was unheated, indeed unheatable. The piano was wedged into a corner, one wall of which consisted of crisscrossed boards protecting the unwary from tumbling into space through a gaping hole but offering no protection against the wintry blasts of February or March. One afternoon, tired of alternately massaging my fingers, blowing into my cupped hands, and practicing scales, I got up to warm myself by making a few kneebends, when I spotted through the cracks between the boards a strange-looking column of dark figures shuffling with hunched shoulders past the garden fences on the other side of the street two floors below. When my eyes had adjusted themselves to the wintry brightness outside, I recognized men wearing the greatcoat of the infantry but no other military insignia. Some wore on their heads woolen caps; others, bandages of a dirty white; others, what looked like turbans fashioned from shawls. Some were bareheaded, and their heads were closely shaved. Many limped, some had an arm in a sling, a few stumbled along on crutches or sticks. All the heads looked like skulls over which a brownish parchment had been stretched tightly to give them the appearance of a human face.

It was the first group of German prisoners-of-war I had seen returning from Russian camps. The sight, although my eyes were accustomed to the multifaceted appearance of death, horrified me; it numbed me to the tips of my fingers so that I was unable to continue my practice. The image stayed with me. I kept thinking of ghosts, of skeletons that had risen from the graves to take their revenge on the living for something, some unspeakable injustice, some horrible crime. After returning to my lessons a few more times, I quit the exercise altogether. It suddenly seemed senseless, ludicrous.

Was there, objectively, a *Kollektivschuld,* a collective guilt of all Germans that made them metaphysically, morally responsible for the rise and the atrocities of the Third Reich, no matter what, if anything, an individual had contributed to its existence? That question dominated, of course, the newspaper columns and radio programs during the extraordinary, unprecedented Nuremberg Trials that began in November 1945 and concluded in October 1946, and for years afterward. The assumption of a collective guilt certainly influenced the attitudes and policies of the Allies toward the defeated country, at least for the first few postwar years. The Russians avoided any public debate of the question. Their propaganda, proclaimed on hundreds of posters erected at strategic points in the city immediately after Berlin had fallen into their hands, was that "the Hitlers come and go, but the German people remains." For most Germans the question was largely rhetorical—the tasks of the present were too overwhelmingly pressing to allow for that kind of soul-searching that began to take place in earnest when conditions had stabilized. For others, the question caused resentment and bitterness.

One evening, during the trials, my landlady and I were listening to a radio program in which some former inmates of a concentration camp described their life in the camp and afterward engaged with the moderator in a discussion of collective guilt.

"What guilt?" the young woman suddenly exclaimed, switching off the receiver. "My husband had just made his carpenter's master when they sent him to France, and I have had my hands full with kids from the day I got married at eighteen. We never had time for politics; we hardly ever had time for each other."

"But you must have known something about concentration camps," I said. "That knowledge alone must have forced you and your husband to take a stand, not publicly, of course, but in your conscience, on the Nazi regime."

"I didn't know anything about concentration camps," she snapped. "You as a half-Jew probably knew a lot more about these things than we did. Besides, I still don't believe that things were as horrible under the Nazis as everybody now says they were. Even if they were, I am sure Hitler didn't know what was going on. He only looked out for Germany, and like all idealists, he was deceived by the people he trusted. He didn't want to kill you or your mother. He wasn't a murderer. And who are those so-called judges in Nuremberg," she continued, getting angrier as she talked. "The Russians who killed my husband? Yes, I am sure he was killed. The Americans and the British who destroyed our cities and killed innocent women and children? The French who now kill the people in their zone by slow starvation?"

It was a standard argument, one I would hear countless times in different versions for the next few years. The Nazis had vanished, but their legacy of suspicion, doubt, and hate continued to fester in the body politic like organisms inflaming the tender tissue that begins to cover an open wound.

In the spring of 1947 I delivered the finished manuscript to the publisher and, with a substantial advance payment in my pocket, decided that the time had come to fulfill another desire I had had ever since I was graduated from the gymnasium ten years earlier: to enter a university. I managed to obtain permission from the French Military High Command to attend the University of Tübingen, which was in the French-occupied zone, and in May enrolled there in a program of study in Greek philosophy, theology, and history. This experiment, too, like the piano lessons, proved that the experiences and needs of my real life had overtaken the dreams and desires of a life I had imagined under the constraints and deprivations of my growing-up years. When I listened to a lecture on Aristotle, Heraclitus, or Kierkegaard, my mind was engaged and stimulated, but the moment I left the classroom I felt isolated among the crowd of young men and women for whom the world seemed to turn on the paper they were preparing for next week's examination. In the picturesque medieval town of Tübingen, which had survived the war unscarred, I felt out of step with an environment that seemed to have closed itself against the sharp but invigorating winds sweeping through the ravaged streets of Berlin.

When, in October, my publisher sent me the first copy of my book, and with it some clippings of favorable reviews, I packed my suitcase and boarded a train for Berlin within hours after I had received the package. In my haste I even forgot to obtain the required transit visa for the Russian zone; luckily, the train, as all trains in those years, was packed to the point of forcing passengers to ride in-between and on top of cars, and the visa inspection at the Russian checkpoint was mercifully cursory.

In Berlin I moved into the little villa in Zehlendorf that had once belonged to Edith and now stood like a ruined testimonial to her unhappy marriage with Father and her shattered dream of a reunion. Edith was living in America, and the ownership of the house had become uncertain. It had survived the bombings with no greater damage than a caved-in roof, blown-out windows, and cracked walls, but most of its precious furnishings had been removed by the Russians. When Zehlendorf became part of the American sector, American soldiers had occupied it for a while but obviously found it too uncomfortable. I installed myself in the kitchen where I fed the stove—it was now winter and bitter cold—with pieces of the furniture the Russians had left behind. Occasionally I would join Stephan, whose apartment was within walking distance of the villa, in a nightly expedition to one of the wooded areas of the southern suburbs to cut down a tree that we would chop up for firewood. The venture was not without risk; to prevent just such expeditions, the parks and forests were patrolled by American soldiers, but we usually managed to outwit them.

I had to keep warm because, unlike most Berliners who survived the cold by spending as much time in bed as possible, I wanted to finish a translation of Joseph de Maistre's *Les Soirées de Saint Pétersbourg* (The Evenings of Saint Petersburg) that I had begun in Tübingen. Father, who had suggested the book on the angels, had also suggested that a German edition of this Catholic classic was long overdue and would be most timely. However, the book never appeared. While I was reading the galleys, the drastic currency reform of June 29, 1948, which laid the foundation for West Germany's gradual economic recovery, brought the publisher near to bankruptcy, and the book's production was postponed. By the time the crisis was over I had

. . . .

left Germany and was preoccupied with other matters than seeking publication of a German book.

I also went courting. I had met Regina in the winter of 1946, at the State Library of Berlin, where she was in charge of the reading room. I had gone there to consult the *Acta sanctorum,* the monumental critical compendium of documents on the life of the saints, and while I was waiting for her I noticed on her desk a framed print of Botticelli's *Dance of the Angels.* We became friends on sight, sharing not only our views on the sad state of the Church and the healthy state of the theater in Berlin but also the slices of dry bread she used to bring for lunch and which we toasted on the gigantic potbellied stove that labored ineffectually to warm the provisional reading room. This was the time, in January 1946, when the General Assembly of the United Nations was holding its first session in London, and we waxed enthusiastic about the prospect of a new world order from which we expected the emergence of a United States of Europe guided by Christian principles of justice. Our friendship was close, but guardedly platonic. She was engaged and I was tied to one of those troubled liaisons that are held together more by a shared desire to escape the pain of loneliness and emotional deprivation than by genuine affection and harmony of spirit. By the time I returned from Tübingen we each had ended our engagement, and we now began what neither of us would have admitted to be a courtship.

Although we saw much of each other during the winter of 1947–1948, neither of us ever hinted at the possibility that our relationship could amount to more than that kind of close friendship between men and women that seems to be much more common in Europe than in America, and particularly among Catholics with strong ties to the institutional life of the Church. Then late one evening in March, Regina, who lived with her parents in the Russian sector, appeared at my door, carrying a small suitcase and asking for shelter. She explained that she had been warned by a friend that the Russians were about to arrest her because of her popularity with the members of the French Cultural Mission in Berlin and because of her frequent trips to West Germany under French diplomatic immunity. We were married two months later.

For the next three and a half years, I led the kind of life that would, if

. . . .

hindsight can assess such things, have brought me success, recognition, and financial security in the field of Catholic literature and journalism had I not left Germany when my career seemed firmly established. Besides the ill-fated translation of de Maistre's work I wrote a collection of biographical sketches of Catholic priests and laymen who had been executed by the Nazis or had perished in concentration camps, and a biography of Cardinal Mindszenty, whose trial by Hungary's Communist regime was then in progress. I began to contribute articles to Berlin's Catholic diocesan paper and became its coeditor. Simultaneously I became the editor of a diocese-sponsored tabloid designed primarily to publicize the Catholic viewpoint on the social and political issues that now emerged in the East-West conflict with increasing clarity. I frequently participated in the programs that the radio station RIAS (Radio in the American Sector) devoted to an analysis of that conflict, and I wrote articles for *Sie* (She), one of the first German consumer magazines to appear again after the war, and for several Berlin dailies as well.

I was now thirty-one and it seemed that, five years after the war, I had come into my own. Regina and I lived with our first child, a daughter who had been born in the final days of the airlift that broke the Russian blockade of the city's western sectors, in a large apartment in one of the first apartment buildings built after the war. Father and I were again on the familiar visiting status. Since my position as a publicist clearly identified with the policies of the Western democracies made it too hazardous for me to visit him at the priory, now situated in the Russian zone, he came occasionally to West Berlin to visit with us and supply himself with books and with cigarettes we had bought for him on the black market. Once Mother came from London to visit us and Annemarie and to see her grandchildren, our daughter and Annemarie's. Father joined us on this occasion, and for the first time in my remembered life I saw my parents together. I had last seen Mother in 1939, eleven years ago when she fled Germany, and now her ever-restless nature drove her to seek, together with Aunt Minna, yet another chance for happiness—she and Aunt Minna, she told us, were about to immigrate to New York, where her brother, Uncle Willi, had settled after his flight from Germany. She had made inquiries about the fate of Aunt Walli and that of her youngest sister, Aunt Clara. Aunt

Walli had died during transport to a concentration camp. Aunt Clara, who had been arrested shortly after the death of her mother, had disappeared without leaving a trace.

If I had any misgivings or reservations about postwar Berlin, they rarely troubled me, and the thought of leaving the city never occurred to me. Of course the war had left scars—Aunt Clara's and Aunt Walli's fate, Mother's and Aunt Minna's restless life as refugees—and there were lacerations that were still festering. The sound of a factory siren or a sudden detonation would reawaken in me the terror of the bombing raids, a terror I managed to keep at bay in daylight but that found me defenseless at dark and in my sleep. The daytime ghosts of the Third Reich stalked more cautiously, were less visible, and filled me not with anxiety but with occasional resentment. Throughout the Nazi era I had felt uncomfortable in the Catholic community of Berlin; the visions of my fellow Catholics, especially of those who belonged to the Catholic youth organization New Germany, all too often fed on the same spiritual streams that nourished the ideologies of the Nazis. Now that I no longer felt threatened by this spiritual kinship my doubts and reservations about the Teutonic cast of German Catholicism vanished and I was able to write about the faith and the Church according to my own vision and with a zest I would never regain. But the past was not to be silenced simply because abstract notions of German glory had, for a time at least, become unfashionable. The past wore recognizable faces; it appeared in the men and women who had, at least outwardly, accepted and in some cases openly supported the regime, and among whom were those who only five years ago had ignored me or treated me with contempt or open hostility. Now they smiled at me, but their smiles were too broad and their handshakes too cordial, and in their words an edge of sarcasm revealed envy at the few advantages I enjoyed as a "Victim of Nazi Legislation," as my identity card put it. Yet I had no inclination toward bitterness, no time to nurse grievances. All of us were paying some price for omissions and commissions, for loyalties and disloyalties in the long *Walpurgisnacht* (the witches' Sabbath) of our lives, and the mood, by and large, favored reconciliation. Besides, what did these few echoes of the past matter in an environment that not only ac-

cepted me fully but for which I had now in many important ways become
a voice and often a spokesman? Whatever annoyed or troubled me did not
add up to a desire to leave Berlin. I was immersed in my work, where I
found release for all the talents and energies that had been choked off for
so long, happy in my marriage, and comfortably settled in the city in
which I had spent most of my life. America was three thousand miles
away, a place where some of my Jewish relatives had found a new home
and from which they sent an occasional CARE packet and other splendid
things for birthdays and for Christmas.

Then, in the spring of 1950, I was unexpectedly invited to visit the
United States under the Cultural Exchange Program, whereby selected
German opinion leaders visited the United States for a period of study and
travel, and vice versa. My assignment was to study American mass communications techniques, particularly from the viewpoint of the Catholic
publicist. What was meant as a study tour turned for me into something
like a binge, an uncontrollable overindulgence of the mind and the senses
in sights and feelings that overwhelmed me and kept me on the brink of a
heady exhaustion. From early childhood I had lived under stress and confinement—my parents' broken marriage, a hostile political environment,
war—and even now memories and images of which I was often unaware
still fettered my inner freedom. The moment I spotted the Statue of
Liberty from the deck of the boat that had brought us to New York I was
transposed by an environment whose character, temperament, and appearance were so totally new that they made useless, overnight, all the
dictates of experience and the subtler signals of formed attitudes that hith-
erto had guided my steps.

To my own surprise and elation, I responded to this invigorating new-
ness immediately and with enthusiasm. In Washington, D.C., I spent
many hours of the night stretched out on a lawn near the banks of the
Potomac, simply to give myself over to the mesmerizing sight of silently
gliding cars that, in the distance, seemed like luminous serpents circling
unendingly the pristine whiteness of monuments erected, I knew, in honor
of some long-forgotten gods. In New York I was embraced by Mother,
Aunt Minna, and other German Jewish refugees, their victim and celebrated guest as they made me, for a week or so, a part of *their* New York,

the city of *their* life, *their* amusements, and *their* hopes and aspirations:
Radio City Music Hall, the Palisades Amusement Park, Coney Island,
Times Square, the Automat, Howard Johnson's, and Loew's cavernous
movie palaces done up in Moorish style. In Milwaukee I was feted by
German and Irish Catholics, in Chicago I was initiated into the America of
the black urban ghetto, in St. Paul I went on fishing trips with Swedish
Protestants. On my own initiative I took a Greyhound bus from St. Louis
to Denver and, in the company of an atomic scientist whom I met by
chance in the local YMCA, climbed Longs Peak. Without yet knowing
the cliché—without knowing or understanding much American English—
I sensed that I was walking tall, that my gait was springier and my movements were freer than I had ever known them to be. I dropped inhibitions
and long and carefully cultivated protective mannerisms, and I became
spontaneous and even voluble in dealing with strangers and friends, oblivious of my broken English, my heavy accent. In three months, between
June and September, I had become a new man inspired by something akin
to the "new freedom" that for Saint Paul was the essence of a life in
Christ.

"Let's go to America," I said to Regina when I returned to Berlin. The
city seemed to have shriveled and aged during my absence. Returning
from a world exuberantly intact and alive, I realized as one discovering an
ancient burial place that we were living among ruins and among people
whose faces bore the indelible scars left by unspeakable terrors, and that
my and my family's *Lebensraum,* our living-space necessary for well-
being, consisted of a few square miles that I could not leave except on the
rare occasions when an American cargo plane took me to some conference
in West Germany. I had, for a moment, glimpsed a new world and tasted
the possibility of a totally new life, and now, while the elation of my
experience still sang in my blood, the Old World seemed bleak, listless,
resigned, and stiflingly narrow. I found few listeners who were genuinely
interested in my tales, who understood my enthusiasm. Was it envy because I had been favored with an experience that for most Germans at that
time was unattainable? Was it the old, deeply engrained prejudice against
the barbarisms and vulgarities that Europeans often associate with American civilization? Lingering resentments against American bombs that had

turned the city into rubble, against American generosity that had fed half of the city during the Russian blockade, against American soldiers that occupied the city as conquerors and as protectors?

Surprisingly, Father urged me to grasp the opportunity. To my argument that I would be breaking off a promising career as a writer, he replied, "You are young enough and talented enough to find a new home—an intellectual, a spiritual home—in another country. You may even learn to be a writer again, in another language, but writing isn't really all that important. There's no future for you here or in West Germany." When I asked him how such a dim view was compatible with his high expectations of Germany's renewal, he shrugged. "Look," he said, "the war has been over for nearly six years. I see no signs that we have learned anything. Worse, Europe is exhausted. We are thought-out, written-out, felt-out. Why do you think I have been interested in republishing the old masters— Hello, Henri Bremond, Christian Stolberg, de Maistre? They still carried the idea of a Christian Europe in their blood—not only on their lips—and they wrote with strength and clarity about their vision. We have nothing to add to what they have felt and said. No, the push for renewal will come from America. It's a young country and perhaps, to us, a savage country, but it has the savageness of innocence, not the savageness of corruption."

Yet as I readjusted myself to my daily routine, the impressions of my American holiday faded. Without being at all certain that we wanted to leave Germany, Regina and I applied for immigration. We knew that we did not have to come to a decision on this matter for at least three years, the waiting period we had to expect before our application could be considered under the constantly oversubscribed quota for German immigrants. Emigration, we reasoned, would be a last resort if the political situation in Berlin deteriorated during the next three years and I could not find another job in West Germany, which was flooded with refugees from Soviet-occupied territories. Having made our decision dependent on future exterior developments over which we had no control, we promptly put the matter of emigration out of our mind.

In the summer of 1951, some six months after we had applied for immigration and completed the customary interviews and tests, Regina called me in Cologne, where I was attending a conference of journalists, to tell me that our immigration visas had been approved and that we had to leave Germany by the end of the year or face a waiting period of several years before we could reapply for visas. Nobody at the American consulate had ever told us that, because I had been born in Switzerland, our request for immigration would be processed under the Swiss quota, for which there was never a waiting list. Now we had to make a decision, unexpectedly and immediately. I believe we realized during that brief telephone conversation that we had been ready to leave Berlin the moment I had returned from America and that all subsequent discussions of the matter were simply attempts to articulate a fait accompli. Within days I had quit my job; within weeks we found passage to America and dissolved our household. The reaction to the news among our friends, relatives, and colleagues ranged from surprise and sadness to disbelief and thinly veiled anger. Nobody except Father supported us in our decision; many expressed their conviction that we would return, disillusioned, within a year.

On a bleak November day in 1951 Father came to Berlin to say farewell to Regina and me, and to his two infant granddaughters. It was a final farewell; by the time I visited Germany again, twenty years after my emigration, he had died. Over coffee and cake we talked about the arrangements for our trip and other trivial matters, careful to keep the conversation light and easygoing. I accompanied him to the city railway station and, on an impulse, offered to ride with him to the last station within the boundaries of the western sectors. The train was packed to suffocation, and for twenty minutes we stood chest to chest, chin to chin, trying to avoid one another's eyes. We did not speak. When my station came, I quickly pressed both of his hands and fought my way to the exit. He followed me, stopping just short of the door. When I had gained the platform I turned, and for a brief moment I saw nothing but his eyes. Glistening with tears, they seemed like a luminous abyss drawing me into a vortex of unspeakable suffering. Now the curtain, which all his life had veiled the gateway to his innermost self, was open, and his soul lay bare, at the mercy of my love. Then a burly man, impatient to reach the exit and finding his way blocked by Father, shoved him aside. Father stumbled, and as the door closed and the train began to move, I saw him fall. Instinctively I stretched out a hand to support him. The train pulled out and I stood, hand outstretched, motionless, dry-eyed, until the red taillights had disappeared in the darkness of a driving rain.

A week later we were on board the Italian liner *Vulcania* in Genoa. Regina, in her seventh month of another pregnancy, was pushing a baby buggy with our youngest daughter, Birgitta. I carried the older daughter, Angelika, and a suitcase. All of our possessions were in that case and in the three footlockers stored aboard. The sea was shrouded in fog, and the mountains embracing the city had disappeared in low-hanging rain clouds. We would not see the sun again until we landed in New York two weeks later, on the last day of my thirty-first year.

Epilogue:
English Lessons

· ·

Early one morning in the winter of 1952, while I was shaving
myself in the bathroom of our small flat in Milwaukee, the
doorbell rang. Before I could answer the door I heard it open, and the
voice of my daughter, who was three years old at the time, rang out,
"Good morning! I am Angelika. Who are you?"

"I am the milkman, young lady," a man's voice answered. "I would
like to speak to your dad."

"You can't," Angelika's little voice replied. "He is in the bathroom."

"But I must," insisted the man. "It's about the milk bill."

"That would be useless anyhow," Angelika said firmly. "You better
talk to *me*. You see, my dad really doesn't speak English very well."

The matter of the bill was eventually settled between the man and me,
but Angelika had been correct: I didn't speak English very well at the time
of this incident. It had been only four months since my family and I had
left Germany to begin a new life in America, and while Angelika during
this short period had become almost flawlessly bilingual, I was still struggling with the basic elements of colloquial English. In Germany, during

194

the six years between the end of the war and my emigration, I had made
my living by the word: as a journalist, essayist, and author of several
books. Now, overnight, I had become one among untold millions who, as
a result of the psychological, emotional, and geopolitical consequences of
the Nazi era and the war, had to learn not only how to adjust themselves to
the living conditions of a country foreign to them, but also—in the radical
sense of the word *communicate*—how to make themselves known to their
community.

My past had not prepared me well for English as my second language.
My father, who was a Francophile, had taught me a love for the French
language, and one of my books was a translation into German of Joseph de
Maistre's classic, *The Evenings of St. Petersburg*. The man who taught me
English for three years in the humanistic branch of the German gymnasium was a fanatical Nazi, and my hatred of him filled me with indifference to, if not dislike of, the subject he taught. Moreover, whatever
English I did learn under duress in school was the English of the British
Isles, a facility that proved more of a hindrance than a help when I tried to
use it on American soil. More specifically, the place where I now tried to
use it was a factory that manufactured copper wire and other copper prod-
ucts, which I helped to load on trucks if I was not busy sweeping floors or
washing windows. Even though it was a place compatible with my background and talents—at least according to the Wisconsin State Employment Office that had referred me to the place because my aptitude
tests had shown a very low IQ and unusually high manual dexterity—it
was decidedly not the environment where I could learn the kind of English
I wanted to acquire.

The French word for "to learn" is *apprendre,* from the Latin *apprehen-
dere*—to seize, to take possession of. Yet after a day's labor in the factory
I was much too exhausted for any serious reading, let alone for a systematic effort at "seizing" a language. Still, what I did learn, whether I
wanted to or not, in the hot, dark, dusty, and noisy halls of that Milwaukee
factory was more than what a tourist may pick up in the hotels, restaurants, and railroad stations, or, for that matter, in the bordellos of a foreign
city. It was the language I recognized and appreciated later as basic American idiom: the stark, direct, uninhibited idiom related to food, money,

sex, sports, and work. It was, literally, body language (a term that had not yet been coined), a way of communicating stripped of all embellishments and saturated with references to parts and functions of the human body. It was a language that sometimes shocked, sometimes amused me, that I could use neither at home nor with my neighbors, nor in the circles in which I moved after hours, but a language that I would hear again, as my Americanization progressed, in environments infinitely more refined than that of a factory.

The circles in which I moved after working hours and where my wife and I had found welcome and generous support consisted for the most part of successful advertising executives, lawyers, and businessmen who were college-educated, involved in the activities of the community, and knowledgeable about and sensitive to political and social issues. In the spacious, thickly carpeted, and elegantly furnished homes of Wauwatosa, Wisconsin, where most of these men and women lived, I seized upon, took possession of, English, the English of the educated upper middle class of the Midwest. It was in these homes, too, that two strikes in my favor came into play: my resolve to become fluent as quickly as possible in written and spoken American English so that once again I would be able to "live by the word," and my extensive knowledge of Latin.

I studied no textbooks, I went to no language courses for immigrants; I only listened, listened with all my senses, attentive to the meaning of words and the configuration of phrases, and to pitch, cadence, and tonality of the voices around me. Understanding the meaning of a word did not imply that I could pronounce it correctly. Understanding and speaking had to fuse at some point, and the only way to achieve that fusion was to speak with abandon, in spite of the fear natural to newcomers that by opening their mouths they would be making fools of themselves.

Given the severe limitations imposed on my social life by long days and weekends in the factory, and by the time I wanted to spend with my growing family (we were then expecting our fourth child), my fierce determination to learn English, good English, as quickly as possible would have yielded meager results had it not been for my knowledge of Latin. The two sets of two-volume dictionaries—German-Latin and Latin-German—I had used in school and had brought along to America were useful at

home, where, when I was reading a magazine or a book, I was more likely
to look up a strange word in the Latin-German dictionary than in the
English-German dictionary. Unfortunately, my volumes were not porta-
ble. Therefore, one of the first purchases I made in America was a pocket
edition of a Latin-English/English-Latin dictionary, a not insignificant ex-
pense when I was supporting a family of five on an hourly wage of sixty-
five cents. Using this dictionary habitually—to the point where I lost all
shame about taking it along and looking up words at parties and on other
social occasions—proved eminently rewarding. No matter how thickly an
English word had been encrusted with different meanings or bleached out
by endless repetition, the image evoked by the Latin root instilled in me,
at this critical time of my linguistic novitiate, a sense for precision and
clarity I have never lost. I never reflected on my almost instinctive reliance
on Latin as my primary teacher of English until, many years later, I read in
Robertson Davies's *Fifth Business* the following sentence, "[My father]
was an intelligent man and well educated in an old-fashioned way. . . . It
was he and he alone who made the study of Latin anything but a penance
to me, for he insisted that without Latin nobody could write clear English." When I read that sentence recently, I realized that it was the writer
in me who, thirty-five years ago, sent me to the bookstore to buy that
dictionary when I should have bought new socks for the children instead.

The writer in me may instinctively have dug for the roots of his new
language, but for the speaker and listener there remained the problem of
tuning his ear and bending his tongue to what makes English a living
language and American English a language bubbling and overflowing
with boisterous life: idiom, jargon, slang, cant, or what I came to refer to,
for want of any sharper distinction, as plain Americanisms. Books, including dictionaries, were of little help for the linguistic novice when he
was bombarded with expressions such as *bunk, chicken feed, up the creek,*
or *off the bat,* or when his friends admonished him to cease playing
hookey and to start bringing home the bacon. Yet Americanisms such as
these I learned quickly: it was a matter of perceiving the image underlying
them, and fitting the image to a given situation. At home, in our walk-up
flat in Milwaukee's black neighborhood, I readily picked up the slang and
idioms of domesticity, family, and neighborhood. Here I learned, for ex-

ample, that a baby shower is not a gadget with which to rinse our newborn who had arrived a couple of months after our immigration, nor an American ritual mimicking the religious ceremony of baptism, and that a washing machine on the blink is not an appliance turned inexplicably into a Christmas tree.

My difficulties began when it came to English words that are blood relatives of German words but took on completely different meanings in the course of their development, such as *become* and *bekommen, flesh* and *Fleisch, mist* and *Mist,* or *map* and *Mappe,* or of words such as *pearl, girl,* or *hurl,* which are pronounced alike but whose spellings differ. Most perplexing to the newcomer, however, were those words that can have virtually innumerable meanings, depending on their connection with other words, such as *run, off, go, up,* and *get.* I made lists in those days of words I found particularly stubborn in their refusal to yield to my grasp. I came across these lists recently and found that for the word *get* alone I had noted seventy-six different meanings—a still-incomplete list, as I know today.

Happily, after the first few weeks in America I had completely overcome my dislike of English instilled in me in the German gymnasium. To my own surprise I found that I took to American English like a duck to water, exhilarated by its directness, its richness of imagery, its vividness, and particularly its innate casualness that made it a wonderful instrument for social intercourse. What did it matter that I told my hostess at a formal dinner party that I had gotten screwed by the cab driver (the fifties, mind you, still observed a verbal etiquette) or startled my coworkers in the factory with words such as *procrastination* and *subterfuge.* What did it matter that I referred to my wife, when she suffered from a bout of arthritis, as a lame duck, or told the automobile mechanic that my car had flown off the handle.

The secret of my excited openness to the language was, I believe, a liberation of psychological and emotional forces in my nature that had been suppressed during my youth and adolescence by the atmosphere of hatred and violence in which I lived as a half-Jew during the Nazi regime. America had made me, literally, breathe freely again, and in the language of its people I found the medium suitable for making my breath articulate.

This was not only a linguistic phenomenon; it was at its root an existential one. I could not have expressed in German this new, deep, joyful consciousness of being a free man. German, conversational German, suddenly sounded harsh, clipped, aggressive, and cantankerous. It evoked sad images and painful emotions that I thought had begun to lose their destructive force.

When an insurance company hired me as a salesman one year after my immigration, I resolved never to call on German prospects even though "prospecting the German market" was a condition of my employment. My desire to keep myself emotionally at a distance from everything that might evoke a troubled past was probably the chief reason for this resolution, although I did not admit it to myself at the time. I was, after all, still dreaming about the Night of the Broken Glass and bombing raids. Moreover, I feared that any close or regular association with fellow-German immigrants would impede the progress of my Americanization. I did not want to live in the divided world of so many hyphenated Americans for whom the hyphen separates the "we" from the "they"—in customs, sentiments, and above all language. Whatever my wife and I retained from our German heritage, we wanted to pass on to our children in the secure knowledge that we had become Americans.

When I left the insurance business three years later, in 1956, counting among hundreds of clients not more than perhaps a dozen who were first-generation German immigrants, I had become as fluent in spoken English as I could ever hope to be. Moreover, calling on prospects at all hours of the day or night; discussing insurance with people representing all social, intellectual, and economic strata had been an introduction to America of a breadth and intensity available to few native Americans, let alone immigrants. Judged from the viewpoint of business, however, my success had been modest at best. I never learned the art of getting people to say yes, no matter how many company seminars I attended or how many manuals I read on the art that "keeps America's wheels of progress and prosperity turning." For me, the language of salesmanship, so widely touted as the Socratic method, had little to do with true dialogue. I came to think of it, rather, as a weapon, a weapon molded, chiseled, polished, and honed to perfection, but a weapon nevertheless. I am a peaceful man who hates weapons. Only by approaching my prospects unarmed, as it were, could I hope to break through their defenses and have them engage in true dialogue.

During my years as a salesman I may have contributed little to keeping America's wheels of progress in motion, but I did penetrate deeply into the numerous ways in which a people lives in its language, not only in its spoken language but also in its literature. As demanding as the insurance business was, it did allow me what the exhausting work in the factory had made nearly impossible: reading books. There was nothing about my reading that remotely resembled a college curriculum in American literature or history; being able to place authors or events in the context of epochs or movements would still take years. Besides, I was never very good at Trivial Pursuit, in *any* category. But whatever I read—by Bernard de Voto, Mark Twain, Oliver Wendell Holmes, H. L. Mencken, Emily Dickinson, Hawthorne, or Ogden Nash—aroused in me the excitement and satisfaction that only true discovery brings. The books I read at night or on a quiet Sunday afternoon illuminated and vivified what I saw and heard, or sensed, in offices and homes on my daily rounds. Without literature, America would have remained for me an enigma on those levels where, in the words of Hawthorne, "the gloom and terror may lie deep; but deeper still is eternal beauty." Without the daily experience of America in the course of a prosaic and often abrasive workday, reading Hawthorne or Dickinson or James Agee or, for that matter, Ogden Nash would have remained, at this stage of my Americanization, an enjoyable but ultimately academic exercise.

At the end of my fifth year in America I was ready to take the Oath of Citizenship. I was also ready for a job more congenial to my nature than selling. More than anything else I wanted to write again, in any capacity, but having no samples in English to produce, my search for a position that would have offered me this opportunity proved fruitless for a long time. One day, however, the manager of the public relations department of a trade association in Chicago, which had an opening for a staff writer, offered me a chance. Commenting that I spoke English exceptionally well, he added a sentence that I can still hear today as if it had been spoken an hour ago: "Let me see what you can do on a typewriter or with a pen." He then asked me to write an article about a national project for which enabling state and federal legislation had just been passed and which was of critical importance to the association's member companies. I spent the next few weeks at the Milwaukee Public Library doing research on subjects about which I knew nothing, then spent another week writing a twenty-five page article and mailed it to the manager. A month later I moved with my family to Chicago to begin a new career.

Yet was it a career in the true sense of a chosen pursuit, of "life work"? I soon realized that it was not, notwithstanding the approval, indeed praise, with which my writing and editing were accepted by my employers. Consequently, after a few months I joined the ranks of those curious people—and they are numerous—who spend their days "writing for a living" and their off-time writing poetry, working on the great American novel, or trying to place articles with *The New Yorker* or *Playboy*. After a few more months I had my first essay published, a reflection on my and my family's experience as immigrants about to take the Oath of Citizenship. Soon another article appeared, and from then on my life was ordered in a style, a pattern, a routine that has governed it to this day: writing and editing "for a living" and writing as the Muse, the Spirit, or the Force moves me.

I should be tempted to say that my romance with the English language—a writer's romance—ended, or turned into a complacently happy marriage, once I had mastered the skills, the techniques, the concessions, and the demands of systematically writing on two planes of creativity. In reality the romance, with all of the turbulence of adolescent infatuation, had just begun. It would never cease. Would I have returned to Germany if Dame Language, to stay with the metaphor, had scorned me on either plane? if, as it seemed for a while, I had remained locked into selling? or if my "serious writing" had produced only rejection notices? I could understand myself only as a writer, and failure to be accepted as one would have struck me with the all-too-common ailment called identity crisis. Mastering English and accepting myself as a true American seemed to me inseparable, and I might well have refused the demands of the Oath of Citizenship "to support and defend the Constitution and laws of the United States of America against all enemies, foreign and domestic," and "to bear true faith and allegiance to the same" if the language of the United States had refused me.

I did take the citizenship oath six years after my immigration, and then a moment came when I would realize for the first time how radically a new country, a new life, and a new language had re-formed my identity. Sitting in a sidewalk café in Berlin on my first visit to my former country in twenty years, I struck up a conversation with the waiter who had just handed me the check. We had talked for a while about the fine spring weather and other trivia when he interrupted himself, saying, "Excuse me. If I may ask, you are an American, aren't you? Where did you learn your impeccable German?" "On my father's knees in a little town in Pennsylvania," I was about to answer, but he had already turned and disappeared among the tables to wait on another guest. How had the man guessed I was an American? My clothes, my haircut, my appearance were not different from anybody else's sitting in that elegant café or walking past it. I had spoken with him not only in German but in the dialect peculiar to Berliners, a dialect into which I had fallen easily, indeed lovingly, the moment I stepped off the plane. If the incident had remained an isolated one I could have shrugged it off as a chance occurrence. Yet it happened again on the same trip, and unfailingly it has happened once or twice on every visit I have paid Germany since.

Language—American English—had taken possession of *me*. It had molded me in an indefinable way, unrecognizable to most but apparent to those who have an exceptionally high sensitivity to what I call the character of language. For them, my language was my American passport, no matter how skillfully I tried to disguise myself with my native tongue.

Being possessed by language is, I am sure, an experience common to good writers anywhere. What may not be as common is the high value that those who, like myself, learned and managed to master a new language in mid-life place on an acquisition for which they paid dearly and for which they must continue to pay with virtually every sentence they write. Suffering from and, by the same token, delighting in the possessiveness of the word—an affliction comparable to that one suffers at the hands of a jealous mistress—was a totally new experience for me, one I had not known as a writer in my mother tongue. It was more than the effort to write well;

it was different from the painful search for *le mot juste*. There is in this experience an element of protectiveness that worries about the purity, the nobility, the sacredness of something on which my unequivocal commitment to a new country, a new culture, and a new allegiance depends critically.

Is it for that reason only that I can never take my possession of English for granted? Would I, had I remained in Germany and there continued my career as a writer, eventually have looked upon, felt about, my native tongue in the same way in which I came to think and feel about the language I had *made* my own? Probably. The time during which I took possession of English coincided with a rising awareness in both countries that their language was in jeopardy. The seriousness of this threat did not strike me particularly on my first visit to Germany after twenty years. Having paid little attention to German in those two decades of my Americanization, I had missed almost a generation in the life cycle of a living language, and I was busy mostly with catching up on new vocabularies that had penetrated all levels of communication under the influence of rapid advances in science and technology. I had read the latest novel by Heinrich Böll and the latest play by Max Frisch, but I did not know the German equivalents for *angioplasty, jet propulsion, atom smasher, data retrieval,* or, for that matter, for *magic marker, ballpoint pen,* or *cassette player.* Yet something else had penetrated the language besides vocabularies: a new *Lebensgefühl,* an awareness of life reflecting preoccupation with money-making, pleasure, self-fulfillment, and unprincipled expediency. I had grown up in a Germany whose language, still reflecting the heritage of the nineteenth century, was characterized by interiorized culture. I had become a man in the Hitler era, when a people went berserk and their language turned shrill, aggressive, and threatening. Now the character of the language had changed again, reflecting new modes of living, feeling, and thinking.

When I had occasion recently to read contemporary German literature almost exclusively for two years, I recognized the full impact of this modern awareness of life on language: the language of Goethe, Uhland, Schiller, and Heine, a language infused with beauty, elegance, veracity, and, above all, openness toward the metaphysical core of all existence had

vanished together with the world it had articulated. A new language dominated the works of popular German poets, novelists, and playwrights, a
language that impressed me as narcissistic, emotionally sterile, often re-
ductionist to the point of absurdity, and devoid of any sense of mystery. In
its crassest manifestations it was *Kloakensprache,* "sewer language," a
term coined by German linguistic purists.

Much the same has happened to English. I keep thinking of the language of most contemporary writers, German or American, as a joyless
language governed by a vision of the world in which all roads lead to only
one gigantic sign, NO EXIT. Why did modernity, which gave rise to so
much we treasure and are willing to defend with our life, lead inexorably
to the corruption of language? Does our very language now accuse us of
the way in which we live our lives? In defense of our linguistic chaos and
corrosion, much is being made of language as a living thing that takes on
the character perfectly proper to the culture it articulates. Yet for me Golo
Mann, the eminent German historian, speaks for many when he questions
the achievements of a people if they jeopardize the integrity of its language. "We hope," he concludes his exhaustive *German History of the
Nineteenth and Twentieth Century,* "that our beautiful language does not
turn barren and vulgar but renews its nobility together with everything
finding expression in the word. Without such a renewal, what would avail
us the power, real and illusionary, we have regained?"

I have no recipe for a renewal of "everything finding expression in the
word." Who has? I can speak only for myself. Even in the routine of the
workday, at the most pedestrian and mundane editorial task, I remain vulnerable at the core of my being to one of those piercing glances of my
mistress, telling me that with this word, this sentence, this construction,
my very life is at stake. My life? Indeed. I find increasingly that in this era
of instant communication, of verbal overload, a distinct mode of living
must support and nourish my habit of speaking and writing. Emily Dickinson (who still makes me feel ashamed of my verbosity and my clumsiness
in the choice of words) would have understood me; few of my contemporaries will. Yet the vocabularies of science and technology, of pleasure and
profit, and—most painfully felt in the realm of the religious—of senti-

mental emotionalism have penetrated popular culture so deeply that I have to place myself at a distance from that culture merely to protect my most prized possession. If I lived in the closed environment of a university, if I lived by the word at home, at my desk, I might find it easier to keep the invaders of my verbal territory at bay. Yet I live in the midst of popular culture and I worship in the midst of popular culture. Consequently, for the industries selling communication, information, entertainment, and religious edification, I have become, in the words of Ogden Nash, a "self-centered nonconsumer." More positively, when it comes to television, radio, newspapers, magazines, and books, I make a special effort to practice those Benedictine virtues I try to observe in all my affairs: moderation, prudence, discretion, and discipline. More than anything I avidly seek and jealously guard every opportunity for silence, a commodity as rare nowadays as spring water in the desert of Canaan.

Besides being protective and defensive, I have resolved to treat words with attention and respect where I used to neglect them readily and frequently: in casually scribbled notes, in memoranda and letters, in documents and reports, and, above all, in conversation, an art that is virtually extinct. I cannot rid myself of the feeling that words are in a crisis of identity, that their meaning, their inner self has been eroded, altered, or perverted. Every word counts. Not even during my initiation into English thirty-five years ago did I consult dictionaries as frequently as I do now. But then, living a life of linguistic virtue is in no way easier than living a life of virtue under any human condition. Sometimes I succeed; more often I fail. How to practice verbal asceticism graciously and consistently—lacking as I do the Benedictine monk's support from a community—may yet be my final and most difficult English lesson.

Yet I am not discouraged. Signs abound that there is abroad a deepening concern for the state of what most of us take for granted: words. Books are still being written—and read—that excel in felicity of expression and whose content opens another door to an understanding of the human condition instead of nailing shut the last escape hatch. Interestingly, too, the very media that have implicated themselves so heavily in the corruption of language seem to have discovered that the subject of language has become popular among their readers and viewers and now instruct or entertain them with offerings ranging from spelling and grammatical accuracy to linguistic history and philosophy.

Most encouraging to me is the fact that I find myself engaged with increasing frequency in spirited discussions about topics as varied as the reliability of Fowler's *Modern English Usage* or the merits of looking up a word in the 1947 edition of "the Webster." Language as a subject of serious conversation no longer is confined to the editorial offices. Perhaps this renewed interest in language signals a first turning-away from the barrenness and vulgarity of modern life, an attempt to find in the symbols that are language some of the values we have lost or forgotten in life. We are, I believe, rediscovering the existential union between life and language, a union that goes much deeper than accuracy of grammar, the choice of the right word, or elegance of style. Something is happening reminiscent of my own discovery of English, a language I learned and learned to love, that became my truly native tongue, the tongue of my nativity into a new life.